T0265667

John B. Denton

The Bigger-Than-Life Story of the Fighting Parson and Texas Ranger

by
Mike Cochran

Number 6 in the Texas Local Series

University of North Texas Press
Denton, Texas

©2021 Mike Cochran
All rights reserved.
Printed in the United States of America.

10 9 8 7 6 5 4 3 2 1

Permissions:
University of North Texas Press
1155 Union Circle #311336
Denton, TX 76203-5017

The paper used in this book meets the minimum requirements of the American National Standard for Permanence of Paper for Printed Library Materials, z39.48.1984. Binding materials have been chosen for durability.

Library of Congress Cataloging-in-Publication Data

Cochran, Mike, 1949– author.
  John B. Denton : the bigger-than-life story of the fighting parson and Texas Ranger / Mike Cochran.
     Pages cm
  Includes bibliographical references and index.
  ISBN-13 978-1-57441-840-8 (cloth)
  ISBN-13 978-1-57441-850-7 (ebook)
  1. Denton, John B., 1806–1841. 2. Texas Rangers—Biography. 3. Peace officers—Texas—Biography. 4. Circuit riders—Texas—Biography. 5. Frontier and pioneer life—Texas. 6. Methodist preaching—Texas—History—19th century. 7. Indians of North America—Wars—Texas. 8. Denton (Tex.)—History. 9. BISAC: HISTORY / United States / State & Local / Southwest (AZ, NM, OK, TX) 10. BIOGRAPHY & AUTOBIOGRAPHY / Historical. 11. LCGFT: Biographies.

  F390 .C655 2021
  976.4/55505092 [B]–dc23
                    2021034650

Number 6 in the Texas Local Series

The electronic edition of this book was made possible by the support of the Vick Family Foundation. Typeset by vPrompt eServices.

Contents

Preface and Acknowledgments

In 1988, I found an old, battered and water-stained, typescript of an article about John B. Denton,[1] which had been printed in the *Frontier Times* in 1931. The article, by former Red River County Clerk J. M. Deaver, was a good, but brief account of the life of Denton and the Battle of Village Creek. In Deaver's article he mentioned that Denton's estate had never been closed out and was still pending in the Red River County Probate Court. Intrigued by this, my wife Linda Lavender, and I decided to make a trip to Clarksville, in Red River County to investigate. It took County Clerk Mary Hausler a few minutes to find the records, but finally she brought out an old box and within it were dozens of musty old documents, from old folded legal instruments to small scraps of paper with scribbled notes written on them. The old rag paper was in surprisingly good condition. Because none of the historical accounts had ever referred to any of the information contained in the file, I believe that we were the first to look at this in a very long time. Among the legal descriptions and promissory notes, we found what seemed at the time like the Holy Grail: John B. Denton's Last Will and Testament.

That experience launched me onto my quest for the true history of John B. Denton. From the will, I was able to determine that his middle name was not Bunyan, but Burnard, which settled an old question. From the deeds and promissory notes I was able to get a good idea of the extent of his estate, and his unpaid whisky bills caused me to question why he was so famous for his eloquent temperance sermons. Each piece of information generated more questions, and with these questions my interest deepened. Over the intervening years, I gathered a large collection of clues to the mystery of John B. Denton, but early on I found that the data I was collecting was often at odds with the official record. Every few years I was asked to give talks on Denton, and each time I did more research and developed the story bit further. About four years ago I found myself temporarily alone for several winter months in a four-hundred-year-old Tuscan farmhouse, with time on my hands, a huge file of collected information about Denton, and no excuses. That's when I finally started to write this book.

One of the things that struck me about Denton, his family story, and their trek to Texas, was how similar it seemed to the stories of countless other Anglo-American families who settled North Texas. I personally felt some kinship to the movement of which Denton was a part. Only years after starting on my Denton research did I realize that one of my great-grandfathers is buried in Arkansas, just twelve miles from where Denton crossed the Red River on his move to Texas. The area where my family settled was in territory once contested between Arkansas and Texas and precisely within the area where Denton had preached as a circuit riding Methodist preacher twenty years before. On the Texas side of the border, my grandfather, Tex Cochran, the Cowboy Evangelist, in his own way, a circuit traveling Methodist preacher, was born just twenty miles east of where John B. Denton moved when he came to Texas. In the end I became an example of a point that I was trying to make—that people are part of movements and by singling out one person to study in detail, you gain a larger understanding of the movement of which they were a part.

This book is partially about a cultural movement, but the large number of people who have helped me over the years is practically a movement of its own. The process has taken so long that there is no question that I will have forgotten people to whom I owe thanks and for that I apologize. Some of these people are no longer with us and I regret that they are not here to share this with me. Yvonne Jenkins, an early Director of the Denton County Historical Museum was encouraging and very helpful in my first efforts to understand John B. Denton. Lonn Taylor, a virtual Google of Texas history, was kind enough to give me many tips and leads over the years and was patient enough to listen to each new discovery I shared with him. Peggy Riddle, current Director of the Denton County Historical Museum, has been invaluable in her help for this project by opening up the museum files and offering assistance whenever needed. Kim Cupit of the Museum was always helpful in answering numerous questions and providing resources. Laura Bradshaw Douglas at the Emily Fowler Public Library is keenly interested in local history and has been very helpful with documents from their collection. Bruce Hunter helped me with maps of the waterways of North Texas. Ruth McVey, of Montisi, Italy, knows very little about Texas history, but knows how a good book should be organized, offered sage advice. A few friends read the manuscript and offered suggestions and encouragement: I am indebted to John Lawton, Dan Foster, John Swenson and Scott Parks for their feedback. I can't think of anyone who knows more about Northeast Texas history than Skipper Steely. His numerous histories of the area were valuable resources, but his editorial comments have made the final product much better than it would have been without his considerable help. Particular thanks go to Karen DeVinney at UNT Press for her encouragement and good advice in helping guide my rough manuscript into a book. And to my wife, Linda Lavender, without whom, none of this would have been possible. She has been along with me every step of way, offering her deep knowledge of Texas history, her good advice and sound criticism as well as listening to me talk about John B. Denton for thirty years, without complaining.

Introduction

On the lawn of the courthouse in Denton, Texas, there is a gravesite, surrounded by a metal fence; at its head stand two Texas State Historical Markers. The first, a granite site-marker placed there in 1936, during the Texas State Centennial states simply:

> John B. Denton: Born in Tennessee July 26, 1806, came to Texas in January, 1836. As a Methodist circuit rider killed in the Village Creek Indian fight May 24, 1841, in what is now Tarrant County. Named for Gen. Edward H. Tarrant who commanded the volunteers. Denton city and county were named for the pioneer lawyer, preacher, soldier of that name.[1]

The second, a metal, pole-mounted marker erected in 1977, informs us that he was a pioneer preacher, a lawyer, and Indian fighter, who died fighting to protect settlers on the prairie. These meager facts have become a shorthand version of the life of John Burnard Denton,[2] and are generally all that the public knows about the man for whom the County and City of Denton are named. But if the community is to bear his name, there is value in learning more about who he was, and why he matters.

The story of the early life of John B. Denton is a muddled and confused tale filled with competing and often contradictory bits of information. It is a veritable jigsaw with missing pieces, and bits from other puzzles added in to make it interesting. There are many questions concerning his lineage and life that remain unresolved. The simple questions of his middle name, where he was born, and who his parents were, have eluded historians looking for definitive answers.

This haze surrounding the life of John B. Denton has created a blank slate upon which some previous biographers have felt free to project their own prejudices and interests. When written about by warriors, his valor was without equal. His bravery in the last moments of his life would serve as inspiration for a generation that followed in his steps. Though he lived but a few years in Texas, to the Texas patriot he exemplified all it meant to be a Texan. At a time when every Anglo was an immigrant, length of residence was less important than commitment to the cause, and for his sacrifice, Texans took Denton for one of their own.

When preachers described his life, great emphasis was placed on his ecclesiastical oratory, his piety, and especially his sobriety. Reports of his sermon against alcohol became legendary. He was celebrated as a powerful "exhorter," one who could spellbind with his words. Accounts of his near saintly life were literally compared to the life of Christ; his martyr's death was a virtual crucifixion on the prairie.[3] Accounts of his log cabin days, and his quest for education, seem lifted from a biography of Abe Lincoln.

In his 1905 biography of Denton, Rev. William H. Allen seemed bent on crafting an origin myth for Denton County, in which his entwined valor and piety were emblematic of the characteristics that made Texas. True to the myth of the frontier, he was the quintessential, self-made New World Man, and his achievements seemed all the greater for the humbleness of his beginnings. Allen wrote that from being an orphan, abused and alone, his life was a demonstration of what grit, faith and character could achieve.

John B. Denton stood out in history, and the story of his life has been described many times, with varying degrees of accuracy. Unfortunately, in the 1850s, the first written accounts associated with his life were by a defrocked Methodist minister and pulp-western writer, Alfred W. Arrington. His fanciful story of the life of a fictional "Paul" Denton was confused with John B. Denton, and helped create a myth that served as a template for many biographical studies that followed. He was remembered as a "bigger than life" character, who thanks to Arrington, became even bigger than his own life after his death.

Denton became a symbol, an everyman who stood in for countless others who had come to Texas, and his story, the story of how he came to be here, and the stock from which he came, is remarkably similar to many of the early Anglo settlers who came to North Texas. By telling his story, we are, with a broad brush, telling the story of many, and in turn describing how America was settled, and how North Texas evolved into its present form.

Denton residents have long been interested in the man for whom their county and city are named, and there is a natural curiosity to find out the facts surrounding his life and death. Some have assumed that Denton was the founder of the community, but the naming of Denton County was an honor bestowed upon a fallen comrade. He was killed in 1841, in a battle with Indians five years before the county was created. When he passed though North Texas on his final journey west, it was a vast and uninhabited open prairie, divided by the dense Cross Timbers and coursed by unnamed creeks. Though he is credited with preaching the first sermon in Denton County, his connection to the physical area of the county was only coincidental. After Texas joined the Union in 1845, new counties were created from some of the old, larger ones. Legislators in Austin remembered their old comrade and honored his memory by giving his name to the newly designated 900-square-mile patch of North Texas prairie.

With the exception of Arrington, these early tales of the life of Denton were as true as the available sources would allow, and the tellers honorable men engaged in an honorable enterprise. But history evolves as values change and more sources become available, thus with that caveat, what follows is what we think is the real truth about John B. Denton, his move to Texas, his untimely death, and the rich body of myths that followed.

Chapter 1

The Obscure Early Life of John B. Denton

I t is unfortunate that the family of John B. Denton knew so little of their history, for the Denton family in America is an old and illustrious one dating from colonial times. But a family line is like a chain, and only as strong as its weakest link; all it takes is one or two generations with no records and only the vaguest of family memories, to break the link and the line of continuity can be lost. The problem of continuity in the Denton family line is compounded by the similarities of Christian names from one generation to the next; the fact that Denton's parents died when he was young; and for at least three generations, his family had been frontiersmen who left no convenient paper trail of documentary evidence for genealogists and historians. Consequently, Denton's children knew very little about their ancestors, a fact which they always regretted and which complicates the telling of his story.[1]

There are dozens of family trees which maintain that John B. Denton was the son of Reverend James and Sarah Clarkson Denton, of Jennings County, Indiana, but the evidence is anecdotal and often contradictory.[2] John Woodson Denton, living in Southwest Arkansas, wrote that he had been aware of cousins who had also settled in the Red River Valley. One of these cousins was "a Methodist preacher and Clarksville lawyer named John B. Denton," a son of his Uncle James who lived in Indiana.[3] Owing to the fact that families on the frontier tended to move in clusters, with neighbors and families settling in the same area, it seems likely that these Dentons could be related, and his father's name could well be James, but there is no solid evidence confirming the link.

John B. Denton's father was originally from North Carolina but later moved to Tennessee where he married and started a family. A son, William C. Denton was born on February 20, 1802, and four years later a second son, John Burnard Denton was born on July 27, 1806. Johnathan F. Denton, the son of John B. Denton's with the most knowledge of their family history, wrote:

My father was born in Tenn. lost his Mother when an infant. My grandfather moved from Tenn. to Indiana, and when my father was still a small boy, moved to Arkansas, then a territory taking his family with him. My father had one brother Wm. Denton and three sisters Charlotte, Jane and Eliza.[4]

Denton's mother died when he was an infant, his father died when he was eight, and as orphans, John and his brother William C. Denton were put in the care of Jacob Wells,[5] on his farm sixteen miles southwest of Arkadelphia, in Clark County. Family lore had it that Wells was a blacksmith who had immigrated to Arkansas with them, and that the boys were taken on as apprentices. From the various conflicting reports, it is believed that they immigrated to Arkansas between 1810 and 1815. Little is known of the fate of the three Denton sisters, save for Eliza who was living in Llano County, Texas, in 1895.[6]

According to an often repeated tale, Denton's life with Jacob Wells was an abominable situation, the Wells family being, "destitute of moral culture, and who hardly observed the decencies of life."[7] Under these conditions of "squalid poverty," his life was "a hard one, spent in slavery under his blacksmith master."[8] He was treated so poorly, that at the age of twelve, he had never owned a hat or a pair of shoes, yet what seemed to have tipped the scales for young Denton was what he perceived to be preferential treatment for his older brother William. Though they were both taken on to be apprentice blacksmiths, young John was too young to work at the forge and was delegated to help Mrs. Wells with the housework.[9] Angry over what he saw as a demeaning position, young Denton ran away from Jacob Wells and took a job on a river boat, which at the time, was the only means to moving goods and materials in frontier Arkansas.

However, there is a small conflict between this popular legend, and the history. Jacob Wells (1790–1844), had arrived in Clark County in 1811,[10] immigrating from Mercer County, Kentucky. He was listed as a farmer and stockman rather than a blacksmith, though there is some evidence he may have done some blacksmithing on the side.[11] "The region was wild and unsettled at that time, but Mr. Wells' farm was of fine black soil, and as he was a thrifty and energetic farmer and stock-raiser he became wealthy."[12] A well-respected member of the community, he was on the first grand jury convened after Clark County was formed in 1818,[13] he was made a Colonel in the Arkansas Militia and in 1836, was elected Clark County Treasurer.[14] It seems unlikely that a man of his stature could be accurately described as degenerate, degraded and poverty stricken.

That there are small discrepancies in a family history is normal. Loose recollections, passed down from one generation to the next, become hardened over time and pass from lore to fact; but they are not always correct. It is not unusual that a family history would be at odds with fact, but what is unusual in the Denton case is that many of these contradictions are not just the result of faulty family memories, but can be traced back, and directly attributed to a single source: the scoundrel Alfred W. Arrington, of whom we will hear more, later in this work.

Chapter 2

The Dentons
Move to Arkansas

The Dentons, like most of the frontier American settlers, had been slowly pushing their way westward for more than a hundred years. In 1735, when the descendants of Reverend Richard Denton, of Hempstead, Long Island, New York, left the eastern seaboard and bought land in the Shenandoah Valley, the Dentons started on their westering trek and did not look back. What followed was a pattern of pushing to the frontier, just past the edge of civilization, acquiring cheap land and then when the frontier advanced westward, they followed it. Every generation pushed the line just a bit further west. These were the bold ones, the stock that created the American West. Around 1811, when young John B. Denton and his family moved from the relatively tame Indiana to the wilds of the Arkansan borderlands, it took some boldness, but the lure of cheap, abundant land made it appealing to those with an adventuring spirit and a westering instinct. This was near the edge of civilization at the time, as Spain still controlled Texas, and the United States had only just acquired what would become Arkansas with the Louisiana Purchase in 1803. Arkansas had fewer than five hundred European inhabitants, mostly French, but the lure of cheap land drew the attention of thousands of Americans. Public land in Arkansas was being offered for sale at $1.25 per acre, and yet even at that low price, a majority of the residents were squatters.[1] What started as a trickle became a deluge as the thousand residents in 1810, became fourteen thousand in 1820, thirty thousand in 1830, and by 1840, Arkansas had over ninety-seven thousand inhabitants.[2]

When Arkansas became a territory in 1819,[3] it was huge and encompassed both Arkansas, a corner of present-day Northeast Texas and most of present-day Oklahoma. Clark County, where the Dentons settled, had barely a thousand people in it, few settlements, and no real towns or villages. The county was much larger than it is today, taking in all or part of ten counties in Arkansas, and for a few years it included a narrow strip extending as far west as the Texas Panhandle;[4] but the sparse Anglo-American population before the mid-1820s, was concentrated in the east.

Land that would comprise Clark County, where the Dentons settled, had originally been in the Territory of Louisiana until 1806, when it was divided off into the newly created Territory of Missouri. In 1818, this was further divided and Clark County was created from this subdivision, named for the Governor of Missouri.[5] The county was rich with resources and game was plentiful. These early settlers lived in log cabins and provided for themselves by subsistence farming, hunting and some trapping for animal furs. In 1809, William Blakely, a blacksmith, established one of the first permanent settlements along the Washita River, called Blakelytown, later changed to Arkadelphia.[6]

In 1811, just a few miles to the northwest on the banks of the Caddo River, Jacob Barkman settled and established the community that would become Caddo Township. Barkman was considered the "Father of Clark County" due to his industry and entrepreneurial nature. In 1815 he built a two-story home of adobe bricks on the banks of the Caddo River and it became "the first county court, the first post office, a stagecoach stop, a racetrack, and an ill-fated textile mill."[7]

In 1812, he had established a shipping business between Clark County and New Orleans enabling the settlers to get their goods to market, but perhaps more importantly, to bring back supplies to the wilderness, which he sold in his store. This shipping business started with a crude *pirogue* made of hollowed tree trunks, later replaced by a flat-bottomed boat and in 1830 he built a paddle-wheeled steamer. It was likely on Jacob Barkman's flat-bottomed boat that young John B. Denton worked in the years after setting out on his own.

When John B. Denton was nineteen, he married sixteen-year-old Mary Greenlee Stewart.[8] They wed on June 23, 1825, in Clark County, Arkansas,[9] in a ceremony performed by the Reverend Green Orr.[10] Mary Stewart was born on December 12, 1808, in Natchitoches Parish, Louisiana. Her father was Jonathan Stewart, born in Washington County, Virginia, and her mother was Mary Polly Yoast from North Carolina. As in Arkansas, in 1808, Louisiana was at the sharp, cutting edge of western expansion and these early settlers were a different breed from those who would come later:

> North Louisiana, at this time, was covered with a dense mass of brush-wood and interlacing vines—the home of the wolf, the bear, and the panther ... The few earlier settlers that ventured into these wild regions had to fairly hew their way, for only a few devious trails and paths were to be found.[11]

Her family moved to Clark County, Arkansas, sometime before 1820.[12] Clark County at that time would have been slightly more civilized than the far northern reaches of Natchitoches County, Louisiana, with more people and better opportunities for earning a living.

In 1824, when newly appointed Governor George Izard assumed office, he was not pleased with the state of the territorial militia. In his effort to reorganize the military, he ordered that each county should have its own unit and records show that Jacob Wells was appointed Colonel, while William Denton and John Stewart were Second Lieutenants in the First Regiment of the Arkansas Territorial Militia.[13] Thus, John B. Denton's older brother, his future father-in-law, and the man to whom he had been apprenticed, were all officers in the same unit. The First Regiment was ordered to report to Fort Towson, Indian Territory, along the Red River in present-day Oklahoma. They were charged with patrolling the border to keep Anglos from poaching in Indian Territory, and to prevent the tribes from stealing from settlers in Arkansas.[14]

Not much else is known of Mary Greenlee Stewart's family, but there
are anecdotal reports of her having being a strong influence on her rough-
hewn, unlettered husband. She was known to have been educated, or at
least literate, and to have taught Denton to read, "at night by the light of
blazing pine-knots."[15] Of this scene, biographer Rev. William Allen has left
us a poetic image:

> angels look with joy when the evening hour has come. In those days
> family altars burned with spiritual life more than now. In the hush of
> birds and repose of nature, the pine-knot fire was kindled to fresh glow.
> The young wife reads a lesson that came down from the skies; they
> kneel in recognition of the God of nature, and their God; and young
> Denton leads in prayer and supplication.
>   It was a school of two in the log cabin, a teacher and one pupil,
> the young wife and her young husband. The wife was not superior to
> the husband ..., but she had the advantage of art.[16]

In 1830, the Dentons were living in Caddo Township, Clark County,[17]
and had started a family. Sarah Elizabeth Denton was born May 18, 1826,
when her father John was not yet twenty years old; five more children
would be born to the Dentons over the next fourteen years.[18]

Although some early descriptions would not be so complimentary of
Denton's appearance and demeanor,[19] once he had reached his full measure
he was described by an old friend,

> In person Capt. Denton was rather below the medium standard, but
> with a face at once handsome and beaming with intelligence. His eye
> was large and gray; his forehead broad and high; his hair dark and
> standing in ringlets on his head.[20]

These conflicting descriptions are testimony to the fact that, as he matured
he transformed himself from an awkward, unlettered backwoodsman with
limited "attainments,"[21] into something considerably more than that.

Chapter 3

The Call to Preach

Rev. Allen supposed John B. Denton got the "call" to preach prior to his marriage and that his efforts to become literate were part of a larger plan to enter the ministry. Although there were no real educational requirements to enter the ministry it was understood as a foundational principle of early American Methodism that preachers were "*called* to the work of the ministry by the Holy Ghost. [italics mine]"[1] It is natural that those with superior oratorical skills would seek and be sought out for positions of leadership. Denton's considerable powers of oratory have been widely reported; if one were an intelligent but poor frontiersman, and there were few opportunities available for advancement, entering the ministry would become a viable choice for many articulate men of faith. Although poorly rewarded financially, the ministry provided a way for many to support themselves while attaining a position of authority and respect in their communities.

Prior to the Louisiana Purchase in 1803, the entire Louisiana Territory under the Spanish and French had been exclusively Catholic. When it became a territory of the United States, Protestantism became legal and it opened up a floodgate of immigrants pouring into the newly acquired lands.

At this same time, the United States was experiencing the Second Great Awakening, a national Protestant revival which greatly expanded the rolls of the Baptist, Methodist, and Presbyterian churches. Rev. Francis Asbury, the Father of American Methodism, was so moved when he saw thousands of people "toiling along on foot and horse" across the Allegheny Mountains, he wrote in his journal, "We must send preachers after these people."[2] The river of Protestant settlers heading west into the former Catholic colonies of France and Spain, coupled with the religious fervor of the Second Great Awakening, would nicely complement the concept of "Manifest Destiny" for America and Americans.[3] The idea took hold that white Protestant Americans had a God-given mandate to push westward to the Pacific Ocean, and neither Catholic Spaniard nor "heathen" Native American would stand in their way.

The Methodist-Episcopal Church was particularly successful in this Great Awakening, having devised a system to send hundreds of circuit-riding preachers into the wilderness to serve the isolated settlers. By 1820, it was the largest denomination in America, and by 1844 had over a million members, with 695 circuit riding preachers taking religion to the widely scattered and often isolated communities of the west.[4] It was in this period that the "Camp Meeting" or "Revival" became popular. The first big Camp Meeting on record was in Cane Ridge, Kentucky, in 1801, and by 1820 the Methodists were holding almost five hundred a year. It was in this format that flowery and powerful oratory became so effective, mesmerizing the attendees with the intensity of their language, and it was just this that John B. Denton did so well.[5]

Rev. William Stevenson is credited with having brought Methodism to Arkansas. In 1814, Stevenson, then living in Missouri,[6] went to visit his brother James, living in Caddo Township, in Clark County, Arkansas. He was greatly impressed with the land but saw in the settlers a great hunger and need of religious instruction. He noted:

> ... a vast region sitting in darkness and the shadow of death, scat-
> tered like sheep on the mountains, having no shepherd to guide their
> feet into the way ... I felt a great desire for the salvation of the
> people.[7]

Acting on this, Stevenson spent the next several years working to establish new Methodist circuits in northeastern Arkansas, serving the clusters of Methodists he had worked to develop in his earlier travels.

In 1816, the Missouri Conference of the Methodist Church was founded after separating from the Tennessee Conference; William Stevenson was given a new appointment to create a Hot Springs circuit. Removing to Arkansas, he brought with him a large number of fellow Methodists who made the month-long journey in a wagon train. Pushing yet further towards the frontier, Stevenson and his band of followers moved on to Mount Prairie,[8] in present-day Hempstead County, Arkansas.[9] By 1818, Methodism in Arkansas had grown to the point that Mount Prairie warranted its own circuit.[10] "Methodist circuit riders became a regular feature of life on the Arkansas frontier. 'If you hear something lumbering through the canebrake,' went one common saying, 'it's either a bear or a Methodist preacher, and either one's bound to be hungry!'"[11]

Mount Prairie soon became densely settled with Methodists, and with Stevenson the presiding Elder of the Methodist Church, an active center of Arkansas Methodism. In addition, Hempstead County was a hotbed of Methodism due to its position as a gateway to Texas. People were on the move, agitated by a sort of "Texas mania" and their own westering instincts.[12] It was Stevenson's job to interest and enlist men to pursue the ministry and as a result many moved to Mount Prairie to be nearer the seat of Arkansas Methodism; among them was John B. Denton.[13]

Denton's first official connection with the Methodist Church did not come until 1833 when he was admitted on a trial basis assigned to the Mount Prairie circuit.[14] Being a Methodist circuit-riding preacher was a difficult, grueling and often dangerous job:

> These settlements were often small and widely-separated, from ten to thirty miles apart. It required from six to eight weeks for the preacher to make one round upon these immense circuits. The custom was for the preacher to stop and preach in a settlement at night, for several nights, until all the people for miles around had an opportunity of hearing the word.[15]

Initially there were few standards for Methodist circuit-riding preachers but they were typically paired with more experienced ministers from whom they were expected to learn. After 1816, a two-year self-study reading curriculum was devised for ministers on trial but this was not always effective due to a shortage of materials. Even past their trial period the church "urged itinerants to study five out of every twenty-four hours. Reading was the most important activity in this regard."[16]

Entering the ministry as a circuit-riding preacher on the frontier was not something to be taken lightly. This was a physically demanding job, requiring long rides on horseback between communities in the circuit, in good weather and bad. Some suffered from physical exhaustion and others even died while on the job. There was a status category in the church for "Worn Out"[17] preachers, which served to acknowledge the effects of years riding the circuit. For a family man like John B. Denton, with four children at home, this was a particular burden. Since his first child, Sarah Elizabeth had been born in 1826, three more children had come along: Jonathan in 1828; Narcissa in 1830; and Eldridge in 1833. That same year, in 1833, when Denton first entered the ministry, the pay for a preacher with a wife was just $100 per year. He was expected to support his family as well as his ministry on this meager salary:

> Younger ministers who married were subject to financial difficulty and the husband often retired to care for the material needs of his family, "Many, very many, pious and useful preachers, were literally starved into a *location*,"[18] one Methodist declared. Younger itinerants often remained settled for a season and recovered health and financial stability; but, then they eagerly rejoined the traveling ministers.[19]

"Located," or "local" preachers were an important part of the Methodist strategy for spreading their creed to the religion-hungry settlers in the Western backwoods:

> The Methodist system of relying on local preachers (who farmed or otherwise supported themselves and preached on Sundays) proved to be ideal in Arkansas [sic] ... These men carried much of the responsibility for nurturing the young congregations that the

circuit riders planted ... Local preachers also made it possible for many communities to have "resident" ministers who could represent the church.[20]

Life was difficult on the frontier and civilization had been left far behind. One of the goals of the Methodist Church was to bring a civilizing influence to the frontier. Attesting to the character of the backwoods inhabitants of Arkansas, English naturalist Thomas Nuttall observed:

These people, as well as the generality of those who, till lately, inhabited the banks of the Arkansa, bear the worst moral character imaginable, being many of them renegades from justice, and such as have forfeited the esteem of civilized society. When a further flight from justice became necessary, they passed into the Spanish territory ...[21]

Besides opposing the Southern aristocratic practice of dueling, the church promoted temperance and after an incident in which five gamblers had been hung in Vicksburg, anti-gaming associations were formed throughout the region. Among his other duties, Denton was also a leader of the anti-gaming association in Hempstead County, Arkansas.[22]

As has been stated, Denton was taught to read by his wife Mary in the early days of their marriage.[23] Observers would later remark on the depth of his knowledge and the quality of his oratory, which would seem to belie the humbleness of his backwoods education. But Clark County Judge A. H. Rutherford, writing of young Denton forty years later, offers an explanation for this transformation:

He [Denton] remarked one day in conversation with the writer about the study of geography, grammar and ancient history in the course of which he said that the pleasure of studying either of them had been denied to him, in consequence of the low state of educational facilities at that early period in the history of the territory ... And for the reasons above assigned had not even examined one of the books mentioned but desired very much to have use of such books for examination and study. He asked the writer if he knew where he could procure them. The books mentioned were among the few the writer had the use of which he willingly offered him and he readily accepted. They consisted of the *Smiley's Geography, Murray's English Grammar* and an ancient history with *Wester's Epitome of History*; only a part of the books were taken at first. But as soon as they were studied and understood were returned and others taken. Upon the return of the first books borrowed the whole man appeared to be changed. He spoke of them as one who has spent days and months studying and pouring [sic] over their pages. His application was so great that he proved himself not only apt but studious in the strictest sense of the term. In consequence of his good success there was a glow of animation about him truly fascinating. Much of his former reserve and stiffness of manner was thrown off when a pleasing smile lighted up a mind at once strong and clear. Often have the thoughts of the writer followed upon the impressions made upon the mind of this rather extraordinary man. He then left with *Rollin's Ancient History* and *Murray's English Grammar* but only taking one volume of ancient history at a time as his home was nearby. This loaning of books to him gave frequent and often occasions for conversation and inquiry about his progress.[24]

Rutherford reported that this educational transformation was immediately applied to his ministry and that his sermons became "more profoundly eloquent in a high degree."[25] His oratory was notable and highly educated ministers "were electrified and astonished at his profound logic and eloquence."[26]

In spite of his considerable abilities, Denton withdrew from the traveling ministry in 1835, not from a crisis of faith, but from financial pressure, the rigors of life on the road, and continual absence from his wife and children. The meager salary of the itinerant preacher and the incidental costs of being on the road forced him to *locate* to better provide for his family.

This was a real problem in the church because many of the itinerant preachers were poor and the salary insufficient to cover the costs required of the position. Some preachers received offerings from the members of food, clothing, and shelter, but passing the plate for offerings was not always successful. Whether it was due to losing able preachers like Denton, or just the better financial position of the Methodist Church, in 1836, the salary for preachers was doubled to $200.00.[27]

By 1836, Methodism in Arkansas had taken root so successfully that it merited its own conference, and the Arkansas Conference of the Methodist

Episcopal Church[28] had its first meeting in May of that year. This new conference consisted of Arkansas, Northern Louisiana, Indian Territory, and a part of the Sulphur Forks area in Red River County, Texas, claimed by Arkansas.[29] The membership at this time consisted of 4,557 Methodists, of whom 1,225 were Indians, and 599 were African Americans.[30]

In the Methodist Episcopal church considerable efforts were made to convert and minister to the Native American population. There was a continuing problem of unscrupulous and illegal traders exchanging liquor in return for pelts as well as other trade items, but the evangelistic fervor brought forth in the Great Awakening made these un-christened "heathens" a ripe target for their missionary zeal. This was difficult, sometimes dangerous work which required "great prudence"[31] and diplomatic skills:

> In many instances they had been cruelly treated by the whites, and were wrought up to such a pitch of desperation that it required more than ordinary skill to enable our preachers to retain the hold they had gained upon the affections of the Indians. The influence of these godly men in restraining the violence of these poor savages has never been fully appreciated by the government.[32]

Chapter 4

The State of the Church in Texas

After the end of the Mexican War of Independence from Spain in 1821, federal support for the State of Coahuila y Tejas waned and the legal settlers, both Anglo and Mexican, began to chafe at rule from afar from which they received little benefit. The population of Texas was small and the newly constituted Mexican government had larger issues to deal with than a few disgruntled Anglo immigrants on the frontier. More restrictive laws enacted in 1830 prohibited further immigration from the United States, increased taxes, and re-emphasized the prohibition on slavery.

With the existing prohibition on Protestantism, these laws served to increase discontent among the largely Protestant, southern American immigrants. Because of the attraction of the land, the remoteness of the government, and the independent nature of the frontier settlers, most of these laws were ignored, as slave-owning southerners continued to pour across the ill-defined border into Texas. So too, the Mexican prohibition against Protestants was ignored and though most Protestants practiced privately in their homes, an occasional Protestant preacher slipped across the line to preach a sermon to the Anglo immigrants. In 1834, Henry Stephenson, a Methodist circuit rider from Arkansas, entered Texas, settled in present-day

Newton County, and established McMahan Chapel: thus the first seed of Methodism was planted in Catholic Texas.[1]

Further exacerbating the problem among the settlers was the lack of Catholic priests assigned to the Texas settlements. Even if the residents had been inclined towards Catholicism, no priests were available to perform marriages so that their informal marriages were not sanctified by a church or recognized by law.[2]

Stephen F. Austin opposed Protestant preachers, fearing discord in his relations with the Mexican authorities. His contract with Mexico had included a provision to bring only "Catholics ... of good morals," into his colony in Texas.[3] Austin observed that "one Methodist preacher" could do more harm to the colony "than a dozen horse thieves."[4] Austin was in favor of a softer approach for introducing Protestantism into Texas and felt that some of these Methodists and their revival style of evangelistic preaching would be provocative to the Mexican authorities.

Mexican opposition to the spread of Protestantism added a revolutionary component to the practice of the religion, and possibly in that spirit, in 1835, Col. William B. Travis wrote an appeal for "spiritual reinforcements in Texas."[5]

> About five educated and talented young preachers would find employment in Texas, and no doubt would produce much good in this benighted land. Texas is composed of the shrewdest and most intelligent population of any new country on earth; therefore, a preacher to do good must be respectable and talented. In sending your heralds in the four corners of the Earth, remember Texas.[6]

In May of 1836, news of the Texian victory at San Jacinto reached the General Conference of the Methodist Episcopal Church meeting in Cincinnati, Ohio. Remembering the appeal from William B. Travis, who just two months before had been slain in the battle of the Alamo, a call went out for volunteers to take up the cause of Methodism in the new nation of Texas. At that meeting Dr. Martin J. Ruter, President of Allegheny College in Meadville, Pennsylvania, was the first to volunteer.[7] Around the same time Rev. Littleton Fowler, the Financial Agent for La Grange College of Tuscumbia, Alabama, and Rev. Robert Alexander of the Mississippi

Conference also answered the call.[8] Finally in 1837, "the Board of Missions of the Methodist Episcopal Church resolved upon a vigorous prosecution of the missionary work in the new Republic of Texas,"[9] and the three volunteers were sent into the field.

Robert Alexander arrived first on August 19th. Rev. Littleton Fowler made his way from Alabama, coming through Arkansas, to visit his brothers, John H. and Bradford C. Fowler, who lived in Jonesboro on the Red River.[10] The Methodists were on the way.

Chapter 5

Littleton Fowler, John B. Denton, and Texas Methodism

L ittleton Fowler, often called "The Father of Methodism in Texas,"[1] played a pivotal role in the life of John B. Denton, and their association increased Denton's status in the history of Texas Methodism. Fowler was born in Tennessee in 1802, and with his parents and three brothers moved to Kentucky in 1806.[2] Fowler was called to the ministry at an early age, and began to preach when he was just eighteen, but owing to poor health he was forced to resign after a few years.

By 1828, Littleton Fowler was back in the church holding various assignments in Bowling Green, Louisville, then after a relapse, in several smaller communities and less stressful positions. A beloved figure, Fowler was described as "One of the sweetest spirits that ever belonged to the Methodist ministry in the west."[3] Still sickly, in 1833, he was given a position as a financial agent at La Grange College in Tuscumbia, Alabama. In spite of his poor health, his role at La Grange College still required some travel, but for the next four years, he worked on behalf of the college and the Methodist Church.

Two of Fowler's brothers had been early pioneers in the borderlands along the Red River. John H. and Wiley P. Fowler had ventured into this

Rev. Littleton Fowler (1803–1846). Fowler was one of the first Methodist preachers to answer the call of Col. William Travis, for Methodist preachers to come Texas. He engaged young minister John B. Denton for his first trip into Texas and became for Denton a friend and mentor. Littleton Fowler is considered one of the founders of Methodism in Texas. *Courtesy Bridwell Library Special Collections, SMU.*

untamed frontier as early as 1817, joining their uncle Claiborne Wright's family who had immigrated the year before. Wright's journey, recounted in Skipper Steely's *Six Months from Tennessee*,[4] tells of Wright having built a flatboat, floating down the Mississippi, and then up the Red River to Pecan Point. The journey took them past the limits of civilization, through the Red River "rafts," a hundred-mile natural dam of fallen trees and maze of waterways, dragging a flatboat filled with tools and provisions.

Littleton Fowler's health restored, the new mission to Texas had revitalized his spirits:

> Tuscumbia, Ala., August 22, 1837. This day I start for the Republic of Texas, there to labour as a missionary ... The impression on my part and the call to go to Texas were as strong and as loud as was my call to the ministry; consequently I go fully expecting the blessing and presence of God. While viewing the labors and privations that await me, my soul is unmoved.[5]

Martin Ruter, with more status and seniority, was named the Superintendent of the mission to Texas. He had warned Fowler what he might expect: "The town of San Augustine is said to have many rough & wicked people loitering in it day & night. Instead of tarrying there, some are in the habit of stopping near it, but not in it."[6] Fowler was instructed to take a direct route from Alabama to Texas but he chose a more circuitous route which would take him through Arkansas where his brothers lived:[7]

> From Washington, Hempstead County, Ark., I went to Jonesboro through the Choctaw Nation, riding with fever two days; at J. [Jonesboro] I met my two brothers [John and Bradford?] and other relatives [the Wrights?]. After two weeks of fever I returned to Hempstead to unite my brother, J. H. Fowler, in marriage with Mrs. Elizabeth Alexander, Sept. 26, 1837.[8]

Officiating at the marriage of his brother John Hopkins Fowler was the likely explanation for Fowler's detour through Arkansas to Hempstead County. While visiting, he met John B. Denton, who he engaged to accompany him on his journey into Texas. John H. Fowler had been previously married in 1825, to another Elizabeth, the widow of Thomas Denton of Miller County, Arkansas, who was possibly John B. Denton's uncle.[9]

Denton had applied for reinstatement in the Methodist Episcopal Church but had yet to receive confirmation or an assignment. Though still associated with the church, with no specific appointment he was essentially a "minister without portfolio," so to accompany Littleton Fowler would be an opportunity to both revive his career and serve the church by being in the advance guard of Methodism in Texas.[10]

Because of his stature in the history of Texas Methodism, Fowler's entry into Texas became an important event: the following journal entry has been quoted in most histories of Texas Methodism and helped put the name of John B. Denton in a place of prominence by association:

> On my departure from Arkansas I employed Rev. John B. Denton, a local preacher, to labor in the Texas mission. Sept. 30 we reached the Sulphur Fork prairies. Travelled up the [river] sixty miles, where I preached at Bro. (William) Duke's to fifteen hearers ...[11]

Fowler and Denton left Hempstead, Arkansas, on September 28 or 29, 1837, and though their exact route is not known for certain, the most direct and logical route crossed the Red River near Fulton, Arkansas, where a ferry had been established in 1836.[12] There they would have joined Trammels Trace, a trail blazed by Arkansas trader, horse smuggler, stock rustler, and slave stealer Nicholas Trammel, who was known to kidnap "slaves with assurances of freedom in Texas."[13]

Though Trammell was expelled from Texas in 1822 for his illegal activities, his name would attach itself to this wilderness trail.[14] Giving the rough trail a name like Trammell's Trace offers it a certain legitimacy as we might think of a well-traveled route or a road today, but the very name of "trace" indicates that it was at best a trail, identified by "blazes" cut by axes on tree trunks to show the way. The path evolved from animal trails, to Indian paths, and was finally discovered by Anglo smugglers and early settlers, as the easiest way to make their way through the wilderness into Texas. In the relatively flat, densely vegetated plains of the Red River watershed, the serpentine course of the river is a slow meandering series of twists and turns. Over time, with the changing course of the river, a maze of oxbow lakes was created which could confuse anyone without a trail to

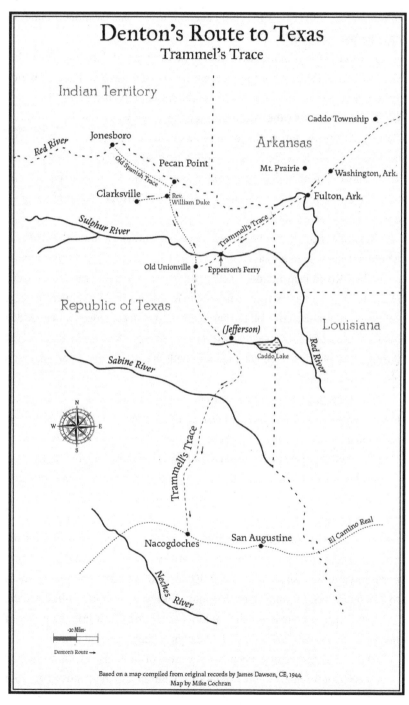

Denton's Route to Texas
Trammel's Trace

Indian Territory

Caddo Township ●

Red River   Jonesboro

Arkansas

Old Spanish Trace   ● Pecan Point

Mt. Prairie ●   ● Washington, Ark.

Clarksville   ● Rev. William Duke   ● Fulton, Ark.

Sulphur River   Trammell's Trace

Old Unionville ●   ● Epperson's Ferry

Republic of Texas

Louisiana

(Jefferson) ●

Sabine River   Caddo Lake   Red River

N   W—E   S

Trammell's Trace

El Camino Real

Nacogdoches ●   San Augustine ●

Neches River

-20 Miles-

Denton's Route →

Based on a map compiled from original records by James Dawson, CE, 1944.
Map by Mike Cochran

Map of Denton's Route to Texas.

follow;[15] "the unwary visitor could become lost ... and wander around for days before escaping."[16]

Denton's biographer, the Reverend William Allen, declared that Denton was a Texan from the moment he crossed the Red River,[17] which although it has a fine ring to it, is geographically incorrect. The land where he crossed to the south side of the river was actually Lafayette County, Arkansas, but it did serve as an accurate characterization of who he became and how he was regarded ever after. Technicalities aside, Texas has claimed him for their own. Fowler and Denton arrived at the Sulphur Forks prairie on September 30, 1837,[18] which was their official date of entry into Texas.

Regardless of where the precise boundary line was, the trip into Texas would not have been an easy one. Commencing on the high northern bank of the Red River, near Fulton, Arkansas, early travelers on Trammell's Trace recall arriving on the southern bank of the Red River and encountering deep, soft sand. A thin dry crust on the surface would conceal a deep muck hidden below which ensnared wagon wheels and horses. Not impossible to get through, but physically demanding, and both man and horse often ended up covered in red mud.[19]

The bottomlands at the Great Bend in the Red River at that time were ringed with dense canebrakes: seven miles of cane, sometimes thirty feet high and bent over, forming a darkened, breezeless archway. Only when travelers reached the rise at edge of the flood plain did they get any relief.[20]

Following the Trace past the site of present-day Texarkana, the path veered away from the Red River in a southwesterly direction crossing the Sulphur Fork at Epperson's Ferry. They would have continued on a few miles further to Old Unionville, where the road intersected with the Spanish Trace. The roads formed a "Y" at Unionville, with one leg leading north towards Jonesboro on the Red River, and the other continuing south to Nacogdoches.[21] From there they most likely went north following the Spanish Trace, a course which would have led them towards the home of their colleague, Rev. William G. Duke, where they stayed the night.

Duke had previously been a colleague of John B. Denton's in the Arkansas Conference of the Methodist Church but had moved to Red

River County in February of 1837.[22] As Methodism crept across the border from Arkansas into North Eastern Texas, many of the same characters appear in the histories of both states. Joining Duke in Red River County were Rev. E. B. Duncan and Rev. Green Orr, Denton's friend who had been the preacher at his wedding. It was in the home of Reverend Duke that Littleton Fowler preached his first sermon in Texas.[23]

From Duke's home,[24] Fowler and Denton traveled southwest a few miles to Clarksville where they held their first camp meeting. Clarksville had been founded in 1833, and the previous April the first Methodist Quarterly Conference had been held there with many of the newly immigrated Methodist clergy in attendance.[25]

After spending almost a week in the Clarksville area, Fowler and Denton resumed their journey, most likely traveling east from Clarksville rejoining the Spanish Trace and continuing their journey south towards Trammell's Trace.[26] From there they rejoined the established trail which wound its way south, through the dense East Texas Piney Woods towards Nacogdoches. Along the way they would pass near the site of present-day Jefferson. The journals of Littleton Fowler described the rough untamed country:

> In company of three others, with provisions packed for four days' travel, we struck out across Texas for Nacogdoches. On the way we passed the unburied body of a man who had been shot six weeks previously for horse stealing. We slept in the woods four nights, using our blankets for beds … Reached Nacogdoches Oct. 16, preached two sermons, one by J.B. Denton, one by the missionary. [27]

From Nacogdoches, Fowler and Denton traveled on to St. Augustine, where they arrived on October 19, 1837. There they preached for four nights in succession and Fowler began a subscription campaign to raise money to build a Methodist Church.[28]

San Augustine was an important early eastern gateway to Texas near the border of Louisiana, along the El Camino Real de los Tejas. This road, which ultimately extended twenty-five hundred miles from Natchitoches, Louisiana, to Monclova, Mexico, and eventually to Mexico City, was initially established by the Spanish in the 1690s. Having become concerned by smuggling and French encroachment on this distant frontier of their empire, the Spanish sought to establish a presence there by settling a mission, and a road to supply it. The French had established a trading post at Natchitoches, Louisiana, in 1714; in response, in 1716, several Spanish missions were established in lower East Texas, in addition to one at Los Adaes,[29] in Louisiana, a few miles to the west of Natchitoches, and a small garrison of soldiers were stationed there in 1821.[30] In 1795, Louis Chabinan[31] started a ferry service over the Sabine River,[32] on the Camino Real, and this became a popular route taken by many immigrants into Texas from the American South. By the time of Denton's arrival, St. Augustine was a prosperous town with long-suppressed Protestant inclinations, and their campaign to raise money for a church was successful. Within two weeks they had received a donated lot and $3,500 in pledges for the first planned Protestant church in Texas.[33]

While in San Augustine, Denton became a Mason and was "initiated as an Entered Apprentice on October 23, 1837, passed to the degree of Fellow Craft on November 3rd, and raised to the Sublime Degree of Master Mason, on November 6th."[34] On the same day Denton was accepted as a Master Mason in the McFarland Lodge No. 41, at St. Augustine, the lodge in Nacogdoches changed their rules to allow him to preach in its lodge hall "every other Sabbath."[35]

By resolution of the lodge on November 6, its two principal officers could allow the lodge room to be used for any religious purpose, "Not, however, to interfere with the business of the Lodge." This toleration recognized that the membership represented many faiths. Although most were Protestant, at least Sterne and Weiss were Jewish, and Nixon, Roberts, and Taylor were Roman Catholics.[36]

Although San Augustine was not as sinful as predicted by Martin Ruter, Texas had earned its reputation as a wild and wooly place where the work of the Lord was sorely in need. Dutifully answering William B. Travis' call, these early Methodist ministers had an almost Sisyphean battle, trying to push these Texian back-sliders back up the hill of righteousness. Writing to his fiancé, Mrs. Missouri Porter, Fowler could not conceal his disgust for the customs of the people he encountered:

Our hostess scolds worse and worse. I told her she would wear her tongue as thin as a six pence, break her constitution & kill all the shade trees round the house if she did not quit scolding. Told her that she could out scold creation. She laughed at all that was said. On yesterday she got so drunk she could not walk or even stand without holding to something. Saw her fall out of a high bed several times on the floor; she is much bruised. She at length became quite sick cast up her accounts and got better, today looks mean, mortified and has scolded but little. God knows if [I] had such a wife I would leave her and be an exile or hermit of the mountains all my days.[37]

In early November, having laid the groundwork for the ministry in Nacogdoches and San Augustine, Fowler left Denton behind to minister to the two towns, alternating between the two, just thirty-five miles apart along El Camino Real. Fowler then continued his circuit through Texas arriving at Washington-on-the-Brazos on November 12th. There he met his colleague, Robert Alexander, where together they held a two-day camp meeting.[38] Continuing, Fowler went south to Houston, which he described:

Here I find much vice, gaming, drunkenness and profanity the commonest. The town is ten months old and has 800 inhabitants: also many stores, and any number of *doggeries*.[39]

The state of religion was such that Fowler encountered some prejudice against ministers. As it was described, "… Texas had perhaps more than its share of imposters, or would-be ministers whose character did not comport with their pretensions."[40] This became such a problem that a group of Protestant ministers in Houston formed a "Committee of Vigilance" to develop a system of accreditation to help weed out the charlatans.[41]

In spite of his disdain for many of the leaders of Texas, as a senior member of the Methodist Mission to Texas,[42] Fowler was made the Chaplain of the Texas Senate.[43] The position did not require much action on his part, but in the Spring of 1838, during the second session of the Senate, he was invited to accompany some of the state's leaders on a tour to Galveston by boat. He wrote with barely disguised disgust of the outing in a private letter:

So soon as I recovered from my serious illness I took a trip to Galveston Island with the President [Houston] and the members of Congress, and saw great men in high life. If what I saw and heard were a fair representation, may God keep me from such scenes in future. On our return on Sunday afternoon, about one-half on board got wildly drunk and stripped themselves to their linen and pantaloons. Their Bacchanalian revels and blood-curdling profanity made the pleasure boat a floating hell. The excursion to me was one of pain and not pleasure. I relapsed from this trip and was brought near to the valley of death.[44]

Though Littleton Fowler was only four years older than Denton, they had the relationship of a mentor and apprentice, with Denton continuing to report to Fowler his successes or failures after their close association ended. Though few of Fowler's own letters remain, and none to Denton, we know that he continued to be apprised of Denton's travails through the letters of Fowler's brothers and Denton's letters to Fowler. As Fowler went off to sow the seeds of Methodism in Texas, planting churches wherever he went, Denton stayed behind to tend the garden.

As his junior, Denton held Fowler in high esteem and expressed his shock just a few days after they parted when he heard a rumor that Fowler had been speculating in land:

Nov. 15, 1837
San Augustine
On yesterday I received the intelligence that Bro. Alexander had commenced to speculate in land and that he was purchasing rapidly and more my Brother that you had bought 2,000 acres as you went out west. Now my dear beloved Brother, if this is true I wish you to let me know it for if you have purchased half a league that together with the land you got from your Brother and your headright and your town purchase I think will go some distance towards land speculation. Now my brother as soon as I heard this I went immediately and gave up my share in Aurora ... with a firm resolve to leave texas without having entered into any plan of speculation. You know something of my nature and therefore will condescend so far as to excuse the plainness of my speech a subject that so nearly concerns both you and me. Brother Fowler the man is not within the dominion of the almighty that I love as well as yourself, and yet I would not hesitate to forfeit your friendship forever before I would remain in the mission if what I deem next to impossible should take place. I mean that you and Bro. Alexander should commence speculation. Write me my dear Bro. by the first opportunity and let me know of it is false as hell and that you are yet my best brother. Pardon me

> Bro. fowler, the information stung my feelings almost to madness and the oath of the best man in the community should not convince me of its truth unless you yourself have told me it is true.[45]

Because one could easily interpret the entire early history of Texas as one vast real estate deal, it is surprising to read this idealistic, almost naive letter in which the recently reinstated junior minister chastised his church superior. Although a circuit-riding frontier preacher took no literal vow of poverty, there were some expectations that one would not use a ministerial mission as an opportunity for investing. It took both nerve and a sense of righteousness to address Fowler thus. Denton came from a background of the lowly circuit-riding preacher, where poverty was the norm and almost a symbol of piety, whereas the more sophisticated Fowler, had been a financial agent for a religious institution and had a different perspective of money. Denton later apologized, but the notion of his land speculation seems to have been reinforced when a month later Fowler received a letter from Bishop Robert Paine reminding him that, "[y]our one and only business [in Texas] is to save souls."[46]

In fact, Denton was correct about Fowler's real estate acquisitions. In just a few years he had amassed an impressive portfolio of land in at least five East Texas counties as well as numerous town lots. Just in the Nacogdoches-San Augustine area he owned more than 12,500 acres of land.[47] Denton's opinion of Fowler's land acquisitions would soon become a moot point in light of his own business dealings and land acquisitions in the new republic.

While Denton was laboring away as a local preacher in Nacogdoches and San Augustine, on November 1, 1837, he was formally appointed to the Arkansas Conference of the Methodist Church and with E. B. Duncan, was assigned to the Sulphur Forks Circuit.[48] Because news traveled slowly, and because of his work in Texas, this appointment did not immediately affect Denton who remained temporarily at his post. Six weeks later Superintendent of the Texas Mission, Rev. Martin Ruter, wrote of him in a letter to Littleton Fowler, implying that Denton had already vacated the mission and returned to Arkansas.

Brother Fowler,
… [If] brother Denton comes back, either as a local preacher, not by
appointment of Bishop Andrew, it may be expedient for him to labor in
the vicinity of San Augustine and Nacogdoches, if he can be supported
by means of what he receives where he labors, [and] if what we can do
for him from other sources.[49]

It seems Denton's service in San Augustine and Nacogdoches was
deemed useful, but not essential. Rev. Martin Ruter was willing to keep
Denton on, but the funding for his position was not assured. The choice
between this uncertain role with Fowler, and a solid position, with salary,
in the Sulphur Forks Circuit, was an easy one. The Sulphur Forks position
would allow Denton to be able to be with, and better support, his family,
which was the reason he had temporarily retired from the ministry three
years before. In spite of the great honor of being associated with Littleton
Fowler in Texas, his family obligations prevailed. Denton returned home
to Hempstead County, Arkansas, in December and reported that his family
was in good health, and his "wife in better health than I have seen her
for years."[50]

In a letter to Littleton Fowler, Denton sought to apologize for his earlier
accusations of financial impiety concerning land speculation. Referring to a
letter from Fowler:

Your mildness and patience have been a check on my wayward
impetuosity. I owe you the gratitude of my heart my Bro for your
Greate Kindness to me and I hope that so far as a lively sense of
Gratitude to God for Granting me such a friend and to you for bearing
with my follies can go[,] you will not be quit unpaid.[51]

Reporting on the state of religion in Hempstead, Denton informed
Fowler it had "waxed cold, and others have backslidden, & so our Divine
Master has suffered in the house of his friends."[52]

Chapter 6

Settling in
the Sulphur Forks

The Sulphur Forks region of Texas played an important early role in the history of the state. Physically, it is an area between the Red and Sulphur Rivers in northeast Texas, of roughly thirty-five hundred square miles, comprising the area of present-day Lamar, Red River, and Bowie Counties in Texas and present-day Miller County, Arkansas. Since the time Europeans first came to the region in the 1500s, it had been part of a poorly defined frontier between the colonial empires of France and Spain, and after 1836, between the nations of Texas and the United States.

Its importance in Texas is based on its position as the gateway for immigrants from Kentucky, Tennessee, Arkansas, and points east. Countless numbers of settlers passed through the area on their journey to Texas and as their first impression, the Sulphur Forks did not disappoint. The naturalist Josiah Gregg observed:

> So I met with no country which I deemed fit to live on till I reached the vicinity of Sulphur Forks prairie. The prairie is on the dividing ridge between the waters of red River and Sulphur Fork … Here I found a prairie of rich lands—generally a black mellow soil, well adapted to cotton and corn.[1]

Although there had been some French and Anglo settlers along the Red River,[2] the Sulphur Forks area was an almost uninhabited land, save for some anonymous backwoodsmen who came looking for beaver or buffalo, and the occasional nomadic Indian. The Caddos, who had traditionally inhabited this region, had been decimated by contact with Europeans and their diseases since they had first arrived in 1542.[3] Most of the remaining members had moved farther south and east fleeing the Osage tribes after a massacre of the Caddo village in 1795.[4] The first known Anglo-Americans to live in the area south of the Red River around Pecan Point were a band of misfits, stock rustlers, and slave stealers,[5] observed there in 1811.[6] As Dr. John Sibley, the United States Agent at Natchitoches, described the early inhabitants:

> There is a party of Bad Men, fugitives from the different jails in the United States, who have settled themselves at the Pecan Point on Red River about 500 miles by water from this Town … These people are Enemies to all law and good order, and most of them would have been hanged if they had remained in the United States.[7]

In those early years before any boundaries were established, this wild and uninhabited land between two empires was particularly well suited for hiding out.

The first Anglo-American settlements on the Texas side of the river were at Jonesboro, about twenty-five miles northwest of present-day Clarksville, and the area centered around Pecan Point. Settlers were reported there as early as 1815, when a trading post was set up by George and Alex Wetmore.[8] Most early settlers clung to the river bottoms because the rivers provided their link to civilization, ample water, and supplies. As more settlers moved to the territory, they began to move upland to the rich prairies between the Red and Sulphur River watersheds. This higher, dryer land was healthier, and the isolated patches of prairie offered soil that was more fertile than that found in the sandy river bottoms. As George Smythe observed in 1833:

> … A few miles south of this place [Pecan Point] is the beginning of a prarie country, or rather a country of prarie and timber interspersed in about equal proportions. The country is partly situated on what is called

the Sulphur Fork of Red River. The tributaries of this stream which empty on its northern side take their rise principally in the ilevated [*sic*] plain within a few miles of Red River, whence they pursue a southern course. The praries are situated between these creeks. The creeks are skirted by narrow bottoms, with all the growthes common to bottom land, oak, Post oak land, generally of very little value except for the Timber, & then comes the Praries, which are the most elevated part of the country, with black, rich soil well adapted to the cultivation of corn or cotton and producing fine pastures. The praries are of various sizes, from 1,000 to 100,000 acres. Nor is the country confined to the limits here designated, these remarks appertaining more properly to that part which I have seen—its boundaries are much more extensive— it embraces the head waters of the Sulphur Fork which has its source 80 miles above the point which I have seen ... I do not hesitate to give my opinion that this is the best portion of Texas which I have seen ... There are settled on the west side of Red River and above the raft between 200 and 300 families—scattered along the river for 200 miles (by land) but in the portion of the country which I just been describing there are not three families living.[9]

In February 1838, Denton embarked to his new posting on the Sulphur Forks Circuit. After visiting the Methodist Mission near Ft. Towson, in the Choctaw Nation, Denton crossed the Red River, at the Kiamichi River crossing, and entered Texas around February 17, 1838.[10] Writing from Clarksville on February 18, 1838, he expressed concern that his colleague, E.B. Duncan, who lay sick in Tennessee, would be unable to help preach at the first quarterly meeting of his new mission.[11] The fact that it was very cold further diminished the prospects for an auspicious event, "Therefore our meeting will rather drag."[12]

Denton was able to raise "four or five hundred dollars,"[13] to start building a church in Clarksville, but his second attempt at holding a quarterly meeting in April was thwarted when "a short time before the time appointed for the meeting Indian depredations so demoralized the country that the meeting was not held."[14] He reported having made three rounds on his circuit, but that it was all very unorganized in the land of the Sulphur Forks.

There was great anxiety amongst the settlers because of lingering questions about the border survey between the United States and Texas.

As Denton described it to Fowler, "People are much confused here about land, land is the cry."[15] The border between the former Texas and Louisiana had never been permanently established and became a source of conflict between these two nations. Previously, when Louisiana was under French control and Texas was a Spanish possession, there had been great tension along this border. This tension was relieved after 1762, when Louisiana was ceded to Spain; it remained a Spanish possession until 1800, when it was retroceded back to France at the insistence of Napoleon.[16] At that point, both France and Spain had bigger things on their minds than this obscure border at the ends of their empires, but in 1803, the United States purchased Louisiana and the French were removed from the equation. In 1821, after the Mexican Revolution freed Mexico from Spain, the conflict resumed as the new nations had inherited an old problem.

When Texas became a republic in 1836 the issue resurfaced, and in 1838 the United States and Texas held a Joint Boundary Convention to determine the exact limits of their respective borders.[17] Initially this was just concerned with the Texas–Louisiana border, but there also were discrepancies in the area south of the Red River claimed by both Arkansas and Texas. "Not only did Red River County, Texas and [old] Miller County, Arkansas overlap, they virtually claimed the same territory. Even their county seats, Clarksville and Jonesborough, were a mere 25 miles apart."[18] Reflecting the uncertainties of the provenance of the territory, one contract for the purchase of land included the following provision concerning where the deed was to be filed: "to be secured from the Mexican government, or Arkansas Territory as the case may be."[19] This was not finally resolved until 1841, generally in favor of Texas.

There were a variety of obstacles presented to Denton in his new mission on the Sulphur Forks Circuit. The anxiety of the residents because of Indian troubles, poor groundwork by previous missionaries, and the absence of his sick colleague which left Denton alone to perform the work of two, this was not much of an improvement over his previous labors as a circuit rider. Once again, he found himself poor, and away from his family, his job no longer a joy. In that spirit, "Denton closed his labors in this mission with but little success,"[20] to show for his efforts.

Denton had left his wife Mary and five children behind in Hempstead, Arkansas, while he traveled the Sulphur Fork Circuit. His salary, even at the higher rate, was not enough to allow them to follow him to Clarksville. His ministry was not as successful as he might have wished, and all this must have weighed heavily on his mind as he contemplated his bleak situation. In his letter of March 29, 1838, to Littleton Fowler, Denton hints at his plans:

> Since I saw you I have been strongly tempted to read and practice law. I have bought a small library of law books and have devoted a portion of my [text missing] of them, now the difficulty [text missing] practice can be pursued [text missing] with the spirit of the gospel. I have not yet received any intelligence from the north and if it should arrive I can scarcely tell how to act. However I will try to act for the Glory of God and the Good of man."[21]

By "intelligence from the north," he is referring to his wait for a response from the Methodist conference to his request to retire from the traveling circuit and "locate;" "he would not withdraw from the ministry, but would withdraw from the traveling connection. This is the official relation he ever afterwards sustained to the Methodist Episcopal Church until his death."[22] The tone of his letter to Fowler is of one seeking the approval of a superior, almost obsequious, talking up meager achievements, and yet not quite ready to admit that he is thinking of quitting the ministry for fear it would displease his mentor.

It is worthy of note that just six days before Denton wrote his letter of apology to Littleton Fowler for criticizing his land purchases, Denton himself applied for and received a Second-Class Headright Grant for 640 acres to be located in Red River County.[23] These Texas land grants came in several classes. The First-Class Headright was for Texans who had been there on the day of the Declaration of Independence, March 2, 1836, and who had not fled during the war. These grantees, if married, were entitled to a League and a Labor[24] of land (4,605 acres); if single they were entitled to a 1/3 of a League (1,476 acres). The Second-Class Headright entitled men with families who had been in Texas before October 1,

1837, to 1,280 acres; single men received 640 acres. Third-Class Head-rights were reserved for those immigrants who had come to Texas after October 1, 1837, and before January 1, 1840. These Third-Class grantees were entitled to 640 acres if accompanied by their family, and 320 acres for single men.[25]

Having arrived in Texas on September 30, 1837, just one day before the demarcation between Second- and Third-Class Headrights, Denton received 640 acres rather than 320 acres he would have otherwise been entitled to had he arrived a day later. Although Denton was married, the certificate makes it clear that he arrived, "as a man here without his family," and not necessarily an unmarried man; the marriage provision required the wife to be present. This distinction will play a role in a lawsuit that took place long after his death.

The next year Denton reported that the work of the church in the Sulphur Forks had fared no better under Jacob Whitesides, who had been appointed to replace him in 1838.[26] Denton continued to be discouraged by the state of the church work in the area. As Denton told Fowler:

> The church is far from prosperous in this place at present father whitesides is our circuit preacher for the present confer[ence] year and he has already made a whole round of disappointments ... [and] is anything else than popular or usefull so far as I can see however popularity is not essential to piety or usefulness. But sometimes we presume to guess about the efficiency of ministers or those who profess to be ministers or teachers of the people.[27]

Apparently, Jacob Whitesides lacked the oratorical skills or personal dynamism required of a popular frontier preacher. Or as likely Whitesides was just old, having been admitted to the ministry in Tennessee in 1815, and spent twenty-three hard years on the Methodist circuit. In 1843, just five years after Denton wrote of him, Jacob Whitesides would be listed in the Methodist Conference notes as "Superannuated or Worn Out" and qualify for the meager Methodist pension.[28]

By 1839, Denton was no longer listed in the *Annals of Methodism* as an active member of the clergy, but was still involved with the church, as can be seen in his correspondence with Fowler. Fowler was encouraging

Denton to continue with the ministry, but Denton's financial and family woes had taken their toll on his religious zeal:

> My beloved Bro you have kindly given me your opinion with respect to my future course for which I am truly grateful though it is utterly out of my power to be governed by opinions which I need not tel now you I value as far superior to my own. circumstances prevent me from doing as I would consequently must I do as I can. At present you have never yet my Bro been compelled to struggle with the cheerless gloom of poverty and misfortune burdened with a large & helpless family. But I will not complain for my heavenly father has been exuberant in goodness to me ...[29]

As Denton pointed out, it was easy for Fowler to ask that Denton remain in the ministry under conditions of poverty, when Fowler had no wife or children, and enjoyed the support of a prosperous and well-educated family who were in constant contact with one another. Whereas Denton, a family man with five children, a self-educated backwoodsman with few resources, and no family support network, must submit to the practical realities of his station in life.

Many of the early settlers in Northeast Texas had previously lived in South West Arkansas and for all intents and purposes the area functioned as one region, inhabited by one people, and divided only by an invisible line. Those on the Arkansas side had witnessed both the steady stream of immigrants moving through Hempstead County into the new republic, as well as their own neighbors and family members who followed the same call. "Texas Fever" was in the air and that, with the lure of cheap land, must have been a powerful motivator to any Arkansan dreaming of a life above mere subsistence level. Denton, having been exposed to the possibilities for opportunity in Texas, was just as susceptible to the temptations of "Texas Fever" as the next man. With a career change in mind, he returned to Arkansas for his family, and became another of those who had "gone to Texas."

His biographer, Reverend William H. Allen, eager to cast him in the pantheon of Texas heroes, wrote it thus: "He was in love with Texas before he came."[30] It is important to remember that his immigration was not by some great trek or arduous journey, as Texas was just a few miles from where he had lived in Arkansas. Although still nominally associated with the church, by 1838, Denton had started a new life, in which he would aspire to be more than a poverty-stricken, backwoods, circuit-riding preacher. Moving to Texas, where he had already filed for a headright and had plans to own more, he became a true Texan, where, as he said it himself, "land is the cry."[31]

Chapter 7

Clarksville:
The Gateway to Texas

I n 1818, when James Clark ventured onto the Sulphur Fork Prairie and came upon land that would one day become Clarksville, he found Henry Stout, already there camping by a spring.[1] Stout was one of the great characters of Texas about whom people loved to tell tales, but probably not as much as he liked to tell them himself. Henry Stout, whose name would be forever linked with John B. Denton, was an early settler of the region. Born in Tennessee (1799), he walked from Illinois to Hempstead County, Arkansas, when he was eighteen.[2] There he married Sarah Talbot, and soon had a son, Selen, himself a legendary Texas character.[3] In 1819, Stout and his family immigrated to the Pecan Point vicinity on the Oklahoma side of the Red River.

In just one of his famous exploits, he was out hunting alone in the Sulphur Forks, when an Indian crept up on him and shot him in the hip with an arrow. Stout lay low in the grass before dispatching his attacker and then assessed his situation. The arrow was in too deep to pull out, and he was on foot, one-hundred miles from the nearest settlement at Fort Towson, in Indian Territory. He broke off the arrow at the surface of his skin, and after four days of walking, made it back to the fort, where an amazed surgeon tended his wounds. For this and a dozen other reasons he became known as a man "that could not be killed."[4]

In addition to his own adventures on the frontier, Henry Stout had either been witness to, or participated in, many of the big events in the state's history. In 1819 he had been a member of the ill-fated Long Expedition to wrest control of Texas from Spain; he took Davy Crockett on his first buffalo hunt; he was a soldier in the Texas Revolution; he served as a Captain in the Texas Rangers; he was with John B. Denton when he was killed at Village Creek; and he was a Confederate officer in the Civil War. While these events were unfolding, he also served as a sheriff and a state representative, and of importance to this story, he reportedly found and dug up the bones of John B. Denton on Fossil Creek, in Tarrant County, in 1879. Of an extraordinary constitution, "Uncle Henry" Stout died at ninety-three, outliving most of his contemporaries.[5]

In 1823, Stout moved with his family to Texas and on that basis later claimed his headright of 4,400 acres, on land which included the spring on Delaware Creek where he had encountered James Clark in 1818. A claim to land ownership in this area at the time was a precarious thing. In an effort to solidify his claim, Stout registered as a member of Wavell's Colony in 1826.[6] Wavell's Colony was located along the Red River between the Sulphur Fork to the Kiamichi River, an area comprising roughly Red River and Bowie Counties in Texas, and Miller County, Arkansas. Although Wavell's Colony was not a success and was nullified by the Texas Revolution, this early claim would help Stout establish his headright claim of a "league and a labor" of land under the Texas Republic.

James Clark, like Henry Stout, John B. Denton, and countless other settlers of Northeast Texas, followed the same route from the upper South, down through Hempstead, Arkansas, and then on into Texas. In 1824, Clark was manufacturing salt at Salt Licks on the Little River in Arkansas, just north of the Red River. Here, Henry Stout briefly worked for him, boiling water from the salt spring to produce the badly needed salt for settlers.[7] In 1830, Clark with his family moved across the Red River into Texas at Jonesboro, where he engaged in trade and local politics. By 1833, he and his family moved once again, twenty-five miles south of Jonesboro, to the spring on Delaware Creek where he had encountered Henry Stout in 1818. This new location was less prone to malaria and unlikely to flood; there he founded the town of Clarksville, on land purchased from Stout by offering free building sites to settlers.[8]

The community was designated the seat of the Red River Precinct in 1835,[9] and in December of 1837,[10] when the Congress of Texas created Red River County, it also chartered Clarksville as an official "town."[11] Although the tiny village of Clarksville was certainly impressive to the residents of the area, one slightly grumpy English traveler observed;

> Texas, where nothing more is required of a man, woman, or child, than to possess a piece of land, and with a few pegs to sectionize a portion of it, and then tack "ville" or "burgh" to the end of their name, and the city, town, or hamlet is complete, and forthwith placed on the list of flourishing and populous localities.[12]

When John B. Denton first came to Clarksville in October of 1837, he came as an aid to Littleton Fowler and they spent a week there preaching. He returned in February 1838, on his own as the Methodist minister for the Sulphur Forks Circuit, but still, it was a temporary association as his wife and family remained behind in Hempstead, Arkansas. Though today Clarksville is a sleepy little East Texas town with a population of just over three thousand, when Denton first saw it, it seemed inevitable that it would grow and prosper. "From the late 1830s, until the War Between the States, Clarksville was the most important trading center in Northeast Texas."[13]

One hindrance to settlement along the Red River was the presence of the Great Raft, a centuries-old, one-hundred-mile-long logjam that prevented easy commercial transport by boat. Only with great difficulty, could intrepid boatmen wind their way through this maze of tangled logs.[14] In 1835, after Capt. Henry M. Shreve had removed a portion of the hundred-mile logjam,[15] a few "steamboats brought goods from New Orleans by way of the Red River and delivered them to sites such as Rowlands Landing, which is 15 miles north of Clarksville."[16] The early settlers of Jonesboro and Pecan Point were moving to higher ground and the open prairies on the Sulphur Forks. For immigrants coming from Arkansas and the upper south, Clarksville would become a convenient first stop after entering Texas.

Concerned about his financial future, Clarksville's excellent position and prospects for growth must have made it an attractive prospect as a place for Denton to make his mark. By March of 1838, Denton had moved to Clarksville, announced his intention to study the law, secured a headright of 640 acres,[17] and had withdrawn from the Methodist circuit, becoming an inactive minister. By removing himself from the traveling ministry it was possible for him to bring his family with him to Texas and live under one roof while he embarked on his new career.

To become a lawyer in the 1830s, one had only to read and study, usually as an apprentice to a more experienced lawyer. Though there were colleges that taught law, the majority of lawyers, especially on the frontier, did not have the benefit of a college education. The trend in the nineteenth century was towards higher standards and a number of states had bar associations dedicated to this end, but this was not really applicable on the frontier where lawyers were needed and thus standards lax. Abraham Lincoln, himself a self-educated frontier lawyer, said "[T]he cheapest, quickest and best way" [to become a lawyer was to] read Blackstone's Commentaries ..., get a license, and go to the practice and still keep reading."[18] In his letter to Littleton Fowler, John B. Denton mentioned that he had already purchased a small law library, and we know that he apprenticed under attorney John B. Craig.

John B. Craig was born in North Carolina in 1796, and at the age of sixteen had enlisted and fought in the War of 1812, under Andrew Jackson at the Battle of New Orleans. He returned to North Carolina, studied law, and in 1820 was licensed to practice in Raleigh. By 1823, Craig had moved to Huntsville, Alabama, where he practiced law and after converting to Methodism, was licensed to preach.[19] In both the practice of law and the profession of the ministry, the powers of oratory were well appreciated and skillful practitioners were often rewarded with success. It was common on the frontier to see learned men use their skills to serve both

God and Mammon. Of his oratorical and intellectual skills, a contemporary observed:

> Brother Craig was a man of no ordinary mould of mind. Strong in intellect, firm of purpose, resolute and determined, he met opposition and overcame difficulties with manly courage. His mind was well stored with useful knowledge of various kinds: he was a man of reading, had studied theology closely and well understood the doctrines of our Church, and preached it with no mean ability. In fact, in the pulpit he was able and eloquent.[20]

Joining in the steady stream of immigrants, on September 22, 1837,[21] John B. Craig arrived in Texas and shortly thereafter hung out his shingle in Clarksville where he hoped to make his fortune. John B. Denton and Littleton Fowler arrived in Texas just eight days later on September 30, and by October 2 or 3, had also come to Clarksville to preach. With Denton and Craig both Methodist ministers and the population of Clarksville yet small, it is a virtual certainty that they met at that time.

Although Denton apprenticed under John B. Craig from 1838 to 1840, Craig was part of the firm of Craig and Fowler, with Andrew Jackson Fowler as his partner.[22] A. J. (Jack) Fowler, the youngest brother of Littleton Fowler, had graduated from La Grange College, Alabama, in 1836,[23] and studied law in the office of brother Wiley P. Fowler in Kentucky before moving to Clarksville in 1837 to join his brothers John H. and Bradford C. Fowler in Northeast Texas. Jack Fowler and John B. Craig had both traveled in Methodist circles, and lived in northern Alabama before coming to Texas, so it is possible that their paths may have crossed before settling in Clarksville. They were both competent, well qualified attorneys and their partnership continued after Fowler was appointed Chief Justice of Red River County in 1839.[24] Fowler was college educated, from a well-respected Red River pioneer family, and had as "good a law library, perhaps, as any in the Republic;"[25] while Craig had seventeen years of legal experience to his credit. The rough-hewn, self-educated Denton, had signed on as an apprentice, the junior member of the firm.

Much of the legal work from the office of Craig and Fowler concerned real estate: the larger land grants were being continuously divided and subdivided as more and more settlers poured into the region. The headright system of land grants allowed a certain amount of unclaimed public land, virtually free for any settler who arrived in Texas, based on a sliding scale of when they arrived and whether or not they were married. But it was not as simple as just coming to Texas, picking out a platted tract, and settling down. The headright grants in the period between 1836 and 1842 gave each grantee a right to own land; but it was up to them to find an unclaimed tract, have it surveyed, and register the purchase. Not an easy task for the typical settler arriving in Texas during this period, and this became the primary legal specialty of the law practice of Craig and Fowler. Denton, being the apprentice, was required to do the field work and besides his youth, his years as a circuit-riding preacher made him accustomed to the conditions:

> Mr. John B. Craig, being somewhat old, did the home office work. Denton was largely in the saddle, often traveling long distances, and did the work over the large field of their practice.[26]

A typical contract for each grant holder would bind Denton and Craig "to locate the best and most valuable lands possible to be got," arrange to have it surveyed, and the plat registered, with the grant holder paying for the surveying and registration fees. Craig and Denton would post a $5,000 bond to insure the performance of their duties, and receive one quarter of the land for their trouble when the grant holder received the clear title to the land.[27]

During the Republic of Texas period, the government issued grants for almost thirty-seven million acres of land,[28] which besides keeping attorneys busy, indicates how desirable Texas had become for immigrants from the United States. Not all of these immigrants came to settle farms and ranches but their headright claims, whether located or not, could be a form of legal tender and there was a large secondary market for unregistered headright claims.

> Vast acreages in Texas were bought and sold sight unseen, and the spirit that kept the settlers on the road had them shifting about and trading places once they had arrived. Land changed hands almost as often as

horses, and until a man had invested something himself in his property, his claim was as tenuous as the hope of good weather.[29]

The going rate for these at the time was around $1.00 per acre. In theory a person who had come early was the head of a household and who had served in the army before October 1, 1837 was entitled to almost six thousand acres of land; for a person of modest means—a fortune. Early immigrants could come to Texas, claim their headright and instantly have a net worth much greater than would have been possible anywhere else.

Like just about every other able-bodied Texan of the day, Denton (despite his earlier misgivings), Craig, and all of the Fowler brothers were occupied with the acquisition of land, for this would lead to wealth. Bradford Fowler, writing to his brother Littleton reported,

> I see independence of Texas has been recognized by the U. S. and only awaits the signature of the President. This being the case, my lands in Tex. will be worth a double fortune; I have claims for the half of twelve leagues, exclusive of my own head-right.[30]

After the Texas Revolution, Texas had just $55.68 in its treasury and its only asset was land.[31] With independence from Mexico, an enormous amount of public land became available and for the cash-strapped new republic, this was an important source of revenue. Texas offered land as payment for military service in the revolution, and later paid in land scrip for service in the Ranging Companies in the Indian Wars. Land became a sort of currency itself for the cash-strapped citizens, with one settler reporting that he had traded land for a horse—which was stolen a week later. State debt was settled by offering Land Scrip at the rate of $2.00 per acre of land.[32] If vacant land was considered to be wilderness, there was a public interest in encouraging settlers to purchase, inhabit, and become tax-paying citizens in the new republic. The possibility of owning large tracts of land was a very attractive lure for Americans and the trickle of immigrants grew into a torrent as the population grew from about 38,000 inhabitants in 1836, to around 142,000 in 1847.[33] Overnight, citizens from across the United States would pack up and disappear, leaving only the letters "GTT" (Gone to Texas), chalked on their doors.

For those seeking to regain lost fortunes, like Sam Houston or Davy Crockett, or lost reputations like Robert Potter, the opening up of the Texas frontier could not have come at a better time. Between 1835 and 1841, Texas sold 1.3 million acres of land, and despite notions of freedom or liberty, real estate was the lure that drew the flood of immigrants to the republic.

Chapter 8

Conflict with Native Americans

Historically, the Kadohadacho, or the Caddo confederacy, was centered around the great bend in the Red River. Their villages had been mostly vacated in the late 18th century because of disease and frequent attacks by the more aggressive Osage tribe. Many of these Caddo had settled in Louisiana.[1] Thus the Sulphur Forks area was sparsely occupied when Europeans arrived and relations with the scattered bands of Native Americans, with whom they often traded goods, were peaceful. In the early days French traders came to do business with the Native Americans, and later, the scattered subsistence farmer posed no threat to the few indigenous inhabitants in the area.

After 1835, when the Caddo signed a treaty with the United States, selling their Louisiana tribal lands for $80,000 near Shreveport, they agreed to relocate back into their sparsely settled old traditional homeland in Mexican East Texas.[2] Their timing was poor, because having sold their land, they had agreed to leave Louisiana, but with Texas independence in 1836, and a resulting flood of new immigrants coming from the United States, they were being squeezed by forces greater than they could have predicted. As Anglo immigrants moved into East Texas and began laying claim to much of the

49

land, pressure was put upon the Native American tribes who were gradually being pushed west under threat from invading Anglo settlers.

Similar pressures were affecting the Cherokee. A small band of Cherokees moved to Texas around 1807, settling on the Red River, but they too were forced to move on into uninhabited areas near Nacogdoches, now in Rusk County.[3] As Anglo immigration increased, rising incidents of theft, misunderstandings over trade, and the general mistreatment of the Indians resulted in a cycle of murders and retaliation, with each side believing themselves to be the victims. Tensions were increasing between the Native Americans and the Anglo settlers. By the mid-1830s when Sam Houston became the first president of the Republic, he sought to find a solution. Houston had lived for years with the Cherokees before coming to Texas and was especially sensitive to their plight.

> [Houston] believed that the Republic should demonstrate friend-ship with all Indians by negotiating treaties that established trade and promised evenhanded justice. In November 1836 he sent the Comanches, Wichitas, and Caddos an invitation to a council in North Texas, but his agents did not establish contact with these groups. Off-and-on hostilities continued with them in 1837 and 1838. In an attempt to live up to his word and win over the Cherokees, Houston submitted the treaty that he had negotiated with them during the revolution to the Texas Senate in December 1836, calling it "just and equitable." The senate, however, delayed for nearly a year and then, at the urging of Vice President Lamar, rejected it on the false grounds that the Cherokees had aided Mexico ...[4]

Although Houston was sympathetic to the Cherokee, his Vice President Mirabeau B. Lamar, and General Thomas J. Rusk had a hardline policy and had each advocated extermination as a solution to the Indian problem. Houston's position was undermined in 1836, when incriminating papers were found implicating the Cherokee as conspirators in the short-lived Cordova Rebellion,[5] so named for Vincente Cordova, a wealthy resident of Nacogdoches, who was still loyal to Mexico. In August of 1838, Cordova was discovered hiding in the woods along with one hundred armed Mexicans and plans to retake Texas for Mexico. The small force was to be augmented by a force of three-hundred Cherokee who had been promised titles to their land if they were successful. Cordova and his Mexican agents did the Native Americans in Texas all manner of harm, by either enticing them to help them fight the Texans, or merely raising the specter that this might happen. The fear of this coalition added fuel to the anti-Indian sentiments shared by many Texans, and became further justification for driving the tribes from the Republic.

Under the constitution, Houston was only permitted to serve as President for two years and Mirabeau B. Lamar was elected his successor, taking office on December 10, 1838. There was no love lost between Houston and Lamar and however much pleasure Lamar had anticipated from his inauguration, Sam Houston ruined it for him with some elements of mockery. Houston came dressed as George Washington, with knee breeches, silk coat, silver buckles, and a powered wig, and proceeded to defend his administration in his "Farewell Address:"[6]

> that continued for three hours. Indulging in every oratorical trick imaginable, he regaled the audience with a wildly exaggerated account of how successful his presidency had been. When he finally turned the stage over to Lamar, who had spent much time preparing what he considered a literary masterpiece among inaugural addresses, the new president was so upset that he could not deliver his speech. Instead, his private secretary read it. Lamar's only consolation was that he had the presidency.[7]

"Houston loved Indians, if he loved anything; Lamar hated them, but his hatred for Indians was probably secondary to his hatred for Houston";[8] he wasted no time in reversing every one of Houston's frontier policies, and implementing new harsher ones. In a letter to Congress just ten days after he took office, he specifically belittled the policies of Sam Houston, and elaborated on his own opinions of the Cherokee and his intentions as President:

> How long shall this cruel humanity, this murderous sensibility for the sanguinary savage, be practiced in defiance of its tested impolicy? Until other oceans of blood, the blood of our wives and children shall glut their voracious appetite? I would answer no. If wild cannibals of the woods will not desist from their massacres, if they all continue to war upon us with the ferocity of tigers and hienas, it is time we should retaliate their warfare. Not in the murder of their women and children,

but in the prosecution of an exterminating war upon their warriors; which will admit of no compromise and have no termination except in their *total extinction or total expulsion.*[9]

While Houston had advanced a policy based on "Everything will be gained by peace, but nothing will be gained by war,"[10] Lamar advocated ethnic cleansing. One of the first things he did when taking office was to was push for legislation, "creating a new regular army, which was passed on December 21, 1838. This 'Frontier Regiment' was charged with the duty of protecting "the northern and western frontier' of Texas."[11] This frontier regiment was to have 840 men, divided into fifteen companies, and was to form a protective line from the Red River to the Rio Grande, but was never fully implemented due to financial constraints.[12]

Chapter 9

The Texas Rangers: Defending the Frontier

I n the first years of the Republic the frontier had been protected by Ranging companies of volunteer soldiers or Rangers. These Rangers were assembled for short periods whenever a threat appeared, but they were not funded, and by April 1838, had been largely disbanded. General Thomas J. Rusk then formed a reconstituted Texas Militia which patrolled the frontier. These were small bands of mounted volunteers and although they could fight and skirmish, they were not able to eliminate attacks on the Texan settlers. The militias pursued the various tribes, but without much backing from the Texas national government, which because of philosophical differences between Sam Houston and the Congress, was without a consistent Indian policy. It is sometimes difficult to distinguish between the Texas "militia" and the "rangers." The militia, constituting a standing army, were often less effective than the more *ad hoc* rangers, but the militia was also too expensive for the cash-strapped republic, which made the economical short-term Rangers the only option for Texas.

Of particular interest in northeast Texas were the aforementioned Caddo[1] who were being forced out of their Louisiana and East Texas lands and pushed towards the Three-Forks area of the Trinity River.[2] The Standing

Committee on Indian Affairs for the Republic of Texas reported that the Caddos had united with the "hostile" tribes on the prairies, and "were thought to be the greatest rogues and most treacherous Indians on our frontier."[3] Some of the Caddo, with remnants of other tribes, were repopulating Texas and moving into the land around the forks of the Trinity River. Texans were becoming more and more agitated by frequent raids from Indian Territory to the north, as well as from tribes living in Louisiana, and did not trust the Caddoan tribes living in Texas.[4] These Indian villages were well known to the settlers and though they were considered hostile, some Anglo traders visited and did business with them with no apparent difficulty. Mr. Neal, an Indian trader, successfully traded with the Three Fork villages and brought back reports that there were about a thousand warriors in the area.[5] When the 4th Brigade of the Texas Militia was commissioned on September 6, 1838, part of its mission was to find and attack the Caddo village said to be in the Three-Forks region of the Trinity River. General John H. Dyer was in command of eighty soldiers who traveled from the Clarksville area to within two miles of the village, but for lack of supplies were not able to attack it.[6]

Four days after General Dyer wrote his report of the unsuccessful foray into the Three-Forks area,[7] Colonel Hugh McLeod wrote to his friend and current Vice-President, General Mirabeau B. Lamar, venting his frustrations about the poor state of the military on the frontier.[8] Like Lamar, he was against the soft approach of Sam Houston towards the Indians, which he thought made the Texans look weak in the eyes of the enemy. "The time has arrived for a general, prompt and vigorous campaign against the Indians ..." It was time to "exterminate the race," and he then outlined a plan devised by General Thomas J. Rusk for doing just that, at least for the troublesome tribes.[9] Rusk would order General Dyer to organize another militia from Red River County; Rusk would take an armed force from Nacogdoches and with one other force they would rendezvous near the Three Forks and attack the large Caddoan village thought to be there. This village was led by their Chief Tarshar, or the Wolf,[10] who repeatedly proclaimed their innocence and reluctance to either fight the Texans, or join the Mexicans in their plans for re-conquest. But the Texans lived in such fear of Indian depredations that they were not inclined to believe the Indians capable of innocence.

When General Dyer received his orders in Clarksville, he sent out an appeal for volunteers and John B. Denton was among those who answered the call. As a young man set on becoming an important member of the Clarksville community, and who, like his neighbors, lived in some fear of Indian attacks, the call to battle must have been irresistible. Not to be discounted were the social perks for participating in the militia. Rank and titles were easily earned, and for many of the more rural and isolated inhabitants of the area, being a member of an organization with a righteous purpose would have provided some welcome diversion among comrades in arms. Military historian Russell F. Weigley wrote, "volunteer [militia] companies were at least as much a social as a military phenomenon."[11]

Every vivid story of an Anglo family killed in some barbaric fashion, was told a thousand times and constantly in the minds of everyone who lived on the frontier. The frontier was rife with rumor and whether they deserved it or not the Caddos were blamed for at least three attacks of settlers in Northeast Texas between 1836 and 1838.[12] Thus it must have been exciting to be part of a four-hundred-man force of his good neighbors, who were self-reliant volunteers like himself, righteous avengers, heading off to battle. But just as important; it would have been embarrassing for the able-bodied frontiersman to stay behind.

Denton enlisted on November 18, 1838, enrolled in the ranks of Rusk's 4th Brigade of the Texas Militia. Not quite yet a lawyer, and still associated with the Methodist Church, he served as the Chaplain on the General's Staff, along with his law associate Andrew J. Fowler, who served as Judge Advocate.[13]

It was with much anticipation that Hugh McLeod wrote to Lamar of the impending military action. He had been the purveyor of many rumors and much fearmongering about imminent action by the Caddos, and he shared these frequently with the Vice President. On November 23, 1838, McLeod wrote that the Caddo are hiding in the "cane brake, [on the Louisiana side of Caddo Lake] and waiting attack, fully prepared for it."[14] If things go badly;

> this Country will be desolated ... it will be a bloody affair, as the numbers are about equal, & the Indians well armed and desperate. If I fall, please write my mother & send her the year's pay that is due me.[15]

In spite of McLeod's dire predictions, the Caddo were indeed hiding in the canebrakes because they were afraid of the Texans and had no intention of fighting.[16] Just a few years before, a U.S. report on the state of the Caddo at the Louisiana border paints a picture of a tribe that is anything but a threat to the Texans. Major B. Riley had found the Caddo to be "peaceably inclined," however "very much degraded, and addicted to the use of liquor, and if they had committed depredations on the inhabitants, or their property, it was caused by the use of too much whiskey :..."[17]

> They seemed to be "a poor, miserable people, incapable of the smallest exertion, either as it regards living, or any thing else except liquor." The Caddo chief, Tarshar, or the "Wolf", told Riley that they wanted to live in peace with the whites and did not want to go to war.[18]

The 4th Brigade, under the leadership of General John Dyer, left Clarksville on November 24 and marched west towards the Crosstimbers. December 5, they met up with Major General Thomas Rusk at the Clear Fork of the Trinity and Rusk took charge of what would become known as the Three-Forks Expedition.[19]

The Texans had been greatly frustrated by the fact that many Caddos lived on the American side of Soda Lake (Caddo Lake) in Louisiana, just out of their reach, and angry that some were moving into Texas. The Caddo were caught in a bind because, in a treaty signed with the United States, they had sold their land, one million acres for $80,000.00,[20] and were being forced out of the Shreveport area, in Louisiana territory, by the terms of this treaty. Part of the agreement was that they were to receive money and goods from the U.S. government.[21] These goods included arms, ammunition, and liquor provided by the U.S. Indian Agent, Charles Sewall, which incensed the Texans and added to their general fears of the Caddo. According to rumors circulated among Texans, Sewall reportedly said, "he did not care if they [the Caddo] murdered every woman & child in Texas, and that he would arm them and push them across the line."[22] Although this is highly unlikely, it represents the state of mind of the warrior Texans on the frontier.

Before meeting General Dyer in the Three Forks, the Texan Militia, under General Thomas Rusk, illegally pursued the Caddo into U.S. Territory at Shreveport. Local residents defended the Indians and Rusk left U.S. territory promptly, but President Martin Van Buren was so concerned that he sent an urgent message to Congress entitled, "Texas Invasion—Louisiana."[23] Attacking a Caddo village near the Trinity in Texan territory at least had the advantage of being in their own country, and was not likely to create an international incident.[24]

Leading his 450-man militia into the Crosstimbers, Rusk's force was plagued by cold and hunger. John B. Denton's duties most likely included a Sunday service, prayers at meals, and since the militia was on the march over the cold Christmas season, sermons for Christmas and New Year's. One "Old Texan" described the scene one evening when Denton was preaching around the campfire, giving what was undoubtedly the first sermon ever delivered in Denton County:

> Denton ... was chosen chaplain of a regiment of Texas soldiers and left his mark as pulpit orator, through he seldom spoke in a pulpit. I shall never forget the occasion of one of his sermons. We were camped at the mouth of what is now called Denton creek, at Hackberry Fort, and were gathered in the grove to listen to Denton's sermon. As he was rising to begin, Gen. Rusk of Texas fame, walked into the crowd and took a seat. It is one of the preacher's happy efforts. He chained his hearers, and memorialized the woods around with some of the grandest natural eloquence that ever fell from human tongue. Gen. Rusk was charmed. He had never seen the preacher and asked the writer of this what little 'thunderbolt' that could be. Said he had heard some renowned diction of Clay, of Prentiss and of Webster, but that such a deluge of rounded periods had never met his ears before.[25]

It was anticipated that they would engage in battle, and in that case, Denton would have performed funerals as well and offered spiritual guidance for the wounded. It is curious that this is the only military expedition in this period that had a chaplain on the staff and it is not known whether this practice had just been discontinued or that Denton was so eager to participate they made special a provision just for him.

Finally reaching the site of the village, they were disappointed to find it deserted, save for some blankets, a few Buffalo skins, and some guns left behind. The Indians had been warned of the approaching army and Rusk had to content himself with burning the abandoned village.

They did however find a friendly Kickapoo who directed them on to the Brazos where they thought the Caddo might have withdrawn, but there too none were to be found.[26] Dejected from the lack of success, the cold, hunger, and fatigue, they turned back towards Red River County.

> Tarrant ... [had] failed to furnish the beeves for army in time, which caused Rusk to be driven to great straights [sic] for subsistence, & forced him as above stated to abandon his waggons & eat the oxen–no indians were killed–not even one ... The weather was very cold & disagreeable, & the men suffered much.[27]

Hugh McLeod described it upon their return, "We are recruiting our broken down horses, and equally exhausted selves, after a march, in my opinion unparalleled, since De Soto's."[28] That being somewhat of an exaggeration, and in spite of his manly war-talk, McLeod had an accident twenty-five miles west of Clarksville and had to stay behind with some of the supplies. He was not actually able to accompany Rusk to the Trinity, but met up with the force as it headed back to Clarksville. Even though the expedition accomplished nothing, McLeod wanted to put the indecisive campaign in a positive light in his letter to Lamar:

> This Campaign however has had one great effect, which amply Compensates for its expense, The Indians never knew they had an enemy beyond this *neighborhood*, nor did they believe the white man could go to the prairies— and when they find a wide road made from Clarksville to there Brazzos & learn from the Kickapoos that *five hundred men* made that *road*, they will perceive the hopelessness of such a contest.[29]

Chapter 10

The Cherokee War

After the Three-Forks Expedition ended in January 1838, Denton returned to Clarksville and resumed his study of law. During this period when his family was settled in Clarksville, Denton was on the move, engaged in legal work and various business interests.

The Sulphur Forks area of North Texas and Southeastern Arkansas, although separated by an international boundary can for all intents, be considered as one cultural region. The people were virtually of the same stock, with common family names on both sides of the border. Many ex-Arkansans who moved on into Northeast Texas kept up their connections with their former neighbors and communities and movement back and forth across the border was common. During this period we know that Denton returned to Clark County, Arkansas, and purchased eighty acres, claiming it as his homestead.[1]

Meanwhile the fear of and hostility towards Native Americans was increasing as periodic attacks took place on isolated homesteads along the frontier. John B. Denton's next military service took place during the Cherokee War of 1839.

The Cherokee were first reported to have entered Texas from Arkansas around 1807, settling on some of the empty prairies in the Sulphur Forks. Pressure from Anglo colonization in the US had forced them into Texas, and encroaching settlements in Texas caused them to relocate several times, before Chief Bowles led sixty families into an uninhabited area in present-day Rusk County. When the Cherokee moved into East Texas in 1820, they prudently sought to obtain title to the land from the Spanish authorities.[2] The Spaniards believed that the Cherokee could serve as a buffer from the encroaching Americans and agreed in principle with their request. The Mexican Revolution took place before their title could be formalized, and ratification was put on hold, but the Cherokee believed in good faith that the land was theirs. During the Texas Revolution there were rampant fears that the Cherokee would align with the Mexican forces against the Texans and that they would be rewarded by Mexico with the title to their land. To head off any coalition inimical to the interest of the Texans, in November 1835, Sam Houston proposed an agreement with Chief Bowles to give the Cherokee title to their land in return for neutrality in the conflict.[3] In February 1836, a treaty was signed by Bowles and Houston formalizing this agreement and creating a semi-autonomous Cherokee state within Texas.

This treaty became highly controversial as most Texans did not share Houston's liberal views towards Indians and many suspected him of having divided loyalties from his close ties to the Cherokees. The Texans lived in fear of attacks to their isolated farmsteads and having some difficulty distinguishing exactly which tribes were responsible for the attacks, lumped them all together. Land speculators, including David G. Burnet, had their eyes on this prime tract of Texas land and several *empresarios*[4] had already been issued grants in the disputed lands. There were a variety of interests opposed to peaceful accommodation with the Cherokees.

After the Texas Revolution in 1836, David G. Burnet became the interim president and, being not inclined to honor the treaty Sam Houston had signed, ignored it. While Sam Houston was serving as the first elected President of the Republic he was unable to convince the legislature to formally ratify his treaty with the Cherokee and thus their status remained unresolved.

When Mirabeau B. Lamar became President in 1838, he immediately set about undoing any of Sam Houston's peace initiatives with the Cherokee. Lamar had made his intention to rid the country of most Native Americans, "The whiteman and the red man cannot dwell in harmony together. Nature forbids it." He said the two races were separated by the strongest hatreds of color and ways of thinking and that:

> "knowing these things, I experience no difficulty in deciding on the proper policy to be pursued towards them. It is to push a rigorous war against them to their hiding places without mitigation or compassion, until they shall be made to feel that flight from our borders without hope of return, is preferable to the scourges of war."[5]

War then was inevitable. In May 1839, letters from Mexican spy Manuel Flores to Chief Bowles were captured that proved that Mexico was trying to enlist the Cherokee in their efforts to reconquer Texas. Though there was no indication how Bowles and the Cherokee had responded, this was enough of an excuse for Lamar to wage a final war to drive them from Texas. In June, Lamar issued an ultimatum to Bowles and the Cherokee, to either leave Texas voluntarily or be driven out. Although Bowles, at age eighty-three, was opposed to war, the younger men of the tribe were angered by the impossible terms presented by Lamar, so the Chief tried to negotiate a better deal. The lengthy back and forth of negotiations finally came to a head on July 15, 1839, when the Texans, led by General Thomas J. Rusk and Edward Burleson, attacked the Cherokee and their allies in the Battle of the Neches. The first skirmish of the battle was indecisive, but the next day the Texans engaged the Indians again at the headwaters of the Neches River, a few miles from present-day Tyler, and won the day.[6] Bowles, although reluctant to fight, stayed and fought bravely, described by a witness: "He was a magnificent picture of barbaric manhood and was very conspicuous during the whole battle."[7] When the Cherokee were routed from the battlefield, a wounded and un-horsed Bowles was shot in the head by Captain Robert W. Smith. Recalling this incident more than forty years later, Henry Stout admitted: "We did not do Bowles right, and I'll always regret it. Bowles was the friend of the white man."[8]

Also on July 15, Denton reentered the military, not in an ancillary, non-combatant role as Chaplain, but as the head of Captain Denton's Mounted Volunteers.[9] This small troop of thirty men was mustered with the First Regiment Infantry under Major Peyton S. Wyatt. "On July 11, 1839, he [Wyatt] received orders from the War Department to recruit 300 men to fight the Cherokees under Chief Bowl."[10] Denton's Mounted Volunteers were apparently the only men Wyatt could muster; among them were privates Andrew Jackson Fowler, and William B. Stout, brother of Henry Stout.

> Most of the men who fought in the Texas Cherokee war were citizen volunteers who could not properly be called either regulars or militia. Many of them were settlers who volunteered because of the immediate danger to their homes. Others were the footloose elements which Adjutant General Hugh Mcleod called, "the floating chivalry which generally compose our volunteer corps.[11]

They left Clarksville on July 17, undermanned, but ready for battle; and unfortunately for them, a day after Bowles was defeated. The war being over, they did a tour of the western frontier for a month before being discharged on August 15, 1839. Once again Denton had missed the action, but he returned home with his new rank as Captain John B. Denton.

Chapter 11

John B. Denton: Lawyer and Family Man

As settlers continued to pour into North East Texas, property was platted, land was plowed, hamlets grew to villages, villages to towns, and it all became much more civilized. Population of the Sulphur Forks Prairie had increased to around 7,500 by 1840,[1] and the new counties of Lamar and Bowie had been carved from parts of Red River County.[2] Clarksville had evolved from an outpost into a real community. After his tour of duty in the militia ended, Denton returned to Clarksville and resumed his practice of the law with John B. Craig. His family grew with the birth of another child, John Burnard Denton, Jr. on March 16, 1840.

John B. Denton's prospects seemed so bright that he bought property in Clarksville to have a permanent home for his family. The property was purchased from Mr. Jesse Shelton for $980, which he was able to borrow from John B. Craig and John N. Porter. Not having a down payment, Denton paid half the cost by trading Craig "one sorrel horse, one sorrel mare and colt, one bay mare, four cows and calves, and one two year old heifer, one two year old bull, ten head of hogs, worth the amount of five hundred dollars."[3] A number of his other purchases around the same time indicated someone settling in and planting roots. He bought lumber, and sills to enlarge his house, and hired a carpenter, John D. Bloodworth, to do the work. He also purchased two loads of dirt to improve his lot.[4]

His domestic life was improving in Clarksville and with his new career as an attorney, it looked like he would finally be able to provide for his growing family. Mrs. Denton was able to buy fine chintz calico, bed ticking for mattresses, flannel, silk, and fine ladies boots from Sam Fulton on credit.[5] From Willis Dean the grocer, they bought ginger cake, watermelon, and whiskey.[6] It was said that Old Willis Dean:

> had a grocery store in a log house ..., and he needed no sign to indicate the character of his stock for there was an intermission of fifteen minutes between every log in the house, and you could plainly see through these cracks what the old man had to sell.[7]

Though providing some finery for his wife and family, Denton required less. George Gerdes told the story of Denton having retrieved an old drab-colored broadcloth overcoat from the body of a surveyor who had been killed. He brought it to Gerdes' mother, who washed the blood out for him.

> There was a tailor at my father's and Denton had this tailor make him a close-bodied coat out of the overcoat ... (a clawhammer), with brass buttons. That was the style of the day and time.[8]

He must have cut quite a figure there in Clarksville, a young lawyer about town in his blood-free dress coat, brass buttons, tails, and all.

As previously mentioned, Denton as the junior partner in the firm did the traveling and would circulate around the district arranging for land claims and appearing in court as far west as Old Warren, about eighty miles west on the Red River. As settlement increased, the counties were divided into smaller political subdivisions. Fannin County was created from Red River County in 1837, and Old Warren was made its county seat. Denton was a fixture at Old Warren, one of the few trading posts along the Red River, and he was well known to many of the newly minted Texans who settled there. Old Warren, near the current Grayson-Fannin County line, consisted of a stockaded log fort, a few houses, and by 1840, a school and a Masonic Lodge, the thirteenth chartered lodge in Texas.[9] Among the founding members of this lodge were three men destined to have counties named for them, E. H. Tarrant, William G. Cooke, and John B. Denton, as well as Denton's partner John B. Craig.

> Joseph Sowell and John F. Scott built a tavern here that was frequented by the jurors, lawyers and officials who came to the county seat to attend the various courts. Many prominent men were among these visitors. John M. Hansford and John T. Mills presided over the District Court in which William Williams and Jesse Benton, Jr., prosecuted and John B. Denton plead for the defense. Edward H. Tarrant and William G. Cooke, Colonels of the Frontier Battalion and Texas Regulars, respectively, found time from their military duties to assist in the institution of a Masonic lodge.[10]

While in Old Warren for court, Denton, still a Methodist minister, was asked by Mother (Mrs. Catherine) Dugan to give a sermon:[11]

> The Dugan family had known Denton in Arkansas, and upon his coming to Warren in the course of his law practice he was invited by Mrs. Dugan to preach to the settlers. He cheerfully made an appointment for the following Sunday, when, in the little log stable and schoolhouse, the pioneers heard their first sermon in Fannin County.[12]

As Denton moved around the district, practicing law, preaching, joining Masonic Lodges, and becoming a Captain in the Rangers, he was becoming a man of stature, well known and respected by his peers. Virtually every contemporary account of Denton remarked on how eloquently he spoke and it seemed only natural that the next stage in his evolution as a public man would be to run for political office.

Chapter 12

The Regulator–
Moderator War and
the Election of 1840

O ne of the most fractious political controversies threatening the new Republic of Texas was the Regulator–Moderator War, sometimes called the Shelby County Wars. This conflict was centered in Shelby and Harrison Counties, on the Texas–Louisiana border where citizens formed vigilante gangs to dispense justice. The land east of the Sabine River, just over the Texas border, had been disputed territory since the days of the Louisiana Purchase. In a compromise, Spain and the United States had declared it Neutral Ground, governed by neither country and thus it became a haven for lawless elements. After the Texas Revolution "some of these societal outcasts came back west across the Sabine to settle in Shelby County."[1]

As more and more law-abiding immigrants settled in Shelby County they became alarmed at the lawlessness in the Neutral Ground and organized into vigilante gangs calling themselves Regulators. They considered themselves a quasi-legal committee to enforce the law where the government failed to do so. The origin of the Regulator–Moderator War was a land dispute which spun wildly out of control when Charles W. Jackson shot Joseph Goodbread, a fraudulent land speculator who had swindled Jackson's friend, the sheriff. Fearing for his own safety, Jackson organized a gang with Watt Moorman,[2] ostensibly to combat cattle theft, but which also served to protect him from retaliation by Goodbread's many allies. They called themselves "Regulators" assuming the mantle of law-abiding citizens merely doling out justice where they saw fit. By adopting the name Regulators, Jackson's vigilantes were associating themselves with a national movement of vigilantism that had arisen in other regions.[3]

Although most citizens wanted law and order, after a few violent vigilante actions by the Regulators, some felt they had gone too far. Some of those they attacked and hung had powerful friends and not all had been guilty. Some other factions felt that the Regulators' activities should be curtailed, and thus formed their own faction calling themselves Moderators. In the barest of shorthand descriptions of this complicated issue, it could be said that the Regulators wanted to quickly hang miscreants and lawbreakers, while Moderators wanted to give them a fair trial—before hanging them. The two factions became so intractably opposed to one another that whatever decent motives they might have originally held became lost in an escalating cycle of violence. It is beyond the scope of this work to get into the complicated details of this localized vigilante war, but the effects of this civil unrest spread into neighboring counties and many otherwise innocent bystanders were forced to take sides.

This conflict spilled over into the political arena and in the Senate election of 1840, the Regulators put up a lawyer and preacher from Red River County, John B. Denton, as their candidate. Denton, though new to politics, was popular, well-spoken, and an ally of William Pinckney Rose, head of the Harrison County Regulators. In 1837, Rose, a wealthy landowner, moved to northern Shelby County (now in Harrison County) with a large contingent of his family and in-laws, arriving just about the time the Regulator–Moderator War was heating up. He was known as "Hell-roarin' Rose," had been at the battle of New Orleans with Andrew Jackson,[4] and fell in with the Regulators shortly after he arrived in Texas. This was Denton's first bid for public office but he quickly mastered the process. Since no frontier election would have been complete without free-flowing whiskey, and in spite of his widely reported posthumous reputation for abstinence (created by Alfred W. Arrington), records show that Denton purchased at least two and a half gallons of whiskey in August 1840, in the run-up to the election.[5] Denton's biographer, Rev. William H. Allen, described a typical frontier election. "Dubious things became positive truths or positive lies, just to suit the cause. Opinions were emphasized with ungodly epithets, and passion rose on the smallest contradictions. Whisky was drunk by quarts without the money of those who gurgled it down."[6] Denton had the gift of speech, a powerful friend, and just to be sure, a keg of whiskey.

The Moderators had a candidate sympathetic to their cause in the person of Robert Potter. Potter was a man of considerable skills and although a notorious scoundrel, was of the Moderator persuasion and thus had a strong following in the district. He had served three terms in the North Carolina House of Commons, and two terms as a Congressman from North Carolina in Washington.[7] His promising career had been cut short in his home state when he was convicted of castrating two men, both relatives, whom he had accused of infidelity with his wife. This practice became enshrined in North Carolinian legal code as "Potterization."[8]

Upon arriving in Texas in 1835, Potter had joined the revolution, becoming the first Secretary of the Navy and participated in the Battle of San Jacinto. His Texian credentials were solid, having signed the Declaration of Independence from Mexico and being on the committee to draft the Constitution of the Republic of Texas,[9] yet as he had done in his home state, he became embroiled in political factions and resigned when Sam Houston, whom he opposed, was elected President. Houston was no friend to Potter, who was aligned with Houston's political enemies.[10] At the Convention of 1836, Potter cast the lone vote in opposition to Sam Houston's appointment as Commander and Chief of the Army. Not one to mince words, Houston would describe Potter as a man "whose infamy was wider than the world and deeper than perdition."[11] In spite of Potter's many accomplishments, history has tended to take Houston's side on this question.

Even with the backing of the powerful William Pinckney Rose and free whiskey, Denton lost the Senate Election of 1840 to Robert Potter; but by only four votes.[12] According to the writer styled "Old Texan," "Potter himself declaring he had never before seen a man so hard to defeat."[13] It is always said that elections have consequences, but this particular election had repercussions that would prove fatal for Potter. As a result of Rose's strong support for Denton,[14] the enmity between Potter and Rose increased, developing into one of the great feuds in Texas history.[15] This culminated in Potter's murder in 1842, by one of Rose's men at Potter's Point on Caddo Lake. The murder achieved such notoriety that even Charles Dickens wrote about it in his *American Notes*.

Terrible Death of Robert Potter.
From the "Caddo Gazette," of the 12th inst., we learn the frightful death of Colonel Robert Potter. ... He was beset in his house by an enemy, named Rose. He sprang from his couch, seized his gun, and, in his night-clothes, rushed from the house. For about two hundred yards his speed seemed to defy his pursuers; but, getting entangled in a thicket, he was captured. Rose told him that he intended to act a generous part, and give him a chance for his life. He then told Potter he might run, and he should not be interrupted till he reached a certain distance. Potter started at the word of command, and before a gun was fired he had reached the lake. His first impulse was to jump in the water and dive for it, which he did. Rose was close behind him, and formed his men on the bank ready to shoot him as he rose. In a few seconds he came up to breathe; and scarce had his head reached the surface of the water when it was completely riddled with the shot of their guns, and he sunk, to rise no more!

By Charles Dickens[16]

Chapter 13

Indian Conflicts in Northeast Texas

Although relations between settlers and Indians had been relatively calm under the rule of Mexico and in the early days of the Republic, increasing immigration meant competition for existing land and the settlers' anger over the constant horse theft and occasional murder, gradually increased tension to the breaking point.

> "During the year, 1836, the Indians showed a sulky friendliness toward the white settlers. They at times visited the homes of the pioneers, and aside from some petty thieving seemed to be disposed to maintain amicable relations with their new neighbors. At length, however, they began to grumble about the occupation of their hunting grounds ... and complaining about the whites killing their "cows" (buffaloes) and turkeys ... In spite of this, the settlers took no special precaution against attacks until the savages encouraged by their lethargy began to steal horses."[1]

The settlers viewed horse theft as a threat to their lives and livelihoods. In Anglo frontier culture horse theft was a "hanging offense" and not taken lightly by settlers for whom their lives often depended on their horses. In Indian culture, horses were an important symbol of power and stealing horses was almost a sport; they took them from Anglos and other Indian tribes indiscriminately.

> One old chief told Captain Marcy that his four sons were a comfort to him because they could steal more horses than any other member of the tribe. It would seem that in stealing horses and well in other booty, the rules of the game set no restrictions on the course of supply. Texas colonists had to guard their horses carefully. [2]

Relations in the Red River Counties were further poisoned on May 16, 1837, when Daniel Montague led a raiding party which

> without provocation, attacked a band of Kickapoos, Shawnees, Cherokees and Delawares near Warren. Several Indians ... were killed and burned. A truce was arranged after this fight, but the Shawneetown Indians, thoroughly aroused by what they considered the perfidy of the settlers, manifested their enmity by stealing horses.[3]

The Cherokee War and the abrogation of their treaty added to the atmosphere of mistrust between the Texans and some of the more peaceful of the Indian tribes. In March of 1840, the fiercely warlike Comanches were invited to a peace conference in San Antonio with the hopes of settling differences, negotiating for the return of hostages, and forging a lasting peace. This proved to be a fiasco. A party of sixty-five, including twelve Comanche Chiefs with their families, arrived in good faith for the peace council. Instead of bringing all of the Texans held hostage by the Indians as ordered, they had brought only one Anglo girl who showed visible signs of sadistic abuse and torture. When the outraged Texans reacted by taking the Indians hostage, the council meeting turned violent.[4] In the ensuing melee, thirty-five of the Indians, including some women and children, were killed, and the rest imprisoned.[5] This blunder came to be known as the Council House Fight, and effectively ruined any chance for peace between the Comanches and the Texans.

As civilization was creeping westward, all was not peaceful along the frontier. As more and more people came to settle in Texas, they found themselves competing for a dwindling supply of unallocated land.

The rapacious appetite of the Anglo settler for land increased tension with the Indians, many of whom had moved west to avoid conflicts in the first place.

All this did not happen in a vacuum. The Anglo settlers were not Europeans in their first encounters with Native Americans; they had been fighting and killing one another for two hundred years. These animosities had been bred into the bone as each successive generation of Anglo invaders pushed further west into the Indian homelands. The Indian response was essentially a resistance movement against invading foreigners, and they had a point.

There was great resentment among the Indians for their correctly perceived ill-treatment at the hands of the Texans. Many of the tribes moved westward onto unsettled lands around the Forks of the Trinity and the Brazos to avoid conflict and were reported to be in a destitute state.[6] George Kendall, founder of the New Orleans *Picayune*, toured the west and "attributed the warlike nature of the Wacoes to acts of bad faith by the whites. 'They had been deceived by our race once," he said, "and ... looked for another violation of our words."[7]

It was not all one-sided of course. As in most conflicts one offense led to a counter-offense, and so on, until it became difficult to tell who was at fault first. The Indians, outraged by the broken treaties and outright theft of their land, fought back but were being decimated by the superior firepower of the Texans. The Texans were being attacked in isolated farmsteads and whenever caught out without protection. Terrible stories circulated about whole families being murdered, scalped, mutilated, or taken hostage. There were even rare stories of cannibalism among some tribes.[8] Rumors abounded about Indians gathering to attack or aligning themselves with Mexican forces to retake Texas. Even though many of the stories of Indian intentions were exaggerated, people on the frontier lived in fear for good reason. In North East Texas there were about sixteen Indian attacks on isolated farms, travelers or surveyors between 1838 and 1841.[9]

Any sense of peace these settlers may have had was slowly being eroded by the steady drip of attacks on their friends and neighbors in the settlements along the Red River. Theft was rampant and almost normal, but the deaths of friends, acquaintances, and family members hit the community hard, and hardened their resolve to stay put and fight back. Fearing attacks, the settlers often would gather together in fortified cabins with only the men and boys venturing out during the day to plant and tend crops.[10] The planting was done cooperatively, with some of the settlers standing guard as others worked the land in rotation, until all of their planting or harvesting was done. In the Fall of 1839, Denton's friend George Dugan, and a Mr. Cox, were killed and scalped in an attack at Dugan's farm in Fannin County. In 1840 there was another series of attacks in the area of Old Warren starting with the Hunter family in which the mother and one daughter were killed and scalped, one daughter was kidnapped, and one servant was killed. A Mr. Moody was killed, his body burned on a pyre. A boy named Sewell was shot with an arrow while protecting the family's horses. Two McIntyre brothers were killed and scalped and the Cox brothers were captured at Ft. English on the Red River.[11]

By 1841 the situation had become untenable as the anger and hatred towards the Indians had reached the boiling point. On January 4, the Fifth Congress passed a resolution: "That the sum of $10,000.00 which was appropriated for the purpose of volunteer expeditions against the hostile Indians on the upper Brazos river ..."[12] In February they became more specific.

> An act approved on February 4, 1841, authorized the settlers on the frontier borders of each of the following counties to organize company of not less that twenty nor more than fifty-six minute men, rank and file: Fannin, Lamar, Red River, etc. The companies were to elect their own officers and hold themselves in readiness to afford a ready and active protection the frontier settlements. The act provided: "The members of said companies shall at all times be prepared with a good substantial horse, bridle and saddle, with other necessary accoutrements, together with a good gun and one hundred rounds of ammunition; and in addition to this, when called into service such number of rations as the captain may direct ..."[13]

Things were heating up on the frontier and the Congressional Resolution of January 4, was literally "marching orders."

Chapter 14

The Ripley Massacre and the Tarrant Expedition

n the Sulphur Forks the settlers were agitated and on high alert: on March 14, 1841, John Yeary's homestead on the Sulphur River was attacked by fifteen Comanches.[1] Yeary and his family, in a fierce hand-to-hand battle, were able to fend them off using a hoe as the only weapon at hand, with just his wife sustaining a slight injury from an arrow. But it was the "massacre" of the Ripley family that caused the greatest public outrage and a serious military response. Ambrose and Rachel Ripley had settled along the old Cherokee Trace[2] in present-day Titus County.[3] Their farmstead, on what is now called Ripley Creek, fed by Ripley Springs, had been a favorite Native American watering site for thousands of years and the site of many Indian graves and artifacts.[4] On April 10, 1841, a band of Indians attacked their home near present-day Mt. Vernon, killing Mrs. Ripley and seven of their children. One son was shot, Mrs. Ripley and five of her children were clubbed to death, and one infant was burned to death when the cabin was set alight.[5] Two daughters managed to escape and hid in a nearby thicket. According to their neighbor, James D. Clifton, the surviving girls hid in the forests and from their places of concealment heard the shrieks of their sisters as they were murdered. The girls were not discovered until the next day,

half senseless from the shock.[6] Not only were the circumstances horren-
dous, but the Ripleys were well known in the community, and the brutal-
ity of this attack struck a chord with the other settlers. In 1839, Ambrose
Ripley had served under Captain William B. Stout in the 1st Regiment,
4th Brigade of the Texas Militia, along with Green Orr, the pastor who had
married John B. Denton in Arkansas.[7] John B. Denton and Ambrose Ripley
knew each other: Denton's estate noted that Ripley owed Denton $8.00 at
the time of his death.[8]

As the story quickly spread through the Sulphur Forks community,
a group of volunteers were hastily organized by Charles Black and Charles S.
Stewart who followed the trail of the alleged attackers, ambushing them
on the Sulphur River and reportedly killing a few.[9] A larger effort would
be required and word went out for volunteers to assemble a militia to avenge
these most recent killings.[10] On May 4, 1841,[11] volunteers started to assemble
at Choctaw Bayou,[12] about eight miles west of Old Warren.[13] Henry Stout
explained the delay: these frontiersmen being mostly subsistence farmers,
"We could do nothing without provisions, so we made our crop and took
the trail."[14] As it took some time to collect the volunteers from the sparsely
settled district and the supplies they would need for the expedition, the volunteers stayed at Choctaw Bayou for about a week. Many old hands and familiar names were among the volunteers, and in the custom of the Rangers, they
chose their own leaders. The assembled "minutemen" chose James Bourland
as their Captain, but General Edward H. Tarrant, a former member of the
Texas Legislature and member of the Texas Militia, came along, unable to
resist the call to arms. William C. Young, First Lieutenant; Samuel Johnson,
Second Lieutenant; Lemuel M. Cochran, First Sergeant; and McQuinney
Howell Wright, Second Sergeant.[15] John B. Denton and Henry Stout, called
"spies" in the official report, were both chosen to lead small scouting parties.
The relatively high pay scale[16] for the militia allowed $75 per month for
Captain Bourland, $60 for Lieutenant Young, $40 for Sergeant Cochran and
$35 per month for everyone else. For the cash-strapped Republic these were
in effect promissory notes and some were not settled until 1854. General
Tarrant, who had been popularly elected commander of an 1839 frontier
militia force, felt slighted that he had not been chosen to lead, but agreed to

come without pay and serve under whoever the men chose to command the force.[17] Perhaps in deference to Tarrant's rank and experience Bourland was effectively sidelined as leader, but Bourland was still responsible for the paperwork and administration for the expedition.

There was some discrepancy about the exact number of men in the company. First Sergeant Lem Cochran reported that there were eighty members but the official report to the Secretary of War stated there were sixty-nine.[18] Captain James Bourland's official roster[19] of his troops as submitted to the Secretary of War lists seventy-one members but allows that there were likely others missing from the list. General Edward Tarrant and thirteen-year-old Andrew Davis for instance were not included, presumably because they were volunteers and not entitled to pay for their service. Andrew Davis was an orphan, whose mother had died when he was a baby and his father killed by Indians four years previously.[20] By modern standards it seems unthinkable that a thirteen-year old boy would be permitted to accompany the militia, but the orphan Davis was well known, well liked and well experienced as a woodsman and hunter. Davis was allowed to tag along, riding his aunt's old mule, which he described as the slowest beast among the many. Among the experienced members were Tarrant, three Bourland brothers, Henry Stout, Clabe Chisum, father of John Chisum, Daniel Montague, and William N. Porter, and of course John B. Denton. Also listed were the several names from families that had suffered from Indian attacks, among them Dugan, Davis, and John Yeary. It is safe to say that there were around seventy members in the expedition. Most of the volunteers were recent immigrants to Texas from the upper south; but besides one or two from northern states, there were three volunteers from other countries, some experienced soldiers among them. They stand out among their comrades.

Jose Maria Gonzalez, as a former colonel in the Mexican Army, certainly had military experience: he was a former commander of a Mexican cavalry company of convicts,[21] defending Bexar from the rebels. However, Gonzalez was a Federalist, who became disillusioned by the despotic tendencies of General Santa Anna. As his sympathies shifted towards the Texans, he "distributed leaflets within San Antonio, exhorting

Cos's troops to desert and join the fight for freedom."[22] His message to his fellow Mexicans was emphatic:

> The ... declaration made by the people of Texas ... offered assistance and support to all members of the confederation who might wish to take arms against the despotism [dictatorship] of the Centralists. This generous offer has allowed me to raise a considerable army which defends the constitution from the abuses which it has suffered and preserves it in spite of treason and perjury ... for the most glorious contest is that of liberty against tyranny.[23]

Stephen F. Austin and James Fannin thought he could be induced to join their cause.

> I particularly recommend Gov. Viesca and Col. Gonzales to the attention of the executive Govt. I have invited the latter to this camp with his men. If he was here I have no doubt he could draw over two companies at least of cavalry now in Bexar as he once commanded them.[24]

In 1834, Gonzales defected to the Texans side, bringing with him twenty Mexican soldiers under his command.[25] After taking an oath to "defend the republican principles of the constitution of 1834 and the rights of Texas,"[26] he was ordered to take his soldiers and report to General Burleson at Bexar. It is hard to say whether he was motivated by a love of freedom or the fact that he had vast landholdings in Texas; but at one point he owned almost fifty thousand acres.[27] That he happened to be involved in the Tarrant Expedition is likely a result of his owning land in Delta County on the Sulphur Prairie.[28] Gonzalez had previously commanded his own company of Texas Rangers in 1839.[29]

Joseph Dornstin, another of the international volunteers in the Militia, was also an experienced soldier, having been a former captain in the Polish Army during the Uprising of 1830–1831. The uprising; an armed rebellion against the Russian Empire began with a group of officers at a military academy in Warsaw. The nationalist uprising eventually spread to Lithuania, Belarus, and Ukraine, but was crushed by the massive armies of the Czar in 1831. After it became obvious that their cause was lost, most of the soldiers went into exile rather than surrender. Although most of these exiled Poles stayed in Europe forming expatriate communities in many of the European capitals,[30] a few ranged further and Dornstin made his way to Texas. A Polish travel writer in Texas, writing in 1909, observed that Dornstin "came here around 1835 and made a living by hunting deer and wild turkey. Although not yet old, the captain was worn out with life."[31] Northeast Texas was about as far removed as you could imagine from the battlegrounds of Poland, but Dornstin was again caught up in events and took up arms.

Not much is known of the Irishman, Thomas Cozzins (Cousin), other than he arrived in Texas in 1838, owned 320 acres of land in Fannin County, and had spent five months as a Mounted Ranger in 1839, before volunteering for the Tarrant Expedition. All three of these foreign volunteers came to Texas from places where revolution was in the air, and the possibilities for freedom in Texas may have drawn them here.

Hours after the election of the officers, the troops moved a few miles west to Fort Johnston, an unoccupied stockaded enclosure built the year before on a site selected by Colonel William Gordon Cooke. Cooke was in charge of an expedition mapping a new national military road from Austin to Coffee's Station (Preston Bend) on the Red River. Cooke had ordered a fortified enclosure to be built called Fort Johnston,[32] just south of Holland Coffee's store, a few miles from the Chihuahua Trail and very close to the present-day town of Denison. The fort was built in 1840, but only occupied for a few months when the Army of the Republic of Texas was disbanded and the fort was abandoned in April of 1841. The volunteer company stayed for four days at Fort Johnston waiting for a few stragglers to arrive and to finalize details of the expedition. At some point ten members of the company withdrew and left for Holland Coffee's Station; among was them Holland Coffee, and according to some, the famous William A. "Bigfoot" Wallace.[33] That these men withdrew from the expedition could explain the discrepancy in the various reports of how many were in the company.

Although James Bourland had been elected to command this unit of minutemen, General Edward Tarrant, either pulling rank or in light of his previous experience, seems to have assumed control early in the expedition as evidenced in the reports which clearly describe Tarrant as in charge, and the troop became known to history as the Tarrant Expedition. The minutemen

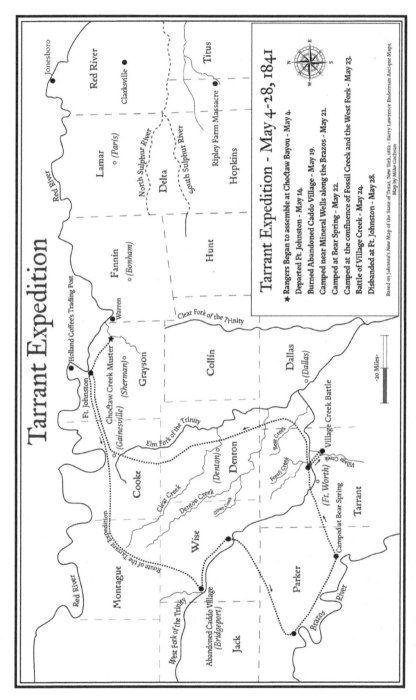

Map of the Tarrant Expedition.

were much more democratic than the regular army and could vote to override Tarrant's decisions, and frequently did, but due to Tarrant's rank, Bourland was effectively sidelined as commander. This was a situation that did not please everyone and opinions seem divided on the subject of Tarrant's leadership. Thirteen-year-old Andrew Davis's account portrayed Tarrant in somewhat heroic terms, while the more frontier-hardened Henry Stout's vivid account of the expedition did not miss an opportunity to accuse Tarrant of cowardice and poor judgement. Somewhat bolstering Stout's account are the results of an 1843 republic-wide election for a Major General to command six newly formed companies to defend the frontier. Tarrant ran for the post and lost the election receiving less than half the votes in his home of Red River County.[34]

On May 14, 1841, the force left Fort Johnston and headed west along the old Chihuahua Trail which roughly paralleled the Red River and far as present-day Archer County, where the trail veered south ultimately leading to Presidio, on the Rio Grande. Jack Ivy, of mixed African and Indian blood, and an experienced Indian trader recommended by Holland Coffee, had joined the expedition to serve as guide. Their intention was to travel west to near the headwaters of the Trinity River, where they had heard reports a large Indian village was located. The company traveled west and a bit south for four days, past where the town of Gainesville sits, then veering southerly, through the Upper Cross Timbers, "crossing the head branches of the middle fork of the Trinity."[35]

> It was believed that the depredating Indians were encamped on a creek which enters the west fork of the Trinity from the northeast side, where the town of Bridgeport now stands, in Wise County... four or five miles up the stream which now bears the name "Village" creek.[36]

On May 19th, they passed into the Western Cross Timbers where they found "tolerable fresh signs" of Indians, and turned a bit more southerly until they found the remains of two abandoned Keechi villages. They were located, as expected, on the "main western branch"[37] of the Trinity, at the fork of Village Creek near present-day Bridgeport (not to be confused with the Village Creek in Tarrant County). Under the cover of darkness, they

approached the villages and found there some sixty or seventy recently abandoned lodges as well as the remains of fields cultivated in corn. Tarrant was
worried that burning the villages, situated as they were in an elevated position, would alert others to their position so the men used axes to destroy as
many of the lodges as they could.

On the next day (May 20) they crossed over the West Fork of the
Trinity and traveled roughly southeast following the general direction of
the river, all the while looking for sign of Indians. On the twenty-first
they left the Trinity, heading south and over the high divide marking the
watershed between the Trinity and the Brazos and camped on the East
Fork of the Brazos possibly near Mineral Wells. As Henry Stout recalled,
they "traveled around hunting for Indians until we found ourselves at
the upper edge of the cross-timbers at a big spring, where we stayed all
night."[38] This was most likely Bear Springs, eight miles southeast of
Weatherford.[39] According to Henry Stout, General Tarrant was of a mind
to end the campaign and return home:

> Tarrant said we should give up the chase. He said he wanted to get back
> before the Trinity raised, but it did not look like rain and we would
> not agree. He was twitted with cowardice and concluded he would go
> along and we continued our search.[40]

Having had no luck in their quest, the next day, they headed east
in the general direction of Birdville (present-day Handley, just north of
Ft. Worth). Crossing over to the east side of the Trinity and Fossil Creek,
they camped for the night at a site just west of Village Creek, in present-day
Ft. Worth.[41]

Up to this point they had not seen a single Indian, but young Andrew
Davis recalled on the day before the battle they encountered a lone Indian on
the prairie and had taken him captive. He was apparently unhelpful and by
sunset Tarrant made preparations to kill him.

> He was placed with his back to an elm tree, his hands were drawn
> around the tree and made secure, and his feet was then tied together
> and secured to the tree. Then twelve men with their guns were ordered
> to take their positions before the Indian. The scene was an awful one in

its solemnity, to me and to all. The men were ordered to present arms. At this moment, the alarmed and terror-stricken Indian became greatly excited, and in great agony of spirit he cried aloud, 'Oh, man! Oh, man!' While he did not utter the above words with distinctness, yet it was more like these words than any other. General Tarrant sent Captain Yeary with an interpreter (Jack Ivy) to the prisoner to see if he would reveal anything, for prior to this he had been sullen, and would not say a word. He was made to understand that if he would tell where the village was and how to find it, he should not be hurt, and he made a full revelation of the whole matter, and closed by saying, "We be friends." He was untied, but kept under guard all night.[42]

Chapter 15

The Battle of Village Creek

They camped a few miles from the ford on the Trinity, near where in 1838 General Rusk and Dyer had attacked a Kickapoo village at Village Creek.[1] Rusk had attacked and burned the village in 1839, routing the inhabitants. After this attack, Rusk ordered troops to march up the Trinity, "destroying, on your route, the villages of all Indians … when you fight exterminate."[2] This village had been thought abandoned at the time, but a few remnants of other tribes resettled there the next year. After the Cherokee War, the Shawnee in East Texas had made a treaty with Texas promising to leave for Indian Territory north of the Red River in return for a cash settlement. Most had complied; but in 1839, a few Shawnees and Delawares, Anadarkos (and others) settled at the abandoned Kickapoo villages at Village Creek.[3] It was obvious that rather than confront the Texans, the remnant Indian tribes of Texas sought refuge on the frontier by hiding out in fairly well concealed creek bottoms where they could farm and hunt. There was no central village site but rather, they settled in "dispersed hamlets strung out along fertile bottomlands; and fields interspersed between their houses, which varied from circular beehive grass houses to wood houses with grass roofs."[4] This traditional settlement pattern is consistent with what the Tarrant Expedition found at Village Creek.

The official report stated that about a mile from the ford near where Fossil Creek joins the Trinity, signs of Indians put them on the alert. Pony tracks and evidence that some of the native grasses had been grazed tipped off Stout to the presence of Indians. After dark Tarrant ordered Henry Stout who, "then, as throughout the expedition,"[5] led the advance scouting party to seek out the village. Andrew Davis recalled that Stout was ordered by Tarrant to reconnoiter, select the point of attack and report back by four o'clock in the morning. With him in the scouting party were James Bourland, Randolph Scott, Elbert Early, and John B. Denton, five important participants who began the day of battle with little or no sleep. "This was done, and by daylight all were in motion under the guidance of our trusty scout, for the village which was reached about nine o'clock in the morning."[6]

They were within three miles of the village and as before Stout led the way through the densely wooded bottoms of Village Creek.

> We passed over a little knoll and around close to where there were a whole tribe of Indians, but they did not see us nor we them. We turned further on to the left there saw two ponies and after two squaws. One of the squaws had a brass kettle preparing something. The only other was an Andargo (Anadarko) squaw and had a baby in her arms. Tarrant learning that Indians were in the brush, kept his men out of the way and let us go it alone.[7]

When the rest of the company got within five hundred yards of the village, still concealed behind a thicket, Tarrant ordered the men to "divest themselves of their blankets, packs and all manner of encumbrances."[8] Asking if the men were ready and receiving an affirmative reply, Tarrant uttered a few solemn words before commencing battle. "Now, my brave men, we will never all meet on earth again, there is great confusion and death ahead. I shall expect every man to fill his place and do his duty."[9] With that, he gave the order to form a line and charge the village.

With Denton, Bourland, and Tarrant in the lead, the men charged, sweeping down on the village, shooting their guns, yelling and causing maximum confusion to the terror-stricken villagers. One of the women screamed and fled to the creek, where she was shot and killed by Alsey Fuller, who had

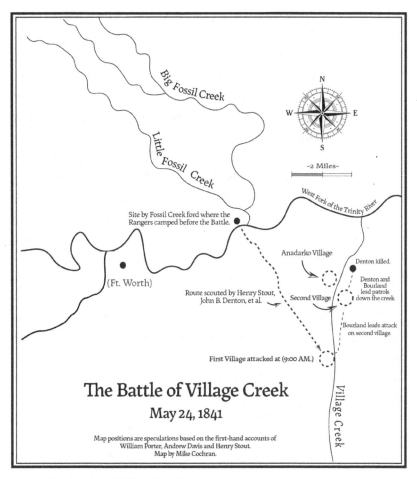

Map of the Battle of Village Creek.

mistaken her for a warrior, while the other woman, the sister of Anadarko Chief Jose Maria, was captured with her child.[10]

Taken by surprise, most of the Indians scattered quickly into the brush or down a trail along the creek but several were shot while trying to make their escape. Most of the Indians killed in the attack had been shot while trying to escape. Tarrant's intentions as stated in the official report: "It was not the wish of General Tarrant to take any prisoners. The women and children alone we suffered to escape if they wished, and the men neither asked, gave, nor received any quarter."[11] After a short while the first village was under the Texans' control. Young Andrew Davis reports having his beloved mule shot out from under him and was then on foot but otherwise unharmed.

Leaving a few men to guard the first village, the rest took out at a fast clip down the trail after the retreating Indians. James Bourland, with a group of about twenty men including Denton and Lem Cochran, crossed the creek and in hot pursuit rode along another trail northwards towards the Trinity River. After galloping about two miles they came upon a second village, larger than the first one. Bourland, with Cochran, took half the men and circled around to the right while the remaining half circled to the left trying to outflank the retreating Indians. Both Cochran and Elbert Early tried to fire on a fleeing warrior but each of their guns broke. Early was fired upon but not hit. Here they met with some resistance but in the main the Indians at the second village sought to flee into the thickets rather than stand and fight.

From this point they could see a third, larger, Anadarko village a short distance away. Some of the men in their zeal started for this third village on foot as many of their horses had been exhausted by the initial attack. The Indians at the third village, having been alerted by the sound of the gunfire and the arrival of their fellow warriors fleeing the Texans, were better prepared and having armed themselves had begun to shoot back. The troops having become scattered over the wide area of the first two villages, Tarrant thought it prudent to stop and called for the advancing soldiers to retreat and regroup at the second village.

> Covered with dust and dirt, and wet with sweat, and almost famished, both for food and water, Tarrant called the company together at a little spring. On roll call it was found that not a man had been killed; a dozen, perhaps, had been unhorsed. Quite a number were hatless, as many as eight or ten were slightly wounded, but none in a painful manner. Many had made narrow escapes from death as their rent clothes abundantly testified. Tarrant commended the men for their good behavior, and said, "Thank God, we are all here. You have had water, repair to the nearest huts and get your hands full of dried buffalo meat, and in fifteen minutes be ready for further advance." My, my how the buffalo meat was used up by those hungry men.[12]

Fleeing the Texans some of the Indians ran north, towards the Trinity River bottoms to hide in the underbrush. After a short interval and eager to continue the attack, Denton asked Tarrant for permission to take ten men and pursue the Indians down a trail by the creek. Permission was granted with the admonition to avoid an ambush. Tarrant then ordered Bourland and Stout to take another small group, which included Andrew Davis, and follow a different trail. The two trails went in different directions but about a mile and a half down the creek they converged in the dense underbrush along the bottoms.

At the point where the two trails joined, a single much wider trail continued through an extremely dense thicket. Bourland had separated from Stout at this point and with Calvin Sullivan and a few others had crossed a *slough*, or low muddy spot, to round up some of the Indians' horses, one of which wore a bell and had attracted their attention. Stout, arguably the most experienced frontiersman in the company, having arrived at the convergence of the trails had, in caution, stopped to assess the situation. He spoke to his men, observing that with the trails coming back together, and with so many Indians having just gone down those same paths in flight, they should be wary. Being so near the creek, and with the denseness of the undergrowth, it was a perfect place for an ambush.

At that point they heard the hooves of approaching horses, and reckoned it was Denton, so they waited to consult with him before proceeding. When Denton arrived he seemed impatient and challenged Stout, "Captain, why have you stopped?"[13] Stout repeated the reasons he had just given his men, that it seemed a likely place for an ambush, but he added, "I'm willing to go as far as any other man." Without uttering a word, Denton spurred his horse on down the trail towards the creek with Stout, not to be outdone, close on his heels.

They rode on a few hundred yards along the path, crossing a cornfield and came to a well-traveled buffalo trail which led down to the creek and a dense thicket. There Denton stopped to assess the situation, possibly recalling his pledge to Tarrant about exercising caution to avoid an ambush. Stout at this point rode to the head of the column and responding to Denton's earlier challenge said, "If you are afraid to go in there, I am not."[14] Denton answered sharply, "I'll follow you to hell. Go on."[15] They rode on, Stout in front with Denton close behind, down a small ravine into the open creek bed and beyond the sheltering thicket. The creek had a high bank on one side covered with dense undergrowth. Denton and Stout had gone no more than thirty paces down the creek when from atop the high creek bank came a barrage of gunfire from a few Indians who were concealed there.

> Just as Denton and I were going down a small ravine ten to twelve Indians fired on us from the thicket. I heard the shots and looked at Denton. He had raised his gun to shoot, but dropped it and fell dead. His horse commenced grazing ... In a moment I received a severe wound in the arm and another bullet struck the lock of my Dutch gun; tore off the spring and knocked the stock against the side of my head with such force as to stun me.[16]

Though Stout was in the lead, he had been partially concealed by a small tree and thus it was Denton who bore the brunt of the attack. He had received three wounds: one in the shoulder, one in the arm, and the killing shot that pierced his breast. Captain John Griffin, who had followed his comrades, was grazed by a ball on his cheek and several had pierced his clothes but no one else was visible to the attackers and all escaped unharmed. The charge had momentarily stopped at this point, the Texans being shocked and confused by the death of their comrade, and Stout incapacitated by his wounds. Still in single file along the narrow trail and fearing further gunfire, Captain Yeary yelled out, "Why in hell don't you move your men out so we can see the enemy? We'll all be killed here."[17] But the Indians had fired their volley and fled the field. Stout had slightly recovered his bearings and said, "Men, I'm wounded and powerless. Do the best you can for yourselves."[18] The other men, realizing that Denton had been killed in the attack, were greatly demoralized, fired a few random shots into the thicket where the Indians had been, then began an irregular retreat to the upper fields where they had begun. As Denton was shot he had remained in the saddle, his gun still clenched in his hand but aimed towards the ground as his muscles gradually relaxed. One member gently removed Denton's body from his horse and placed it on the ground before leaving the battleground. There was a widely held belief that Chief Jose Maria fired the shot that killed Denton, but even if proven

Death of Captain John B. Denton. Although there were no contemporary images of John B. Denton, this image purporting to be the attack at the Battle of Village Creek has been reprinted many times since it was published in 1912. From *Border Wars of Texas*, by James DeShields.

false, seventeen years later, it was to have a profound effect on the life of Denton's son, Ashley N. Denton.[19]

Stout, who had no great love for General Tarrant, said, "Tarrant heard the guns and never made a move to assist us ... As soon as Bowlin (Bourland) heard the shooting he rushed to our assistance."[20] Randolph Scott shouted out the news to Bourland that Denton had been killed and Stout wounded, and though not usually a cursing man, "cursed the stupidity that had brought about the accident."[21] Stout was bleeding profusely and very weak and Bourland thought they should remove him to the spot where Tarrant and his command had rested at the second village. On the way Bourland found a brass pot abandoned by the Indians, filled it with creek water and poured it over Stout's head, which revived him and he credited with having saved his life.[22]

After they regrouped, Bourland asked for volunteers to return and retrieve Denton's body for they feared that he might be scalped or mutilated. Twenty men volunteered, among them young Andrew Davis and Elbert Early, who writing of the experience sixty years later, each expressed great pride in having been among the volunteers. The Indians having fled the battleground, the Texans found the body of their fallen friend unmolested and retrieved it without incident. Early reported that at the creek they found a mare and a colt which they caught and later gave to Mrs. Denton.[23]

When Bourland and the volunteers returned to the main force they had a discussion about their next move. They decided that they should withdraw from the field rather than pursuing the fight into the third, much larger village up the creek. William Porter in his report explains their reasoning:

> From the prisoners we had taken we had learned that at those villages there were upward of one thousand warriors, not more than half of whom were then at home ... We felt convinced that if the Indians could ascertain the smallness of our numbers, they might, with so great a number, by taking advantage of us at the crossing of the creeks with such immense thickets in their bottoms, which we were compelled to cross, if not defeat, at least cut off a great many of our men; and if we had remained in the village all night, it would have given the Indians time to have concentrated their forces, ascertained

our numbers, and with ease have prevented our crossing a stream the size of the Trinity.[24]

The after-battle assessment of the operation in Porter's report lists the casualties: "We had one killed; one badly and one slightly wounded. The Indians had twelve killed," but speculated that many more were likely dead. Of the Indians, "They were a portion of a good many tribes—principally the Cherokees who were driven from Nacogdoches County; some Creeks and Seminoles, Caddos, Kickapoos, Anadarcos, etc."[25] Interestingly he does not mention the Comanches or the Choctaws, the tribes who were actually suspected of being the perpetrators of the Yeary and Ripley attacks that the expedition was intended to avenge.

From the Indian perspective there is an Anadarko account of the battle for the third village, which was led by "the young, charismatic Jose Maria (Iesh), an Indian leader who would make a substantial mark on Texas history ... During Tarrant's attack, Jose Maria rallied his men and halted the attack."[26] Jose Maria was well known as a peacemaker: he signed a treaty with Sam Houston in 1844, and traveled to Washington, DC to sign another with President James K. Polk in 1846. Captain Randolph Marcy would later describe Jose Maria as, "a very sensible old chief ... who feels a deep interest in the welfare of his people; and is doing everything in his power to better their condition."[27] Though Tarrant had kidnapped Jose Maria's sister and nephew from the villages, the sister escaped along the way back, but he kept the boy for another two years.[28] Two years later both Jose Maria and Tarrant would return to the area together, under much different circumstances: each of them were cosigners of the 1843 Bird's Fort Treaty.[29]

The Porter report paints a picture of a well-organized, prosperous, and well-provisioned Indian community. There were over 225 occupied lodges in the first two villages and more beyond that they could not count. The Texans found over three hundred acres of corn under cultivation:

(They) were abundantly provided with ammunition of every kind. They had good guns and had molded a great many bullets. Every lodge had two or three little bags of powder and lead, tied up in equal portions;

and, at one lodge, a sort of blacksmith shop, where we found a set of black-smith tools. We found over a half bushel of molded bullets, and we found also some sergeant's swords, musket flints, rifle and musket powder, pig lead, rifle and musket balls, which we supposed they must have taken from the place where the regular army had buried a portion of their ammunition. They had all manner of farming utensils, of the best sort, except plows. In some of the lodges we found feather beds and bedsteads.[30]

The decision having been made to flee the field rather than face a much larger force, they made ready to leave. The soldiers spent some time plundering the captured villages, the spoils which Porter enumerated in his report: six head of cattle, thirty-seven horses, three hundred pounds of lead; thirty pounds of powder, twenty brass kettles, twenty-one axes, seventy-three buffalo robes, fifteen guns, thirteen pack saddles, three swords, "more salt than mule could pack."[31] As Stout told it, "We were rich in plunder and spoils."[32] Though they eventually discarded much of what they had stolen, the remaining plundered goods were sold for $2,000 in the settlements when they returned.[33]

"At five o'clock, with our poor dead companion tied across a horse we left the village, marched twelve miles back on the trail we came."[34] The troop marched back to the area on Fossil Creek near the Trinity where they had camped the previous night, arriving around midnight. Along the way they had abandoned much of the plunder acquired at the villages, the weight being excessive and the need for speed great. Leaving at first light the next morning they next crossed to the north side of Fossil Creek heading east in the direction of the site that would become Bird's Fort. Perhaps it had been their original intention to bring the body back to Clarksville for a proper burial, but "the men conveying the body discovered that on account of the hot weather, decomposition had set in and they would be compelled to stop and bury the body before reaching the settlement."[35]

Andrew Davis reported: "At about 11 o'clock we halted in a prairie on the south side of a creek with a high bank on the north,"[36] and there they buried the body of their fallen comrade, John B. Denton.

His grave was dug a good depth, a thin rock was cut so as to fit in the bottom of the grave, similar rocks were placed at the sides and also at the head and foot. Another rock was placed over the body and the grave filled up. Thus was buried one of God's noble men.[37]

Henry Stout remembered Denton as "One of the grandest men Texas ever contained … He was a pious good man, and a truer friend or more daring spirit never lived." And with a dig at Tarrant, Denton's "death and my wounds were a result of bad management."[38]

With Denton buried it must have been a sad trip home, battle weary and in shock, mourning the loss of their beloved and respected friend. They traveled north and east, aiming for Bonham riding along the west side of the Eastern Cross Timbers and the Elm Fork of the Trinity.[39] Near the site of the present-day site of Gainesville they came to the Chihuahua Trail on which they had started their journey less than two weeks before. From there they proceeded east, back to Ft. Johnston, near Pottsboro, where they divided their spoils and disbanded. The sad task of informing Mary Denton of the death of her husband fell to Clabe Chisum. He promised her that he would one day go back and retrieve the body of her husband and his slain comrade.[40]

He (Denton) was universally beloved and respected where he was known, especially so in Clarksville, and his death was the occasion for profound sorrow and regret in that little city, to the extent that it made impressions upon the minds of the children of that town that lasted for many years. Dr. Pat B. Clark, though a small boy, remembered in the early morning of the cries and screams that awoke the citizens of that town when the first courier arrived with the sad news that the Indians had killed Captain Denton.[41]

Thus ended the First Tarrant Expedition and the life of John B. Denton. But his story did not end there, not by a long shot.

Chapter 16

Aftermath of the Battle and the Creation of Denton County

The Battle of Village Creek quickly achieved legendary status in the memories of early Texans. It wasn't a decisive battle but the list of the participants, many of whom went on to assume positions of responsibility in Texas, elevated its importance. John B. Denton's life story was entwined with the story of the Battle of Village Creek and his posthumous popularity helped keep the battle alive in the public memory.

Having participated in the Battle of Village Creek was, for those who served, a proud moment and something that would be referred to for the rest of their lives. It would lend them a gravitas as battle-hardened veterans that late-comers could not claim. Biographical sketches and the obituaries of many of the participants make a reference to their presence at the death of John B. Denton on Village Creek and this became an important footnote in their own distinguished lives.

By the same token, there are a number of articles about individuals with claims of having been at the battle, without any corroborating evidence to support them. Dr. D. L. Owings, for instance, the first mayor of Denison, claimed to have been a Village Creek veteran. "We have frequently heard him tell of the fight and hurried burial of Denton,"[1] but there is nothing in the record to support this. John D. Pickens claims to have been fourteen at the battle, and provided some details later used by historian A. J. Sowell in his account,[2] but there is no independent evidence of his participation. Barkley M. Ballard rated a mention in the Dallas paper when he passed through in 1874. Claiming to be a veteran of both the Texas Revolution and with Denton at Village Creek, he received free train tickets and hotel accommodations for his stolen valor.

> On noticing his name on the books of the Commercial Hotel, we felt a thrill as we read the word, "donation," knowing that the proprietors of that house are new comers to Texas.[3]

The results of the first Tarrant Expedition were inconclusive. Like many of the frontier expeditions, they had sought an elusive enemy who was reluctant to engage with them. They set out to avenge the murder of the Ripley family and most likely attacked a group of Indians unrelated to the actual perpetrators. The expedition had been plagued with tensions over leadership and judgment, and they had lost a good friend. John Henry Brown's assessment underscored some of the problems mentioned by Stout:

> The expedition was unsuccessful in its chief objects and, from some cause, probably a division of responsibility, the men, or a portion of them, at the critical moment, were thrown into a degree of confusion bordering on panic.[4]

When Tarrant returned to Red River County he was eager for a more decisive victory and immediately started preparations for another much larger expedition to the upper Trinity. President Lamar, pursuing his policy of Indian extermination, authorized Tarrant's Fourth Militia Brigade to return to the field and clear the Cross Timbers of any remnant tribes. This new force of about 300 minutemen contained many old hands from previous expeditions and among them friends and acquaintances of John B. Denton. One friend, George Gerdes, recalled returning to Village Creek with Tarrant in July of 1841. On that journey, some of the men who had been with Denton in the Battle of Village Creek, pointed out to him the exact place where Denton had been killed, by the creek, and under a large Cottonwood tree.[5]

"Tarrant kept his Fourth Brigade in the field for two more weeks in search of hostile Indians. His men saw no action during this time and ultimately returned home with provisions nearly exhausted."[6] One result of the Tarrant Expeditions was that they served to push the line of the frontier further west as the Indians had moved to avoid confrontation. Only in that sense, by opening up more land for settlements, could it be judged a success; but it didn't really address the putative reasons for the expeditions in the first place, avenging Indian attacks. Pushing the relatively peaceful Indian villages farther away didn't necessarily prevent the raids from Indian Territory, but it reassured the settlers that something was being done and served the economic interests of the region.

Residents along the Red River were lulled into a sense of complacency after the last of the Tarrant expeditions to the Crosstimbers. However, Indian attacks continued from renegade bands across the border in Indian Territory where it is very likely many of the previous attacks had originated.[7] One of the justifications for the attack on Village Creek had been a supposed direct link between depredations on east Texas settlers and the Indian villages on the Trinity. This is highly unlikely, and although at least one of the soldiers claimed to have retrieved his own horses from Village Creek,[8] it is a claim that would be impossible to verify. Very shortly after the Battle of Village Creek, the Sulphur Forks experienced several more violent attacks on settlers living not far from the Red River.

> The Indians responsible for the death of young Dugan and Kitchens and the attack on the Kitchens house were renegade Coushattas from the United States. This group of Indians, and associated bands, were not only a source of constant menace to the white settlers of Texas but also to the civilized Chickasaws north of Red River.[9]

Lamar's policy of ethnic cleansing on the frontier was costly and in the end not particularly successful. In his three years in office he had spent $2.5 million on his Indian campaign driving the republic deeper into debt, while: "Overall, Lamar's approach, although it inflicted severe losses on the western Indians such as the Comanches, did not bring lasting peace to the frontier."[10] Unlike Sam Houston, he opposed annexation to the United States and instead harbored grandiose expansion plans that included extending Texas to the Pacific Ocean.[11] But it was the ill-fated Santa Fe Expedition that unraveled his presidency. Without authorization from Congress, Lamar initiated a commercial and military expedition to set up a trade route and assert Texan control over New Mexico. The expedition got lost, ran out of provisions and finally when they arrived near Tucumcari, were immediately captured by superior Mexican forces. In a humiliating failure, the captured Texans were imprisoned in Mexico, which further tarnished Lamar's reputation and helped Sam Houston regain the presidency in 1841.

In Houston's second presidency (1841–1844) he attempted to reverse some of Lamar's policies: he promoted austerity for the finances of the republic; he pursued peace negotiations with the Indians; he avoided a war with Mexico; and he encouraged the annexation of Texas to the United States. In May of 1844, Houston wrote a letter to Waco Chief Acah-Quash, inviting him and Jose Maria, the Indian hero of Village Creek, to make peace:

> When you come down to see me, we will send away all trouble, and if the whites have done wrong they shall be punished, as bad men should be. You will embrace your red brothers for me. When you come to see me, my heart will be open to receive you and José Maria. (Your brother, Sam Houston)[12]

In 1844, Houston reopened the negotiations with the United States for a treaty of annexation, but because of slavery and internal politics in the United States, this was not finally ratified until February 19, 1846. The referendum held in Texas over annexation was overwhelmingly approved by the voters of Texas. In all four of the Red River counties, opposition to annexation garnered only thirty votes.[13] Very early in the order of business for the new State of Texas was the passage of "An Act to create the County of Denton,"[14] which passed on April 11, 1846. There were thirty-two new counties created in that first year of Texas statehood and most were named to honor someone important to Texas, its history and its development. Four counties were named for men who participated in the Tarrant Expedition: William C. Young; Daniel Montague; General Edward Tarrant; and for John B. Denton. Senator James Bourland is credited with the honor of having suggested the name of Denton for a new county.

> It was doubtless due to Senator Bourland that Denton County, created at this session of the Legislature, was so named, in honor of his neighbor and friend who was slain when they were fighting together.[15]

Chapter 17

John B. Denton's Will and Estate

When John B. Denton was killed at age thirty-four, his community was saddened and his family was devastated. To his wife Mary, now a widow with six children, the youngest just fourteen months old, it must have seemed as if the world had ended. The cries and screams of lamentation filling the night air of Clarksville, when his family learned of Denton's death, were remembered by many residents for the rest of their lives.[1]

Since taking up the practice of law in 1837, Denton had not wasted his time and having acquired a reasonable portfolio of property did not leave his family completely destitute upon his death. His will, executed July 15, 1840, just a few months after John B. Denton, Jr. was born, designated his partners and friends, John B. Craig and William N. Porter as Executors. (John B. Craig became the sole executor when Porter withdrew from the post and by 1844, Porter was no longer living in Texas.[2]) After providing for the payment of his debts, he gave all of his personal property to his wife, Mary Stewart Denton. In addition, he also bequeathed her the 640 acres of his headright and another 320 acres to be divided from land he owned with John B. Craig. To his oldest daughter Sarah Elisabeth, he bequeathed a thousand acres, to be divided from land he owned with Craig. To his remaining children, "Johnothan," Nancysu, Eldredge, Ashley, and Burnard

John B. Denton's Last Will and Testament. Denton's will, signed July 15, 1840, was found in the Probate Records of the Red River County Courthouse. This was signed during his campaign for the Texas Senate, and just four months after his youngest son, John Burnard Denton, Jr., was born. His will demonstrates that he was becoming a man of some means, and for the first time in his life he actually had assets to pass on to his growing family.

(John B. Denton, Jr.) he bequeathed the balance of his estate to be divided equally from land also held in partnership with John B. Craig.[3] The discrepancy between the legacies left to his children can be explained: Elizabeth, though only fifteen when Denton died, was soon to marry Bernard Hill and start a family. Hill, a teacher in Clarksville, had taught Elizabeth as well as John Chisum, who would later figure prominently in the story of the discovery and reburial of Denton's bones. For the remaining heirs, the legacy of an undivided share in land not yet sold, was not exactly a "bird in the hand." Unenumerated land in his estate consisted of four parcels, totaling 1,951 acres, a portion of which was sold at auction in 1843,[4] and the remaining sold in 1848.[5]

A widow with six children, living on the frontier, was in a precarious position. After a respectable interval, Mary Denton found a suitable husband in Abner McKenzie, and on August 11, 1842, they wed. McKenzie was the brother of Rev. John W. P. McKenzie, a Methodist minister and the founder of McKenzie Institute, a college three miles from Clarksville. Rev. McKenzie had been in the Arkansas Conference of the Methodist Church at the same time as John B. Denton and they undoubtedly knew each other. His brother, Abner, managed a farm for the Institute, growing all of the food needed for the college and living there, which likely provided a wholesome environment in which the Denton children would be raised.[6]

Although Denton did not leave his family without property and some resources, with the complications of his business dealings, he left them in a web of entangled debts and receivables that would take decades to unravel. Bear in mind that there were no banks available to loan money for real estate, so most transactions took place with the exchange of personal promissory notes. The Republic of Texas chartered no banks: "The Commerce and Agricultural Bank opened in 1847 in Galveston, and was the only chartered bank in Texas before the Civil War."[7] The bank mortgage, as we know it today, did not exist. Of course, there were some money lenders, but there was no way they could keep up with the vast amount of property being bought and sold in Texas. Merchants often filled in the gap and almost all of them offered credit for goods—as demonstrated by the unpaid bills Denton left upon his death.[8]

To further complicate matters, other than the 640-acre headright Denton left his wife, all of his other land was held undivided, in partnership with John B. Craig. Denton and Craig were both buying and selling property: giving promissory notes for land they bought and receiving notes for what they sold. The very complexity of these entanglements meant that the resolution and final distribution to the heirs would neither be quick, smooth, nor without acrimony.

The records indicate that John B. Craig spent much time trying to attend to the business of the Denton estate, but as he would plead to one judge, "there are debts to a very considerable amount ... which your petitioner has not funds to pay."[9] Some debts owed to Denton were deemed "uncollectible,"[10] and it became necessary for the family to sell personal property, a horse and two pistols, as well as a part of Denton's 640-acre headright to pay creditors. There were numerous ads placed in the *Northern Standard*, Samuel DeMorse's Clarksville newspaper, for the sale of land from the John B. Denton estate. There being no ready buyers for some of the property, Craig was forced to auction off some of the property on the courthouse steps to the highest bidder.[11]

The problem, of course, was that so many people already owned headrights acquired land by grants, that there was an abundance of land for sale. The Dentons, like many Texans, fit the very definition of "land rich and cash poor." New land opening up to the south and west caused incoming settlers to pass through the Sulphur Forks rather than stopping there, as in the early days of the Republic. Things reached such a low point in the resolution of the estate, that in 1847, Craig sued the estate of John B. Denton and a summons was issued for them to appear in court. The next year, and at regular intervals afterward, Craig was summoned to court and ordered to produce a report on the estate, with an itemized accounting of what was owed, what was due and what had been paid. By 1855, the estate had paid off $2,888.00 in claims, but it still owed almost $1,800.00 in unpaid bills (including $5.38 to Willis Dean for groceries and $15.00 to John Bloodworth for repairing Denton's house fifteen years before). By the early 1850s, Craig had retired from the law, returned to the Methodist ministry and moved to Hopkins County, on the Sulphur River,[12] but still had to deal with the Denton estate by answering judges' summonses and reporting to court in Red River County. Slowly the assets and claims were whittled away: Craig resigned as executor in 1858, and the estate, unclosed, is still pending the Red River County Probate Court. The last amended report was filed in February 1880, thirty-nine years after Denton had died.

In addition to resolving the standard issues of the Denton estate, the family had an additional complication when trying to collect one of the debts owed Denton for services he had rendered in his legal practice. Just a week before Denton's death, he entered into a contract with William Davis to acquire an Augmentation Headright of 3,130 acres, for which Denton would receive 640 acres for his efforts. William Davis moved to California for a few years, but returned in 1848, at which time he donated 120 acres, on which the town of McKinney is located.[13] His debt to Denton was never resolved but listed as an uncollected asset in the Denton Estate. In 1860 the Denton heirs filed a suit to recover their share of the Davis headright. In the intervening years the land in question had increased in value from $0.50 to $25 per acre; the Denton heirs had reached maturity and had just become aware of the debt.[14] William Davis responded, denying the claim in February of 1861, but owing to the commencement of the Civil War one month later, the suit was put on hold until 1868 by which time Davis was deceased.[15]

The case took a bizarre turn in 1869 when the heirs of William Davis claimed that the Denton suit had no merit, based on the fact that John B. Denton had engaged in a criminal conspiracy, "by assisting, aiding and abetting ... Davis to wrong and defraud the Government of Texas." The Davis family claimed that he had not been married when the headright application was filed, and thus he was not legally entitled to the additional land he had been granted. This seems like an oddly self-defeating legal strategy, perhaps born of desperation, but the Denton family had hired the legal firm of James W. Throckmorton, former Senator, former Governor, and legal powerhouse to represent them and the ploy was easily dismissed.

In 1870, the Davises amended their appeal with the bombshell accusation that if the contract and debt were valid as claimed, the Denton heirs were still not entitled to inherit from the estate of their father, because Denton had never been legally married and thus his heirs were all illegitimate and not entitled to inherit.[16] There may have been some confusion over the fact that Denton's headright of 640 acres was for a single man, or more precisely, "a man without his family present." Nevertheless, this was a highly personal attack on the character and integrity of the entire Denton family and demonstrates how deep the acrimony between the families had become.

Testimony was presented from both sides. James Baker, whose son was married to Denton's daughter Sarah Elizabeth,[17] had known Denton for many years and had been his neighbor in Clarksville; J. L. Lovejoy, a respected early settler, stated that he knew Denton to have been married by Rev. Green Orr in Clark County, Arkansas.

John C. Bates, a witness for the Davis family, stated that he had known Denton during a period in which he returned to Arkansas in 1839, where he had presented himself as a single man. The Denton family presented their family Bible as evidence of their marriage, but could not find a Marriage Certificate. Considering the state of affairs in Clark County, Arkansas, in 1825, it is not surprising that a proper certificate could not be located.

Although John C. Bates was not believed as to the status of the Denton marriage, there is strong evidence that Denton had returned to Arkansas briefly in 1839, where he received a land grant for eighty acres in Clark County on November 1, 1839.[18] The Certificate states that he was a resident of Arkansas at that time, while his family, law practice and legal residence were still in Clarksville. There is more anecdotal evidence of Denton having traveled back to Arkansas, in the form of a letter from John H. Fowler to his brother, Littleton Fowler. Fowler was married to the widow of Thomas Denton,[19] and apparently no friend of Denton's as evidenced in this letter to his brother containing an explosive accusation:

> "You may feel some ... solicitude to hear about Denton. Public Sentiment has settled down against him. Mrs. Orr has a child corresponding with the time he was suspected. I have seen the child and all I can say about it is, it favors its dady"

> Letter- J. H. Fowler to Littleton Fowler
> Steamboat Mairier, Shreveport, May 19, 1839.[20]

The court did not believe the accusation about Denton's marriage because there was enough circumstantial evidence to prove its validity, and on the frontier not everyone had a marriage certificate. On November 9, 1870, they ruled in favor of the Denton heirs entitling them to 320 acres in Collin County. After a long and particularly nasty legal fight, their award was worth about $8,000;[21] less than what they had sued for, but still a big loss for the Davis heirs.[22]

Chapter 18

Honoring
John B. Denton

I n the 1880s, as the ranks of old settlers and early residents of Denton began to thin, many of these older citizens became nostalgic about the past and yearned to meet again with the friends of their youth. This generation of settlers had come to land that was bare prairie when they arrived, and in some thirty odd years of hard work and determination, had created a thriving community, literally from nothing. It was a community and a legacy they could be proud of. When founded in 1856, it was nothing more than a staked-out grid on the prairie, but by 1871, it had grown into a pleasant little farming town of 361. In 1881, the city became linked to the world when two railway lines came to Denton, greatly reducing the cost of goods sold in the community, and providing an economical way for farmers to take their products to market.[1] This was an economic shot in the arm for the community and by 1900, the population had grown to 2,558.

All this dynamism caused the citizens to start thinking bigger. Although there had been a private teachers college in Denton since 1890, in 1899, a consortium of citizens had worked very hard and persuaded the state to locate North Texas Normal College in Denton. Town spirits were in such bloom that the community decided to celebrate holding a "Mass Jollification"[2] on the square, to honor both the state funding for the teachers' college, and their prospering community.

With a heightened sense of community pride and a feeling that the old ways were passing, a few members of the old families organized the Old Settlers Association of Denton County, "for the purpose of preserving the names of the old settlers as well as the history and reminiscences of Texas."[3] In this spirit they organized a reunion of the families of the old settlers, to celebrate with an old fashioned community picnic and barbecue where the "old timers" could see one another again and reminisce about the old days. They held their first picnic in August 1889, and in their by-laws pledged that henceforth, "the Association ... shall meet on Thursday and Friday on or before each full moon in August at the city of Denton."[4]

As early as 1893, there had been some discussion of compiling a history of Denton County but nothing formally took place until the meeting of the Old Settlers Association in August of 1898. Anticipating the turn of the "New Century" in 1900, the organization, "began to discuss the history of Denton County and to formulate plans to secure the publication of the history at its session in 1899."[5] Much like "Millennial Madness" would affect the year 2000, the change from the nineteenth to the twentieth century would cause people to anticipate the future and reflect fondly on the past.[6] It was a worldwide phenomenon in which people attached an artificial significance to events happening at that juncture in time: "it came in forms many of today's citizens will recognize: Newspapers in December 1900 and early January 1901 ran historical reviews and ... reminiscences of centenarians."[7]

At this same time and in similar spirit another group was organizing efforts to bring a second college to the community which they decided to call the John B. Denton College, after "the pioneer Indian fighter."[8] Huge events were planned in cities around the country and Denton was not going to miss the party. At the meeting in 1898 the committee authorized two big things for Denton. Recognizing that the county was named for John B. Denton and, "Feeling the pride natural with all men when their county and town are fair to look upon ... it was but natural that their thoughts should turn to the source of the name."[9]

And since no one really knew much about him, they sought to correct the record by compiling a history of his life. There had been an ongoing controversy as to the location of Denton's grave, which they sought to resolve if possible, memorialize it, and give John B. Denton a decent funeral. They would give Denton a funeral that would do justice to Denton, the nineteenth-century man, and honor Denton the county, on the cusp of a bright future in the next century.

Rev. William H. Allen (1835–1908), who lived in southeast Denton County, was a Methodist minister, a teacher, a State Senator, and an author upon whose shoulders these tasks would rest. Allen had come to Texas as young man and had written a light-hearted book about his adventures trying to find his way in the world.[10] As a young man he had moved to Clarksville and worked for Clabe Chisum surveying land. It was from Chisum that he first heard of John B. Denton and the grave.[11] He later settled in far southeastern Denton County on the Collin County line, where he preached and operated a small private school. His second literary venture was a book entitled, *Erudia, the Foreign Missionary to Our World; or The Dream of Orphanos*,[12] a bit loftier but less readable than his first book, it was an allegory about the human condition. From this he named the small community where he lived Erudia, which had a post office for a few years on the Collin County side of the line. Allen was a distinguished man of letters and as such was a natural choice for doing justice to the legacy of John B. Denton.

His first task was to find Denton's bones. This was no easy job, because although it seems a settled matter today, at the time there were various and conflicting opinions about their whereabouts, and no definitive answer to the question. William N. Porter's War Department report was inconclusive, merely stating that they had been buried on a creek bank returning from Village Creek. Allen, wishing to gather more information, made a public appeal in the *Denton Record Chronicle* in August, 1900:

> The Pioneer Association of Denton County wishes to hear from anyone knowing anything relating to (1) The spot where John B. Denton lies buried; (2) Whether there is anywhere a portrait of him; (3) his nativity; (4) Every scrap of history of his life and character. Please report to William H. Allen, Rock Hill, Tex.[13]

Rev. William H. Allen. Allen was the author of *Captain John B. Denton,*
Preacher, Lawyer and Soldier, the first book-length biography of John B.
Denton. He became a Methodist minister in 1860, served as a State Senator
from 1887–1891, operated a private school in Southeastern Denton County,
and wrote several books on various subjects. When questions arose about the
history of John B. Denton, the Old Settlers Association of Denton called
upon Rev. Allen to answer them. Image from *Personnel of the Texas State*
Government with Sketches of Distinguished Texans, 1889.

From Denton's death until William H. Allen's appeal for information,
there had been a number of newspaper articles with opinions on the location
of Denton's grave. As early as 1859, James Isham, who was with Denton
at Village Creek, is reported to have found it on Bear Creek in east
Tarrant County, and deposited the remains with Mr. A. G. Clark, at Witt's

Mill in Dallas County.[14] Henry Stout reported that he found the grave on Fossil Creek, near Birdville.[15] One report suggested he was buried on Denton Creek— without much in the way of evidence.[16] John Henry Brown, *Indian Wars and Pioneers of Texas*, follows the Stout version of the Fossil Creek grave, in which the bones were exhumed and entrusted to a Rev. Mr. Lewis M. White,[17] of Grapevine.

When William H. Allen published his appeal for information, it was shared in other papers and broadcast widely around the state. Everyone loves a good mystery and soon the controversy over the lost bones of John B. Denton was featured in a number of articles published in the fall of 1900.

> Every few years the question of what became of the remains of John B. Denton, who was killed in a fight with Indians in 1841, is a matter of discussion in the newspapers. Of late several letters have appeared in the *Dallas News*, and two parties tell different stories of their being found and being reburied.[18]

Allen's appeal was successful, at least in reviving recollections about Denton and his lost grave. It got people talking, and encouraged old-timers to share their memories of Denton and the mystery of his lost bones.

Newspapers were quick to latch on to this human-interest story, recognizing that a little mystery makes good copy and sells papers. Although many newspapers may have published articles about the search for the grave, none devoted as much ink and column space to it as did the *Dallas Morning News*: not even the *Denton Record Chronicle*. The *Morning News* took it up as a cause and from September 9, to November 11, 1900, published fourteen articles about the search for Denton's grave. Their first article on Allen's appeal and the search for the grave, "To Honor a Texas Pioneer," was published on September 9, 1900, where they observed that Denton had been "buried on some spot in Denton County, the exact location of which no man seems to know."[19]

Noted Texas historian James De Shields quickly responded that he was happy to hear of the plan to memorialize Denton; however he understood Denton's remains to have been buried on Bear Creek, in Tarrant

County.[20] Eleven days later in an article headed "Special" to the News, "John Denton's Grave—Clew [sic] to the Burial Place of the Pioneer Has Been Obtained."[21] This article is the first public mention of John Chisum's claim to have found Denton's bones.

> Heretofore the promoters of the monument have had no idea as to the exact location of the spot, but Mr. J. W. Austin, a citizen of Pilot Point, says that he was told by James Chisholm[22] [sic] who had known Denton well, that his grave was on Clear Creek, three miles northwest of Bolivar, ... by a tree ...

Next, Col. John Peter Smith, an early Tarrant County settler, often called "the Father of Ft. Worth," weighed in on the subject and recounted that he had been to the Village Creek battleground with Henry Stout around 1874, and he believed Stout.

> He found the spot where John B. Denton was killed and thought he could follow the route they retreated over and locate the grave ... But the country having been cut up into pastures and trees having been cleared away they despaired of finding the spot where they buried him ... but he was certain that they did not pass Denton or Clear Creeks in the prairie.[23]

Colonel Smith[24] turned up the heat in the discussion by seeming to discount the word of John Chisum. "This occurred in 1841, and John Chisholm [sic] did not move or settle in Cooke or Denton County until 1855."[25] John Peter Smith was one of the "big men" of Fort Worth: well respected and wealthy, he was a tireless promoter of the interest of his community, but big as he was, he was no John Chisum.

John Chisum the cattle baron, was a legend who had gotten his start in Denton County. After leaving Denton in 1862 he moved west, stopping for a few years on the Concho River in West Texas before moving to New Mexico. There he became one of the biggest ranchers in the country, creating a virtual empire along the Pecos River. He claimed almost one hundred miles of the river where he grazed his enormous herds of cattle. He was well known and well respected, and to many who remembered him from his days in Denton County, he was considered one of their own.

Chisum had moved to Texas when he was thirteen, settling in Red River County in 1837, around the same time John B. Denton had moved there. He had attended school with Denton's daughter Elizabeth, and the two families were well acquainted with each other. His father, Clabe Chisum, had served with Denton and been on the Tarrant Expedition when Denton was killed: he had been the one to bring the sad news of Denton's death to his family. Clabe Chisum had often told his son of the battle and burial, describing the location on a creek bank near a tree and of his pledge to retrieve the remains of his buried friend. John Chisum still had many friends in the area and they were ready to come to his defense for any imagined slight by Colonel John Peter Smith.

The response came quickly when the next day the *Dallas Morning News* published an article with statements from two well-known Denton residents: Capt. Robert H. Hopkins Sr. and County Judge I. D. Ferguson. Hopkins recounted details of the events he had heard from John Lemuel Lovejoy,[26] a militia veteran who was with Denton at Village Creek and was a good friend of Clabe Chisum. He corrected a small detail in Colonel John Peter Smith's statement and went on to say that Chisum, the elder, had told his son John, "as near as he could, the exact location of the grave which he thought was somewhere on Denton Creek."[27] Roaming all over Denton County with his herds, Chisum was reported to have come across the place described by his father on Oliver Creek, near present-day Justin, Texas, where he found the grave of Denton. It was, as it had been described to him by his father, near an Elm tree; the old bones wrapped in a blanket; the teeth had some gold fillings and it was buried with a tin cup and some trinkets. Chisum had taken them and placed them in an old wooden box and left them there when he sold the ranch to J. H. Waide in 1863. According to Hopkins, after a few years they started to smell and Mr. Waide buried them near the old Chisum ranch house. Judge I. D. Ferguson, who oddly claimed to be named for Denton's brother William, recounted almost the same story of Chisum finding the bones, determining they were Denton's and reburying them on his ranch near Bolivar.[28] These accounts by Hopkins and Ferguson were at odds with Chisum's own account: he did not find the bones by the description of the burial place from his father, but rather some boys found bones at the confluence of Oliver and Denton Creeks and he assumed they were Denton's bones.

A few days later on October 2, 1900, John W. Gober wrote to confirm the Chisum account and offered the definitive word on the subject, as the paper reported: "The incidents concerning the matter are so fresh in Mr. Gober's mind ... it is believed this statement will decisively settle the matter."[29] Gober related that his knowledge was based on having seen the bones at Chisum's house in September of 1856, just a month after Chisum had discovered them. Chisum had dug them up and bought them back to his ranch in an old grub sack and was absolutely convinced that they were the remains of his long dead family friend.

> The bones were getting musty and beginning to smell, and he asked my advice as to what to do with them. I suggested that he bury them in a box, as Denton's people (who had been notified by Chisum of what he had done) were not coming after them.[30]

Gober then revealed the ultimate confirmation: a letter from Chisum, written in 1880, describing exactly how he found and retrieved Denton's remains, and what he did with them.

Roswell, N. M. July 4
Dear Friend,

The remains of John B. Denton are buried at the Waide place in a small box six or eight feet from the house I lived in, rather at the southwest corner of the yard ... His grave was discovered by some boys who were out rabbit hunting on Oliver Creek. From the description W. H. Bourland, W. C. Young, and Henry Stout had given me of the place where he was buried I knew that that was his grave, and being a friend of Denton's, I took up his remains and carried them home. I notified his children and his brother Masons of what I had done. There being no steps taken I placed them in a box and buried them as I tell you. From many circumstances I can say I am positive there is no mistake in their being Denton's remains. His rib bones were very rotten when I took them up and more so now. He was killed in 1841 or 1842, I believe, which was a long time ago. You will notice one of the arm bones I buried was broken. Some doubted them being the bones of Denton, but I know they are his and no mistake.

> I am as ever, your friend,
> John Chisum[31]

Col. John Peter Smith's mere hint that Chisum's account might be in error had caused an avalanche of reaction in the pages of the *Dallas Morning News*. Old comrades came riding to the rescue like a posse of avengers to corroborate, and occasionally embellish, the story of their old friend John Chisum. Robert G. Johnson, an old cowboy, wrote that he had been with Chisum when they disinterred the remains of Denton.[32] By his recollection, Chisum had known of the grave site and had taken James Bourland and Felix McKittrick,[33] then Sheriff of Denton County, to verify that it was indeed Denton. This done to his satisfaction, Chisum later returned with Johnson, Cristopher Fitzgerald, who brought the pick, Reese Hanna, Newt Anderson, Patrick O'Ferrell, and Phil and Jiles Chisum,[34] and dug up the bones. They found vestiges of a blanket, evidence of a broken arm and a gold-filled tooth. "So far as I know, no one of the party named ever had a reasonable doubt about the bones being those of John B. Denton."[35] Be that as it may, none of these men had actually been there when Denton was buried.

Everyone seemed to have an opinion on the subject and even many of the pro-Chisum accounts were at odds with the facts, but if there had been any doubt left, it had withered under sheer weight of Chisum's gravitas and the passion of his allies. The grave controversy which *The Dallas Morning News* had so enthusiastically encouraged had been resolved:

> It is believed that his (R. G. Johnson's) statement will be conclusive evidence, when brought before the committee of the Old Settlers' Association, which will take steps thereupon for exhuming the remains near Bolivar.[36]

Chapter 19

Rev. William H. Allen's Report on Denton's Bones

With the enthusiastic response to the public request for information about John B. Denton, Rev. William H. Allen had an abundance of material from which to write his report about Denton for the Old Settlers' Association. As for the grave, he was fully aware of the difficulties and expressed his doubts at the outset:

> The territory ... was a vast wilderness and untraversed except in pursuit of Indians. Denton's grave was therefore lost.
> The question now arises: Has the lost grave ever been found? We are inclined to believe that if it has never been found that it never will be. We say this out of due deference to all parties who think they can find it.

Allen had received a large amount of personal correspondence and many were compelled to write letters to newspapers which provoked a considerable amount of public discussion of the matter. This could have made his task easier, but as Allen noted, "The testimony of eye-witnesses is oftentimes not in full accord."[1] Of the various possible scenarios suggested by the public concerning Denton's grave, it quickly became obvious that the testimony received supporting John Chisum's version of events won in the court of public opinion. The narrative of Chisum, with his local connection and impeccable reputation, fulfilling his father's pledge to find the bones of a fallen comrade, was a compelling one. For Allen, the job of weaving his way through the available information to a definitive conclusion was complicated by the fact that the executive committee of the Old Settlers Association was made up of four distinguished citizens: R. H. Bates, Christopher Columbus Dougherty, Robert H. Hopkins, and John W. Gober. Hopkins and Gober were old friends of Chisum, and each had weighed in publicly promoting the Chisum scenario.

With the committee heavily weighted towards Chisum, it looked like the conclusion was pre-preordained, which put Allen in a difficult position. Under these conditions he did the best he could. Here he outlined the problem:

> in looking over the evidence, we have been put to the necessity of studiously extracting the truth out of the half-way chaotic bundle of matter that came under the eye of the writer of this biography. Those who, ... had an opportunity to be agreed were not, some contending that Captain Denton was first buried in the territory of what is now Tarrant County; others that he was buried in the territory of what is now Denton County. These differing reports came from the two or three who yet survive of the Kechi battle, in which Denton was killed, and from others with whom the old pioneers had talked. *These not being in harmony, it became necessary to identify Captain Denton's body on another line of evidence.* [italics mine]

He chose to deflect from having to determine which camp was correct and instead he relied on some sketchy forensic evidence to make the choice, which he then presented to the Committee. The forensic evidence was weak by modern standards or indeed by any standards at all. One of the arms of the skeleton they found near Oliver Creek showed evidence of having been previously broken. Allen asked Denton's son, Rev. Johnathan F. Denton, whether or not Denton had ever broken an arm. Rev. Denton, who had been twelve when his father died: "says that his father once had an arm broken by a fall from a horse. This seemed to me to be good corroborating evidence."[2]

Allen and the Committee seemed untroubled by the fact that no one remembered which arm had been broken in either the recovered skeletal remains,
or by Denton.

Like a good prosecutor Allen laid out his argument, both the pros and
cons, and rather than affirmatively declaring which of the scenarios was
the correct one, he presented the evidence to the committee for their final
decision.

> The pioneer settlers are all convinced, agreed, and satisfied. They
> constituted the jury that sat in the case, and unanimously have rendered
> their verdict that the remains buried on the Chisum ranch are all that
> is left to us, in a material way, of the noted pioneer, Captain John B.
> Denton.[3]

Besides having the authority of John Chisum and the Oliver Creek
burial scenario, this version had the benefit of having actual recoverable
bones that could be ceremoniously re-buried—both lacking in the Henry
Stout and Isham versions. They were planning a big party and the Chisum
scenario assured that the guest of honor could attend.

Chapter 20

The Reburial of a Hero

he photograph is dated November 21, 1901.[1] Looking southeast over the yard of the four-year-old Denton County Courthouse, it shows a large milling crowd; well-dressed men with short-brimmed Stetsons; bearded old-timers; ladies with hats; and a few boys skipping school for the big occasion. In the background you can see a few figures looking out of the windows from the dentist office above the bank, some ranch hands standing on wagons, and one man standing on a window ledge. In the center of the photo are the pallbearers, six old men of distinction gathered around the grave, two of them seen holding a rope as they gently lowered the casket into the ground. It is a big event, but from their faces you can see they aren't celebrating: it is a solemn occasion, being the third burial of John B. Denton, whose bones would finally be laid to rest on the lawn of the courthouse in the county named in his honor.

The reinterment ceremony, which had just taken place in the courtroom, had been imbued with all the dignity befitting the man. His fine casket lay in state, while the main floor and upper gallery of the courtroom were filled with over six hundred good citizens, and old-time settlers who came to pay their respects. Seated immediately in front of the bier on which stood the

Burial of John B. Denton, November 21, 1901. Group of individuals on the
Denton Square for the burial of John B. Denton on the lawn of the Denton
County Courthouse. The pallbearers are E.B. Orr, L. Willis, J.M. Swisher, John
W. Gober, J.H. Hawkins, and W.C. Wright. The Minnis and Curtis Drugstore
can be seen in the southeast corner of the square. The Exchange National Bank
can be seen in the background. *Courtesy of the Denton Public Library.*

casket, were three of Denton's descendants: his sons, Rev. J. F. Denton and
Rev. John B. Denton, Jr., and grandson, Professor William Baker.

The ceremony started at 1:30 p.m. with Rev. William H. Allen officiating.
After a few opening remarks, Allen introduced Prof. O. H. Thurman, President
of the newly formed John B. Denton College,[2] who led the assembly in the
singing of "America." Then a brief invocation from Doctor W. C. Lattimore of
the First Baptist Church, before Rev. Allen delivered his address.

Rev. William H. Allen was a brilliant orator, a scholar, a writer, educa-
tor, and former State Senator with a great command of the English language.
With his year-long pursuit of the grave and facts about John B. Denton, he
had become immersed in the story and was the person most knowledgea-
ble and capable of delivering a proper eulogy to Denton. The Old Settlers
Association had placed their faith in his abilities, and that day, he did not
disappoint.

The paucity of solid information about the life of Denton was no obstacle for a man of many words and in his forty-minute eulogy he painted a beautiful picture of the life of Denton and his contributions to history. The Old Settlers, who had known little about Denton, wanted him to be a man of whom the citizens of Denton could be proud. In his homage to Denton, Allen offered a sort of Denton County origin myth: the tale of a simple man of native nobility who, rising from poverty and deprivation, gave his life that others might live.

That so few had known much at all about Denton, the ceremony was as much a public unveiling of Denton's life as it was a burial of his bones. Allen's address on the life and death of Denton was for many the first real introduction to the man they had become so curious about. Allen quickly reassured the assembled citizens:

> the name of your county and city perpetuates the name of an honorable man, who looked forward with great interest and sacrifice to the civilization of your state, and even yielded his life that you and your children might have a peaceful legacy.[3]

From his humble beginnings; "Orphanage, penury, and the wilds of Arkansas ..."[4] to lofty heights:

> had he lived in the days of chivalry he would have won a silver spur; had he been an ancient Greek he would have won the laurel at Olympia; had he been a Frenchman in the days of Napoleon he would have been a field-marshal.[5]

In the pantheon of Texas heroes he would join those who,

> bravely fell for frontier protection, and in the interest of Texas. He will sleep in an honored grave as do Fannin, Travis, Crockett and Bowie, and all that slumbering and moldering host who yielded their lives, shedding generously their patriotic blood for Texas.[6]

He had died, a "martyr to Texas civilization,"[7] and the peaceful bounties enjoyed by citizens of the day had been paid for with the blood of her heroes. Though Denton County had not existed when Denton fell, "His blood is in her soil and his crumbling body is a part of her dust."

He then introduced the Rev. James W. Chalk, the Chaplain of the Old
Settlers Association, the first man to propose relocating Denton's remains
and erecting a monument in his honor.[8] Rev. Chalk declared, "Denton,
had he lived, would have taken his place with Houston, Rusk, Hemphill,
Bayler [sic], and those others whose names have been handed down in
Texas history."[9]

After Rev. Chalk's "impromptu" and somewhat rambling reminiscences, Allen introduced the sons and grandson of John B. Denton, who
expressed their gratitude in short but heartfelt remarks. A barbershop
quartette sang the popular, "Some Sweet Day." And as the pallbearers,
Messrs. E. B. Orr, L. Willis, J. M. Swisher, John W. Gober, J. H. Hawkins,
and W. C. Wright, lifted the coffin, the quartette began to sing "Rock of
Ages," while they slowly processed to the yard of the courthouse, first
Denton's family, followed by hundreds of spectators to the prepared grave.
Before internment, those present were given the opportunity to view the
bones, crumbling and discolored after sixty years in the ground. In spite of
their poor condition, Allen left an elevated, almost spiritual image of the
last view of John B. Denton's mortal remains;

> about them in the mind's eye was a halo, a spirit of heroic fortitude,
> of unselfish courage, and loyal patriotism to the new country, for
> whose up-building and for whose later civilization he gladly gave
> up his life.[10]

Around the grave, a low brick wall was built and plans were made
for a more ambitious monument to honor the man. A monument had been
in the plans from the very beginning of the discussions about honoring
Denton. There had been serious doubt in the beginning whether his grave
could be found, and the Old Settlers' Association had planned to memorialize him with a stone "shaft," a monumental pillar on the courthouse
lawn. In the late nineteenth and early twentieth century, the country was
experiencing a sort of "monument mania" among civic-minded citizens.
They were being placed everywhere for almost any occasion. Denton was
also the home of other monumental plans: in 1907, A.G. Lee announced
his plans to build a massive six-hundred-foot-tall stone pyramid dedicated

to John D. Rockefeller, "the greatest man the world has ever known;"[11] and around 1910 he announced plans to build a large monument to the greatest living woman philanthropist.[12]

While Lee's fanciful projects barely got off the ground, the Daughters of the Confederacy were raising funds to build a Confederate Memorial on the courthouse square during this period and it is likely that the community enthusiasm for Denton's monument was overwhelmed by the Confederate monument subscription drive. In 1911, the Chamber of Commerce voted to cooperate with any ladies' clubs in building a monument on the Courthouse lawn, "either to John B. Denton or Confederate veterans," to improve the appearance of the square.[13] Because of the dwindling numbers of the Old Settlers Association and the Confederate Veterans Association they merged in 1915 and the bylaws were changed to unite the two aging groups:

> Resolved, That the proposition submitted by Sul Ross Camp of Confederate Veterans, that the Old Settlers and the Confederate Veterans consolidate, is hereby accepted, and that the old settlers of Denton County and the Confederate veterans ... are hereby united and consolidated for the purpose of annual reunions and such other purposes as may be found desirable.[14]

At the same time members of the local Grand Army of the Republic Association (the Union Army veterans) were also invited to join with the others forming Old Settlers' and Veterans' Association of Denton County, and plans for a monument to Denton seem to have been forgotten. It wasn't until the Texas Centennial in 1936 that a substantial granite historical marker was placed on Denton's grave.

Chapter 21

The Martyrdom of
John B. Denton

I n 1905, Rev. William H. Allen published his long-awaited biography of John B. Denton.[1] Having experience as a writer, and having prepared the biographic report for the Old Settlers' Association, he knew as much as anyone did at the time and was well qualified for the job. Allen acknowledged the problem of the biographer: "Hence there remains only a modicum of written data upon which to construct true biography," but proceeded to elaborate with enthusiasm. Though it was an earnest effort, it contained some of the myths told about Denton from the days of Alfred W. Arrington, and carried with it the cultural baggage of the age regarding Native Americans. With a relatively small amount of information it was embellished with all of the gusto that a skilled nineteenth-century orator and southern preacher could bring to the task. In it, he published the address he had delivered at the reinterment ceremony, his report on the grave, as submitted to the Old Settlers' Association, several newspaper articles about the search for the bones, and an additional essay on Denton's life and his significance in history.

The importance of the Allen book is that it codified the story of John B. Denton, bringing together information from widely diverse sources for the first time into one narrative. Addressing the controversies which had surrounded the story of Denton's life and death through the nineteenth century, he had produced a solid canon of information about Denton, which in the public's mind, settled the argument of who he was and where he was buried.

Allen was well aware of the suspicious nature of some of the previous tales about Denton and distanced himself from some of them:

> There are many stories relating to Denton's career as a preacher, a lawyer, and an orator which must be omitted. The object in writing this biography is a faithful and truthful portrayal of this noted and good man. Things that are at all doubtful, or that test the credulity, are not regarded as worthy. Future generations, through this treatise, should know the man in his true character, and they should not be left to guess at what is true and what is fiction.[2]

This is encouraging but somewhat contradicted by the lengthy pages of prose in which Allen cannot escape his ministerial frame of reference. He repeatedly refers to Denton's death as a martyrdom, his blood sacrifice necessary to purify this new land.

> The blood stains of the earth, even as there is something beautiful in the lives of those who freely shed their blood for humanity's sake ... Blood and sacrifice, as with the force of a law, seem to be associated in all things appertaining to man's progress.[3]

His Biblical references to "blood and sacrifice" are not falsehoods, but neither are they biographical data. Denton's blood on Texas soil reminds Allen of the "stained spot at Calvary": Captain Denton "crucified himself on the cross of human love that mankind might be made better, purer in heart and motive."[4]

> The cross is the central object in the Christian religion. The cold, blood-stained body of Caesar, stretched out in the Roman Forum while Anthony spoke the funeral note, has never been forgotten; The pierced Lincoln, Garfield, and McKinley will live as three tragedies in American history. The tragic fall of Captain Denton on the plains of Texas, in battle for his country, is most talked of and most remembered among the things of his life. It was the culminating tragedy in his

illustrious history with its blood stains. People did not forget it, cannot forget it, because of the blood.[5]

This is tall company for Denton to keep, but if Allen's goal was to write an origin myth for Denton County, he could do no better than place Denton in the company of Caesar, Lincoln, and Jesus.

Chapter 22

Who Is Buried in Denton's Tomb?

O   ne of the results of the Allen investigation, the burial, and the biography
     was to place in the permanent record the notion of Denton having
been buried three times. The story of the man with three graves, and his
connection with the ever-popular John Chisum, caught the public's attention and became a lead-in for numerous newspaper articles. Since the bones
were reinterred 1901, it has been an unquestioned matter of fact that
John B. Denton's bones were found by John Chisum, and were eventually
buried in the ground on the Denton County courthouse lawn.

And there they lay peacefully, the controversy over their identity, buried
with the bones; until May 24, 1941, exactly one hundred years after Denton's
death, an article was published questioning the accepted history. L.E. Slawson,
a historian from Ft. Worth, announced his belief that the bones were buried
near Birdville, Tarrant County, and that it would have been "impossible to
carry the body to Denton [County] for burial in that length of time,"[1] to Oliver
Creek. Slawson had likely read Henry Stout's version of the burial of the bones
which had been well covered in the *Ft. Worth Gazette*.

In 1998, historian A. C. Greene brought up questions about the
identity of the bones stating that Chisum himself had had doubts about

their identity as evidenced by his casual treatment of them.[2] This is a reasonable point; throwing the bones of a revered family friend into a candle box, and then burying them in your yard as an afterthought, does not seem like it either honors the sacred remains of a fallen hero, or a solemn pledge to one's father. (But there is no evidence that Chisum ever expressed anything but confidence in their identity.) Greene goes on to cite Henry Stout as a source of an alternative grave scenario and mentions unnamed historians as being in agreement. The unnamed historian Greene cites was most likely the iconoclast Barrot Sanders, who had reprinted Stout's *Fort Worth Gazette* interview in his privately printed book on Dallas history a decade before and speculated that the bones buried on the Denton square were those of an anonymous Native American. Sanders had made a name for himself for his research questioning whether Dallas' John Neely Bryan Cabin had been the work of another pioneer resulting in the removal of its historical marker.[3] In keeping with his penchant for iconoclasm, Sanders questioned the identity of Denton's bones, based on the Stout article, and claimed that he could find them; his efforts were not well received in Denton and they did not get much notice or any acceptance.[4]

Now that we are at the 180th anniversary of Denton's death, and in light of new information not previously available, it might be a good idea to take a closer look at the evidence surrounding the identity of the bones.

It must be remembered that prior to the Allen Report, Denton's burial was regularly referred to as "controversial." One of the first articles announcing the effort to honor Denton with a monument stated, "... he was slain, being afterwards buried on some spot in Denton County, the exact location of which no man seems to know."[5] The headline of the article publishing the Allen Report was "Committee does not think his remains have been or will be located."[6] Allen himself in his report to the committee seems to hedge his bet, mentioning that the first grave had been on a vast unmarked prairie and that there were a variety of opinions on the subject. His report left the question open: "The question now arises: Has the lost grave been found? We are inclined to believe that if it has never been found that it never will be ..." Allen refused to make a determination and left it for the committee to decide: the committee consisting of two old friends of John Chisum who had previously expressed their support for his version of events.

When Allen's book was published in 1905, it reprinted the article from the *Dallas Morning News* of October 19, 1900, about his report to the Committee. The original article had contained statements of doubt about the bones, but when Allen reprinted it he omitted the paragraph expressing doubts and effectively erased them from the general public record, the matter having been settled by the committee, the court of public opinion, and the bones from Chisum's ranch already buried on the courthouse square. He may have felt it was a moot point at that late date. Nevertheless, his book has been considered the authority on the subject for more than a century and any doubts about the identity of the bones have become obscured by history. As a consequence, it effectively stopped further inquiry into the subject.

Forgotten in the intervening years are the numerous accounts from the nineteenth century with alternative reports of the location of Denton's bones. What follows is a review of the various accounts of the site of the grave. They fall into several categories: accounts of the battle and firsthand descriptions of Denton's burial, firsthand accounts of efforts to retrieve the buried remains long after their burial, and secondhand reports by historians or friends of participants.

Col. William Porter, Acting Brigade Inspector, wrote the first account of the Battle of Village Creek in his report to the Secretary of War six weeks after the battle. His report was silent on the location but likely accurate as far as the distances traveled.

> At five o'clock with our dead companion tied across a horse we left the village, marched twelve miles back on the trail we came, crossed the Trinity and camped on an open prairie. The next morning twenty-five miles from the village we buried our friend.[7]

The first published claim about the discovery of Denton's bones was in 1859, by James Isham, a member of the Tarrant Expedition. He reportedly found Denton's grave on *Bear Creek* in eastern Tarrant County near present-day DFW Airport.

> The Remains found by Jim Isham were on *Bear Creek*, in Tarrant County. Mr Isham claims to have found the place where the body was deposited, and after diligent search he found the bones, except the skull, in a hollow. The cattle had made a path immediately over the grave, and the water had washed up the bones, and they were protruding out of the bank of the wash. The head is missing, Mr Isham boxed up the bones and has sent them for safe keeping to a gentleman near Witt's mill in this county- A. G. Clark, we suppose, there to await the action of the friends of the deceased.[8]

William H. Allen was apparently unaware of this forty-year-old article, because it was not mentioned in the Allen Report nor publicized during the public discussion of the location of the gravesite.

Mindful of his old comrade, Henry Stout went back several times to try to find Denton's bones. John Peter Smith reported accompanying Stout in an attempt around 1873 or 1874. Although unsuccessful, it did describe the general area where Stout thought Denton had been buried.[9]

> That night they crossed the Trinity and got out onto the prairie. He was of the opinion that the remains of Denton were interred *not far from where Birdville was then located*[10] ... They went back as rapidly and as directly as they could to Clarksville. Mr Stout could not find or identify any spot or location of the grave, but he was certain that they did not pass Denton or Clear Creeks in the prairie. [italics mine.][11]

In 1879, Henry Stout reported a second expedition to find Denton's bones at the request of James J. Jarvis, Esq. of Ft Worth, a friend of the Denton children. There is a contemporary reference to Stout finding the bones in an 1879 article, in the Bonham *Christian Messenger*.[12] At a slightly different location than on the previous trip, he reported that he found the remains of his old comrade. "We buried Denton in the forks of Fossil and I marked the place as I told you and recollected it and found it thirty-eight years after."[13] After retrieving the bones, Stout reportedly left them in the care of Rev. Lewis M. White, another Methodist minister

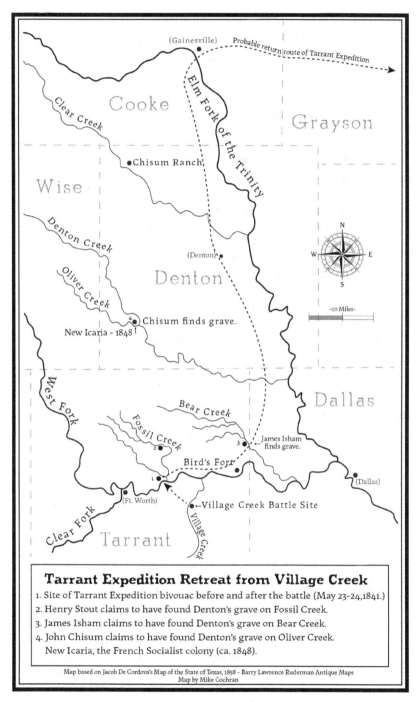

Tarrant Expedition Retreat from Village Creek

1. Site of Tarrant Expedition bivouac before and after the battle (May 23-24,1841.)
2. Henry Stout claims to have found Denton's grave on Fossil Creek.
3. James Isham claims to have found Denton's grave on Bear Creek.
4. John Chisum claims to have found Denton's grave on Oliver Creek.
   New Icaria, the French Socialist colony (ca. 1848).

Map based on Jacob De Cordova's Map of the State of Texas, 1858 - Barry Lawrence Ruderman Antique Maps
Map by Mike Cochran

Map of the Tarrant Expedition Retreat from Village Creek.

and friend of the Denton children, for him to deal with as he saw fit. Rev. White was the founder of the White's Chapel Methodist Church, the first church in northeast Tarrant County.[14] There is some slight conflict between John Peter Smith's and Henry Stout's accounts, and Stout may have confused some events from one expedition with those from another, but nevertheless they are both in agreement about the approximate area where they searched.

Andrew Davis was just a boy at the battle and had some vivid recollections of the retreat and burial of Denton.

> About 4 or 4:30 p.m. the body of Captain Denton was securely tied upon a gentle horse, and the command moved out from the village ... We moved up the river to a point not far from Fort Worth and there spent the night. Early next morning we crossed the river at a point where the timber was narrow. After crossing the river *we traveled in the direction of Bird's Station, aiming for Bonham as our objective point.* At about 11:00 a.m. we halted on a prairie on the south side of a creek with a high bank on the north. On one of these elevations Captain Denton was buried. [italics mine.][15]

Davis, the youngest survivor of the battle, had the best recollection of the events when recounted in 1900. His account established in greater detail the movement of the soldiers after the battle with specific mention of passing the future site of Bird's Fort, and then traveling northeast towards home. Although he later seemed to go along with the decision of the committee, his initial published remarks seem to contradict the Chisum version.

> I have never for a moment doubted but that I could find the identical spot ... I have always wanted to go to Denton's grave, and know for myself, beyond a doubt, that his bones have not been found.[16]

Elbert Early, another veteran of the battle recalled:

> It was decided to leave that night. *We traveled eastward, I think about twenty miles,* and the next morning we buried Denton on the east side of a rocky branch. We had nothing to dig a grave with so we pried out a shallow grave, and wrapped Denton in his blanket and laid him in a

covered him with rocks. We made as few signs as possible for fear the Indians would find the body and mutilate it. [italics mine.][17]

All of the firsthand recollections except Porter's mention leaving Village Creek and traveling eastward back in the general direction of the Red River settlements. They traveled about twenty-five miles before burying Denton by a creek. Andrew Davis reports that they initially travelled back on the trail on which they had come, to the point on Fossil Creek where they had camped the night before the battle. This would have been about ten miles slightly west and to the north. Rising in the morning they traveled east towards the site of Bird's Fort, about ten miles from their Fossil Creek campsite. From Bird's Fort they veered north towards Bonham and around 11:00 a.m., they buried Denton on the high bank of a creek. If one were to travel northeast from the site of old Bird's Fort, the first creek one would pass would be Bear Creek which seems to confirm Isham's account from 1859.

Having attacked and looted the villages on Village Creek, kidnapping the sister and nephew of Anadarko Chief Jose Maria, and having fled from the greatly superior Indian force, the soldiers were justifiably afraid of retaliation. Along the way they jettisoned some of the booty they had stolen from the villages, and all reports indicate that they "went back as rapidly and as directly as they could ..."[18] They traveled north towards the Bonham area and rejoined the Chihuahua Trail where they had begun their adventure a week before. Reading the accounts, looking at the maps and imagining the situation, the Bear Creek burial site seems like the most logical scenario. The expedition being largely unsuccessful, and fear of the Indians being a strong motivator, there was an incentive to return home as quickly and directly as possible.

In 1900, when Rev. Allen began his search for information about the life and death of Denton, it opened up a long-simmering controversy about the location of his remains. A number of firsthand reports from actual veterans of the Tarrant Expedition and a large number of accounts with secondhand information came to light and were the subject of numerous popular news articles. As outlined in a previous chapter, there was a public argument taking place on the pages of the *Dallas Morning News* over the location of the bones.

If we step back and look at the reports, none of the actual participants in the Tarrant Expedition mentioned being anywhere near the area of Oliver Creek. They are at odds with each other over the exact creek name; but this can be explained by the fact that there were few creeks named at the time; it was a vast unmarked prairie, they were fleeing Indians, and all of the creeks looked pretty much alike. But they do agree that they traveled in a north-easterly direction from Village Creek, whereas Oliver Creek is in a north-westerly direction.

Two of the Village Creek veterans, James Isham and Henry Stout, report having found bones they believed to be Denton's, though on different creeks, but both within a reasonable distance from the battleground and conforming to the time and distance reported in all of the accounts. They cannot both be right, but if nothing else, this is at least testament to the fact that there was more than one unmarked grave on the prairie.

John Chisum was seventeen when his father joined the Tarrant Expedition. As a schoolmate of Elizabeth Denton, he most likely felt close to the story, and hearing his father's description of the burial site made a strong impression. As fine a man as John Chisum was, and much as we might want to respect his recollections, it is a lot to ask us to believe that a secondhand account, of an event which took place twenty years before, in an area with no distinct landmarks, should be trusted on the basis of his good name alone. If actual witnesses to Denton's burial were confused about the creek name and location of the grave, it seems that a secondhand description heard long before would be almost impossible to locate. In a court of law it would be called "hearsay."

Andrew Davis reported that they left Village Creek in the late afternoon with Denton's body tied over a horse, and loaded down with plunder. They returned to the area where they had spent the previous night near Ft. Worth: described by Stout as on Fossil Creek. The various reports are in accord that Denton was buried around 11:00 a.m. on the morning of May 25th. The distance from that point on Fossil Creek to Oliver Creek near Justin is about twenty-two miles in a straight line. Allowing for the roll of the land and the various smaller creeks along the way the actual distance traveled on heavily laden horseback would likely be much longer. On their trek westward towards the Bridgeport area, they had averaged about fifteen miles a day. Assuming that fear of the Indians would encourage faster travel, it still would have been an impressive feat of horsemanship for the troop to have traveled twenty-two miles in a morning and buried Denton on Oliver Creek by eleven.

With the 1859 James Isham account, and assuming they spent the night near Fossil Creek, as Davis and Stout reported, moving on the next morning and traveling northeasterly past the Bird's Fort site, they would come to Bear Creek. It is about eleven miles in a straight line past Bird's Fort to where he reports having found Denton's bones. This version has the advantage of being in an exact north-easterly direction from Village Creek and about a twenty-five-mile march from the battleground as reported by Porter. That Isham's Bear Creek scenario was the first published account, and it suggests the most direct route home, it cannot be dismissed or ignored as it was in 1900.

The reference to Birdville and the grave is one of the conflicting points between the Andrew Davis recollection and that of Henry Stout. In his recollection of retrieving the remains, Henry Stout reported that they went up the forks of Fossil Creek and from there to Birdville where they found the grave. In his account of the battle and retreat, Davis indicated that they spent the night near Fossil Creek and then traveled east passing near the Bird's Fort site before burying Denton. The original Bird's Fort, located between Village Creek and Bear Creek, was abandoned around 1844, and the town of Birdville was created a few years later near Fossil Creek, about ten miles to the north and west.[19] The conflation of these two locations (Bird's Fort and Birdville) could have caused Stout some confusion and caused him to remember the burial site as Fossil Creek.

In the end, the more direct route past Bird's Fort and across Bear Creek seems the most reasonable. The shortest and quickest route away from danger and towards safety seems like the most logical course of action, but on the other hand, people don't always behave logically. Fear can focus the vision and produce clear direct action, or it can scatter the brain and cause one to flee helter-skelter. None of the firsthand accounts report anything like panic in their retreat; in fact it seems almost leisurely, although one article by John Henry Brown, written many years later, mentioned there was some poor leadership and panic which affected the decision-making process.[20]

The Bear Creek burial scenario calls into question the true identity of the bones buried on the Denton Courthouse lawn. But, studying the literature and maps of the area, and understanding how the "fog of war" can cloud recollections and cause irrational actions, the Chisum-Oliver Creek scenario, though in the wrong direction and not mentioned in contemporary reports, is at least possible—barely.

Chapter 23

An Alternate Explanation for the Denton Bones

I f there is doubt about the identity of the bones, then whose could they be? There is another possible explanation for the bones retrieved by Chisum at the confluence of Oliver and Denton Creeks in 1861.[1] There is no question that John Chisum found human bones of European descent, wrapped in a blanket at the confluence of Oliver and Denton Creeks in 1861,[2] and that in good faith he retrieved these as the bones of John B. Denton. The North Texas prairie was uninhabited and poorly mapped in 1841, when Denton's bones were buried. But in the intervening period between their burial and Chisum's discovery of bones twenty years later, settlers had settled and the country was no longer just a vast empty prairie. People had claimed the land, lived their lives, and some had died there. It is understandable that Chisum might assume that the bones he discovered, on uninhabited land by Oliver Creek, could have been that of his father's long-lost comrade buried somewhere by a creek on the prairie. But this particular land had not always been uninhabited.

In June 1848, a group of French Socialists arrived in Denton County, after having secured land from the Peter's Colony for a new community. The settlers were followers of Etienne Cabet, a French socialist, activist, and visionary who had written a novel entitled, *Travels in Icaria*, about a utopian colony in America.[3] When the ill-equipped Frenchmen arrived to create their New Icaria, they settled at the confluence of Oliver and Denton Creeks, near present-day Justin, Texas, exactly where Chisum found bones purported to be Denton's. The site for the colony was nothing like the utopian vision presented by Etienne Cabet. They were ill-prepared, lacking in supplies, without basic knowledge of frontier survival, and were soon beset by malaria and cholera. Four of the settlers died, three of disease; one was struck by lightning,[4] and by the fall, defections, internal conflicts, and starvation had all but ended their dreams of utopia. Historical accounts mention that all of the colonists became ill throughout the summer,[5] so it is not certain that all of the deceased were given proper burials at the traditional six-foot depth. It is possible that some of the dead could have been given simple burials by the creek wrapped in a blanket.

It must also be recalled that when Robert Johnson described the state of the bones retrieved by John Chisum, they found evidence of a broken arm and a "gold filled tooth." In the 1830s the state of dentistry was in a primitive state and gold was not a common method for filling teeth. Edward Maynard was one American pioneer skilled in the use of gold foil for building up fillings, but his technique was not developed until 1838. Maynard's patients included US presidents, congressmen, and Tsar Nicholas of Russia. It is unlikely that such a costly and rare dental technique would have found its way to the edge of civilization and into the mouth of a young lawyer in East Texas.[6]

On the other hand, France was the birthplace of modern dentistry and gold crowns had been developed in the late eighteenth century.[7] Although there is no evidence to support the idea that the Frenchmen buried at New Icaria actually had gold fillings, it seems more likely that an educated urban Frenchman would have them than John B. Denton, or any other random European American living on the frontier.

In addition to some of the other conflicts, John W. Gober heard Chisum complain that the bones had begun to smell, and on his advice Chisum reburied them in a whale oil candle box. If John Chisum dug up Denton's bones in 1861, they would have been in the ground for twenty years and less likely to smell, than would bones buried in 1848. Depending on soil conditions it is not impossible that bones buried for twenty years could retain an odor, but it is certainly less probable.[8]

The passage of time, the changing of the physical landmarks, the vagaries of memory, and the variety of opinions make it impossible, without DNA evidence,[9] to determine exactly which version of the history of the bones is correct.

Chapter 24

Art Imitating Life: Alfred W. Arrington— Pulp Westerner

Most of the counties of Texas have been named for individuals who have either helped build Texas or died defending it. Many of these worthies were important in their lifetimes and were honored for their contributions, but not much is heard about them ever after. In Denton's case, he died too young to have contributed much to the building of Texas, but he died in battle and was honored for this sacrifice by having his name given to Denton, County.

Unlike some of the others though, Denton's deeds and his name did not die with him and after his death his story took on a life of its own. Thanks to the creative embellishments of Alfred W. Arrington, who took elements from the real life of John B. Denton, fictionalized them into a fantastic tale of Rev. "Paul" Denton. The story of Paul Denton was published in hundreds of newspapers around the world, and in the process broadcasting the name of "Rev. Denton" far and wide. Alfred W. Arrington was an unmitigated scoundrel, but he was a gifted writer and he put beautiful words into the mouth of Rev. Denton. In the following chapters I have tried to unravel the entangled stories and set the record straight.[1]

About the same time that John B. Denton moved to Arkansas, another young man also arrived there with his father, a minister, and who like Denton was also drawn to the ministry from an early age. His name was Alfred W. Arrington,[2] and though these contemporaries came from similar backgrounds, and for a brief time followed the same paths, first as Methodist ministers, and later as lawyers, their lives could not have been more different. While Denton followed a righteous path as a minister, an honorable family man, a fundamentally decent person, who in his brief life contributed to his community; Arrington took a different tack and became almost the evil opposite of Denton's decency.

Like Denton, Arrington was self-educated, widely considered to be "an intellectual prodigy,"[3] and an extraordinarily gifted speaker who was in great demand in his early days as a preacher. One female congregant breathlessly described his skills: "He seemed to reach up and grasp the stars and set them on his brow."[4] Another contemporary described him as "An intellectual giant— but a moral monstrosity."[5] At the age of twenty-three, he was forced to resign from the ministry for moral lapses, but the next year he asked for and was granted reinstatement in the Missouri Conference of the Methodist Church. Arrington displayed genius through his masterful oratory, but was once again caught with a married woman. As one biographer put it, "his world example did not harmonize with his orthodox teachings."[6] This being a second or third offense the church elders felt compelled to publish a statement of his confession in which he admitted he had been caught with a married woman, "detected by her husband and drove from the house, and when in the street turned on his pursuer, drew his pistol and fired ... He further (stated) that he had been a debauchee from his fourteenth year."[7] He was expelled from the Methodist Church for the last time in 1835.[8]

With the ministry now permanently behind him, but possessing a phenomenal aptitude for public speaking, it was a natural transition for Arrington to take up the law as did many preachers on the frontier. His oratorical skills would serve him as well in the law as they had in the pulpit, but the moral constraints of the ministry would no longer be an issue. Arrington moved to Fayetteville, Arkansas, set himself up as a lawyer and "took the position of a master at once."[9]

Alfred W. Arrington (1810–1867). Arrington was a defrocked Methodist minister and lawyer who wrote pulp western novels featuring several characters with the name of Denton. His writing was so effective that his fictional characters became confused with the real history of John B. Denton. From the *Southwestern Historical Quarterly* 55, no. 3 (Jan. 1952).

In 1845 he abandoned his family in Arkansas and moved to Clarksville, Texas, with his mistress, a married woman. In Clarksville he set up his law practice and at this time turned his hand to writing "pulp westerns." Arriving in Clarksville, just four years after Denton's death, it is easy to assume that the story of John B. Denton was fresh in the minds of the residents and Arrington would have been exposed to firsthand recollections of Denton. He was writing for an Eastern audience which had an insatiable appetite for outlandish tales of the frontier, and the Indian battles and bloody feuds of East Texas provided a rich source of material for his highly embellished fictional accounts in *The Lives and Adventures of the Desperadoes of the South West*, and others.[10] It was said of his stories that "he wrote with more than poetic license, and when he wanted an incident or fact his fertile imagination supplied it."[11] He would often use the barely disguised names of real people to spice up his stories, and with his prodigious skills as a teller of tall tales, he was able to weave borrowed details from the life of Denton into his own fictional creations.

One of his most popular pieces, written as a newspaper article, was about a frontier preacher named "Paul" Denton, with certain similarities to John B. Denton. Unfortunately, the fanciful story of Paul Denton from the pen of Alfred W. Arrington became so popular that it gradually began to overpower the story of the real Denton. Their narratives were so entwined that historians and journalists confused him with the mythical character from Arrington's fiction. One early version, which was later copied by John B. Denton biographers, is likely the source of the myth of Denton's childhood of penury.

> Paul Denton, a remarkable man. Left an orphan, and [was] placed in one of the most degraded families in Arkansas, he performed the meanest work of a servant such as cooking, washing and scouring. Until he was twelve years of age he was a stranger to hat or shoes.[12]

Denton had grown up poor, as most people did in Arkansas in the 1820s: but the tales of his degraded early life, a shoeless victim of the "wretched" Jacob Wells, like many others surrounding the life of John B. Denton, were more a product of the pen and vivid imagination of Alfred W. Arrington than his true situation.

The public perception of John B. Denton, and even what his own children thought they knew of Denton's life, had been heavy influenced by these widely spread tales. It became a case of "life imitating art," as the myth of Paul Denton began to morph into the story of their own father's life.

Chapter 25

Rev. Paul Denton and the "Apostrophe to Water"

E very biographical sketch of Denton mentions his skill as a master-ful orator, with some of his sublime sermons compared to Cicero,[1] and although none of his actual sermons survive, one example of fine speech often attributed to John B. Denton was an "Apostrophe to Water." The "Apostrophe" became a legendary temperance sermon, allegedly delivered by Denton at a frontier gathering, which gained a wide following after his death.

The reason there are no contemporary accounts of Denton's famous temperance sermon is because he never made it. In February of 1850, an article published in the *The Evansville (Ind) Daily Journal* recounted the story of a powerful speech entitled an "Apostrophe to Water," by a Texas preacher and Indian fighter named Paul Denton.[2] This article was published under the name of Charles Summerfield, the pen name of Alfred W. Arrington. In this account, Reverend Paul Denton advertised that he would host a barbecue; all were invited, and he would provide the liquor. On the appointed date a great crowd arrived, attracted more by the food and liquor than the preaching, but he gave his sermon and beside him on the lectern sat a glass of pure water. After he had finished and when no liquor appeared, a crowd of toughs became unruly and started to make a scene. The leader of the rabble was the famous lyncher, Col. Watt Foeman who spoke up demanding, "Mr. Paul Denton your reverence has lied ... Where is the liquor?" Denton pointed to the glass of water, exclaiming, "There, there is the liquor which God the Eternal brews for all his children." In the lengthy Summerfield/Arrington account, another sermon followed which was so spellbinding and popular with the crowd that the ruffian Colonel Foeman was chastened and dared not speak again.

Blending real history with his fiction, Arrington reported that just as the sermon ended, Paul Denton heard of a brutal Indian attack and quickly organized an expedition to hunt down the "barbarians." As in the real life of John B. Denton, this Reverend Paul Denton led a charge against them and was killed. However, unlike the real story, Arrington's Paul Denton was struck, not by an Indian, but rather by the hand of that "incarnate fiend," Col. Watt Foeman, still fuming over his humiliation at the "barbecue." The story ends with Paul Denton being honored by having a county in Texas named for him.

Arrington had no qualms about taking liberties with history in pursuit of a good story and he borrowed from John B. Denton to give his tale a bit of authenticity. Watt Foeman was most likely a reference to Watt Moorman, a leader of the Shelby County Regulators in the Regulator-Moderator War, and a noted lyncher among other things.[3] Aside from all the other absurdities of the story, in the Regulator-Moderator War, Denton, with Regulator sympathies, was actually on the same side as Moorman.

The "apostrophe" as a literary device is not as well known today as it might have been in the mid-nineteenth century when educated people studied rhetoric, and were aware of proper rhetorical nomenclature. In this sense, the *apostrophe* is not a punctuation mark, but refers to an aside, as one might speak to an inanimate object, in this case a glass of water.

The roots of the "Apostrophe to Water" go back at least as far as 1844, when Arrington newly arrived in Texas was in Nacogdoches visiting with some friends. In those days in which ornate speech was greatly valued and was how educated public men spoke, Arrington stood out as being exceptionally gifted. His reputation preceding him, he was urged to make a speech before an informal gathering of distinguished Texans. Being unprepared, his speech was at first rough and his voice harsh, but as he warmed up he launched into the "Apostrophe to Water," in which he railed against the evils of alcohol. His extemporaneous speech, on a subject he did not believe, spellbound his listeners who offered an enthusiastic ovation when he finished.[4] Ever the rascal, Arrington later admitted to a friend, "When I made that big temperance speech, I had a pint under my belt."[5]

The next year at the formation of the Bar Association in Clarksville, Arrington was again asked to speak. There he repeated his successful "Apostrophe to Water," "which he afterward included in one of his fanciful stories as the preaching of Paul Denton ... a methodist preacher, who will, it appears, ever be confounded with John B. Denton."[6] It was a bit bold to tell a story based on Denton, just four years after his death, and in the company of many of Denton's friends, but if deficient in character, Arrington was always well supplied with audacity.

In an age with an active temperance movement, this tale of the "Apostrophe" became wildly popular. Initially the story was republished with the Summerfield byline, but after a few months, this was dropped and the story of Paul Denton and his "Apostrophe to Water" appeared as a regular news item. The story of Paul Denton, the pioneer preacher, was published hundreds of times and took on a life of its own. So great was its range that readers as far afield as England and Australia read of Paul Denton in their temperance leaning publications.[7] Virtually anywhere in the world where there was a temperance movement, the "Apostrophe to Water" of Reverend Denton was likely to have been published. It was so rhetorically well-crafted that it is still being used today (2021) as an example of eloquence for use in a United Nations speech contest for young people of the world.[8]

Due to the overwhelming number of published accounts of the sermon of "Paul Denton," it is easy to understand the confusion over the identity of the man for whom Denton County is named. In 1855 Henderson Yoakum wrote one of the first comprehensive histories of Texas. In it "Paul" Denton is praised for his superior powers of oration, his bravery in battle, having overcome his dramatically humble beginnings, and having a county named for him:

> In his sermons he rose with his subject: his figures were original, drawn from nature, and always apposite. His selection of words was the very best; and in his ornate flights he seemed to test the strength of the English language ... To drive back the savages he raised a company and marched against them. In a battle with them he was killed. Texas has honored his name by giving it to one of her northern counties.[9]

Following the lead from Yoakum, a chart published in *The Belton Independent* in 1858 listed every county in Texas with the name of the county seat, when it was created, and who it was named for. Denton County was listed as having been named for "Paul Denton."[10]

The fact that John B. Denton had been a very early Methodist missionary to Texas, and had died in battle caused him to assume a role in the history of Methodism in Texas that exceeded his actual contributions. He was a fine preacher and a good man, but his death at Village Creek took on the overtones of martyrdom which served to increase his posthumous stature. His story was told in an early and influential book on Texas Methodism by Homer Thrall. In it Thrall rhapsodizes on the life of Denton and his skills in the pulpit, using his correct name, but his account is heavily influenced Arrington's articles on "Paul" Denton.

> Young Denton had a fine personal appearance and a musical tone. His language rose with the grandeur of the theme, until it would remind the classical scholar of Cicero. His action was like that of Roscius—his use of figures most appropriate. We have read an *apostrophe to water* in one of his temperance speeches, which, for impassioned eloquence, is equal to almost anything found in our language.[11] [italics mine]

Thrall's account of Denton and his "apostrophe to water" would be copied in newspaper articles and other history books for years to come and greatly influence subsequent accounts of the life of John B. Denton.

In 1874, John Russell Hutchison, writing in his *Reminiscences*, further confuses things when he recounts an embellished story of John B. Denton, taken from Homer Thrall's history, but in his rendition he calls him Paul Denton.

> One of the most remarkable preachers, whose name appears in the early history of the State, was *Paul Denton*. He was early left an orphan in Arkansas, and lived in a family where he was treated as a servant, and had to cook, wash, scour, and perform other degrading work.–Until he was twelve years of age, he was a stranger to hat and shoes. When he became older, he ran away from his oppressors, and commenced life for himself. At an early age he married, and learned to read and write after becoming the head of a family. He finally became a preacher, and soon showed remarkable powers as a public speaker.–He was a man of fine person, agreeable manners, and although without any advantages of education, displayed a high degree of eloquence. His first efforts as a preacher of the Gospel, were in the Red Lands in Eastern Texas.–He afterwards removed to the Northern part of the State. He was a man of public spirit, and was brave as well as good. He raised a company of volunteers to chastise the Indians, who had become troublesome to the white settlers, and was killed in battle. *Texas has honored him in calling a county by his name*.[12] [italics mine]

By 1880, an article in the *Galveston Gazette* reported that there was even confusion over the story of Paul Denton and the life John B. Denton in a Denton County newspaper.

> Col. T. G. C. Davis, of Denton, in an article in the Pilot Point Post revives the tradition that the county is named for Paul Denton, the mythical character created by the genius of a romancer out of the scant material furnished by a worthy pioneer preacher and Indian fighter, half of whose name the sensational writer adopted for his hero.[13]

Charles De Morse (1816–1887), publisher of the *Northern Standard*, an influential early newspaper from Clarksville, lamented that "John B. Denton (had been) made so famous by Arrington or Paul Denton."[14] And another article stating, "John B. Denton whose name has become noted through the romance of Arrington as Paul Denton the preacher," further demonstrates

Ashley Newton Denton (1836–1901). Dr. Ashley Newton Denton was the fifth child of John B. and Mary Greenlee Denton. He was just five years old when his father was killed at the Battle of Village Creek in 1841. Dr. Denton served as a surgeon in the Civil War and 1873–1874 as a Texas State Representative from San Antonio. In 1883 he was appointed Superintendent of the Texas State Lunatic Asylum. *Courtesy of the Denton Public Library*.

that confusion between the real and the fictional Denton had been a problem for a long time.

Hugh Miller aptly describes how typical characters in fiction become greater in the public mind than any of the real men they represent, and the fact has often been remarked by others. So Judge Arrington's character of Paul Denton, with his wonderful apostrophe to water, written by Arrington himself and declaimed all over the United States and England ... has usurped the place of the real Denton, and will doubtless continue to hold it in spite of the frequent attempts to do justice to the memory of a real hero.[15]

John B. Denton's son, Dr. Ashley N. Denton, had a long and distinguished career as a doctor, first in San Marcos and later as the Director of the Texas State Mental Hospital. In a final indignity to the memory of his father, when he died in 1901, he was honored by the Board of the State Medical Association of Texas with a resolution and celebrating his achievements and mentioning that he was the son of "Paul Denton, a Methodist missionary."[16]

Chapter 26

John Denton and the Murder Trial of Mary Denton

There is another popular myth about John B. Denton and the murder trial of his wife, Mary Greenlee Denton, which should be examined, for it continues to resurface in publications to this day.

Around the time of Dr. Ashley Newton Denton's death in 1901, another colorful story started to circulate concerning the life of his parents. Captain Joseph C. Terrell, a prominent Ft. Worth lawyer, well versed in North Texas history, wrote an obituary published in several newspapers in Texas which included a brief biography of Dr. Denton, followed by an account of a courtroom drama involving John B. Denton and his wife before they came to Texas.

In this story, as told by Terrell, Denton and his wife had separated while still in Arkansas, and Mrs. Denton moved to Fayetteville to establish a millinery store.[1] Although this carries no negative connotations today, in the nineteenth century, a millinery shop was considered low in stature; and "the milliner as prostitute"[2] was a common literary theme. Middle-class moralists, skeptical of the virtue of most wage-earning women, singled out dressmakers and milliners, associating them with loose morals.[3]

In this vulnerable position, Mrs. Denton received an unwelcome visitor late one night, and fending off his unwanted advances, she shot and killed him. Because the man she killed was one of the wealthiest and most powerful in Fayetteville, she was indicted for the murder and put into jail. When it came time for her trial, the consensus was that because the deceased had important friends, and Mrs. Denton, in her lowly position had none, she would surely be convicted.

The murder generated great public interest and the courtroom was packed with the curious and unsympathetic spectators who always seem to swarm around the whiff of scandal. As the trial started, the judge asked Mrs. Denton if she had an attorney present to defend her, and looking down she forlornly replied, "No, I have no attorney, and no friends."[4] At that point a stranger, someone no one had noticed, stood up, approached the defendant, and staring intently into her face said, "No, not without friends. If it please your honor, I will appear for the defendant, if acceptable to her and to the court."[5] She of course acceded and the stranger was allowed to continue, but he was a mystery to the crowded courtroom.

The prosecuting attorney made a strong and compelling argument against her and to the crowd it appeared her fate was sealed. Then it was the turn for the stranger to speak:

> In manner he was as calm, cool and emotionless as if he were an animated marble statue. But every point he made was as clear as the noonday sun, and he spoke as he shot to the center every time. And his very impassiveness seemed to carry conviction. The first emotion he displayed was in his peroration, when, resting his eyes upon the defendant, he said in part: "Gentlemen of the Jury, look upon the defendant. Scan that pure face and behold something dearer to me than life, and more precious to me than all things else under the blue canopy of heaven. Need I tell you that she is my wife. I could as easily believe an angel guilty of crime as my wife. She never had an impure thought in her life. It is true that whilst no woman was ever a gentler or more kind-hearted or more faithful and affectionate wife, she, with a courage born of virtue and innocence, slew the ruffian who would have desecrated my fireside. And for this worthy deed of a noble woman I honor and love her more than ever. Thank God for having blessed me with such a wife."[6]

To the astonishment of all, the identity of this stranger was immediately revealed to be none other than her husband; John B. Denton. When he finished he approached her and said: "No, not without friends little woman." He extended his arms, "Behold, in me you have more than a friend—a husband."[7]

In tears, she swooned into his arms as the spectators went wild with shouts of joy, while the sheriff tried in vain to keep order in the courtroom. The jury, almost without deliberation, instantly leapt to their feet and unanimously exclaimed, "Not guilty!" and Mrs. Denton was a free woman, united with her faithful husband once more.

This colorful story, later published in a book, *Reminiscences of the Early Days of Ft. Worth*, by Captain J. C. Terrell, was added to the lore surrounding the life of John B. Denton, but not widely publicized.[8]

In April of 1957, the Denton Centennial Commission was planning a huge citywide extravaganza and grand pageant celebrating "100 years of progress." The centerpiece of this would be the Centennial Centurama, a pageant involving hundreds of local volunteers celebrating the rich history of the community. In the words of Harwell V. Shepard, Chairman of the Centennial Commission, "our progress has been due in great measure to the pioneering spirit, the courage, and the love of freedom exemplified by such God fearing men as John B. Denton, for whom our county and city were named."[9] Men were encouraged to grow beards and wear a special Centennial bowler hat: Ladies would wear bonnets. As a result of the preparations for the Centennial there was a resurgence of interest in discovering the history of the community and John B. Denton.

In the spirit of the Centennial, Riley Cross, publisher of the *Denton Record Chronicle*, made a commitment for the paper to join in the celebration and, "… mark Denton's 100th anniversary with a memento future generation would treasure." The paper set about the job of gathering the history of Denton in preparation for their Centennial Edition. In a letter to one of John B. Denton's descendants, Miss Patsy Cross (Patterson) outlined one problem.

As it happens, little is known about (John B.) Denton and we are trying to put together a centennial edition for the City of Denton.

Of course, anything we can learn about John B. Denton is of particular interest to us.[10]

On February 3, 1957, the *Denton Record Chronicle* published its "two-pound giant *Centennial Edition*,"[11] celebrating the 100th anniversary of the founding of the town. The 131-page special edition is full of history and was an impressive effort to tell the story of Denton.

In their pursuit of information about John B. Denton, the paper found and reprinted the J. C. Terrell account of the murder trial of Mrs. Denton which gave this almost forgotten story new life. Under the headline, "Denton Won Wife's Murder Acquittal," it recounted the story: "The real and almost unknown reason for Denton leaving Arkansas for Texas involves his defense of a beautiful milliner being tried for murder—his own wife."[12] Since 1957, every few years, the Denton paper and many others have republished this dramatic tale, and though its veracity has been questioned, it is such a good story that it has become enshrined in the lore surrounding the history of John B. Denton. So popular has this story become that during the Denton County Sesquicentennial in 1996, an actor portraying John B. Denton gave several performances of the Fayetteville courtroom scene to great acclaim.[13]

Capt. J. C. Terrell states that he heard the story from John C. McCoy, a Dallas historian. McCoy, a former Peter's Colony surveyor and the first active lawyer in Dallas, was a charter member of the Texas Historical Society, and the first president of the Dallas County Pioneers Association. Captain Terrell mentioned that a full account of the sensational trial had been published by Charles De Morse in the Clarksville *Northern Standard* "forty years ago."[14] Perhaps this is where McCoy first read of it.

But where could this story about Denton's marriage have come from? Historians have long been skeptical of the veracity of this "too good to be true" melodrama involving Denton and his wife, but as in other tall tales about Denton, we need look no further than the hand of Alfred W. Arrington, ever tinkering with the historical record.

Around 1850 there were a series of newspaper articles being published around the country entitled, "John Taylor, the Timon of the Backwoods

Bar and Pulpit,"[15] with a story very similar in its essentials to Terrell's tale of John B. Denton. This story takes place in Conway, Arkansas, in 1838. A beautiful young milliner is accused of murdering Hiram Stone, who "belonged to a family, at once opulent, influential and dissipated. He was himself licentious, brave and ferociously revengeful—the most famous dualist in the South-west." She had rebuffed his advances and he sought his revenge. On Christmas night 1837, Stone had forced his way into the home of the virtuous and incredibly beautiful milliner, Emma Miner. She was only able to fend off this cad's advances by shooting him twelve times with a pair of revolvers: she was immediately apprehended and taken to jail. Because the Judge and Sheriff had been friends of the deceased, the friendless Emma Miner was held without bail, as the Sheriff, "chained her in the felon's dungeon."[16]

At her trial a rough-looking character entered the courtroom, dressed in the buckskins of the backwoodsman. His appearance was so outlandish that it invited laughter from the crowd that had gathered for the spectacle of the trial. This backwoodsman was John Taylor, and as they laughed he turned slowly towards them:

> his lips curled with a killing smile of infinite scorn; his yellow eyes shot arrows of lightning; his tongue protruding through his teeth literally writhed like a serpent, and ejaculated its asp-like poison in a single word: 'Savages!' No pen can describe the defiant force which he threw into that term, no pencil can paint the infernal furor of his utterance, although it hardly exceeded a whisper ... it was the growl of a red tiger in the hiss of a rattlesnake.[17]

As in the story of Denton's defense of his wife, John Taylor, the stranger, stepped up to defend the accused women for she had no lawyer. Like Denton, he dazzled the courtroom with the precision and brilliance of his defense, "like Jove himself hurling red-hot thunderbolts among the quaking ranks of a conspiracy of inferior gods."[18] His summation was so intense, his language so brutal:

> Men groaned: females screamed, and one poor mother fainted, and was borne away in convulsions. ... The jury rendered a verdict of

'Not Guilty,' without leaving the box; and three cheers like succeeding roars of an earthquake, shook the old courthouse from the dome to the cornerstone, testifying to the joy of the people.[19]

The story, "Timon of the Backwoods," portrayed Taylor as a rough and fearsome character and although he did a good thing by representing the accused woman, it was not designed to give a favorable impression of him. After the trial Taylor announced that he would preach that evening at the courthouse. His sermon was in the same raw, brutalist style of his courtroom defense as he painted a picture of hell without the possibility of redemption.

There was in fact a real John Taylor who had lived in Arkansas, who was a brilliant speaker but a terribly unsympathetic person.[20] He had been in a very public row with Alfred W. Arrington; "no one ... ever forgot his terrific excoriation ... of Arrington, who had imprudently ventured with a wealth of barbaric ornamentation to assail him in debate."[21] Arrington rarely missed an opportunity to repay an offense, and took the opportunity to (accurately) immortalize his adversary as an unattractive misanthrope.

In 1856, a different version of the story was published, under the title "Romance of the Backwoods." It was virtually the same as the Timon of the Backwoods, but Arrington changed the name from John Taylor to Will Denton, coincidentally the name of John B. Denton's brother.[22] The location of the trial had changed to Little Rock, but most important change in the story was what happened after the trial:

> They returned to Texas. The husband was a colonel in the revolution and escaped its perils only to fall the next year in a terrible fight with the Comanches. *A new county in the cross-timbers*, a county of wild woods romantic as his own eloquence, and of a sun-bright prairie beautiful as his own Emma's sweet face, *commemorates; the name* of a transcendent star that set too soon ... for he was nature's Demosthenes of the western woods.[23] [italics mine]

In this updated version of the "backwoods" courtroom drama, Arrington had once again dipped into the real history of John B. Denton to give his fictional story some authenticity. Perhaps he had had such success with his account of Paul Denton that he sought to once again capitalize on the interest in the Denton name. As he borrowed authenticity from Denton for his story, he was once again infusing the story of John B. Denton's life with the Arrington brand of romantic western tall-tales.

For the next twenty-five years, Romance of the Backwoods was published with some small changes in dozens of newspapers across the county perpetuating the belief that a fictional character had been the man for whom Denton County was named. Will Denton became William Denton and Emma Miner/Mason had become Emma Greenleaf,[24] which was much closer to the real name of Denton's wife, Mary Greenlee Stewart; but otherwise it was the same fantastic story, a story which by 1900 had morphed into the legend of John B. Denton.

Chapter 27

John B. Denton's Legacy

I t is a historical curiosity that Denton's name would travel so far, wide, and falsely, but if this legacy meant he was not forgotten, then it too could be considered a sort of memorial to the man. Whether or not Arrington did Denton a disservice is open to debate, but he certainly helped spread the name and legend of John B. Denton far beyond their natural boundaries.

The question might arise: does it really matter who is actually buried in Denton's grave? The original intention of the Old Settlers' Association was to create a monument to John B. Denton and place it on the court-house lawn, which is precisely what they did. The grave was really an afterthought, a serendipitous discovery along the way to building a monument. As with the Tomb of the Unknown Soldier, whose bones serve as a symbolic stand-in for all the soldiers killed in battle; we do not honor it any less for the anonymity of the bones it contains. And so it should be with Denton's monument. The bones are a symbol, and doubts about them do not diminish what they symbolize.

Values have changed dramatically since Denton lived, and today we view the Indian policy of the nineteenth century as barbaric. Praising Denton as an "Indian fighter" was an appropriate honorific in 1900 at the reburial, but by today's standards this would be considered a stain on his reputation. In recent years Denton has been disparaged as an "Indian killer;" which from all the hype about his life as an Indian fighter, one might conclude; but it would not be true. Not for want of trying of course, but there is no record of him having killed anyone, and to the contrary, much of his fame came from his having himself been killed by Indians.

Although much of the praise heaped on the legend of John B. Denton was overly enthusiastic, the real accounts by people who knew him, both contemporary, and from those who remembered him sixty years later, were so laudatory that none of the hyperbole was even necessary. As we have seen, Denton's legend was partly fueled by myth with the made-up stories of a pulp-western fiction writer, but by questioning these myths and stripping away the fiction, we do not diminish his reputation, we enhance it. We turn him back from a cartoon character, into the real man he was. A real man of his time, who earned the respect of his contemporaries.

There were hundreds of thousands of anonymous Americans who made the trek over the Cumberland Gap, through the upper South to points west, ever pushing the line of the frontier forward. They were pursuing a primal urge: to own land; to practice their religion; to have no one above them in station; to fend for themselves; and to be left alone. Of these original westering pioneers, there are millions of descendants, whose basic character was forged by their pioneering ancestors. Most of these descendants know little of the trek and travails of their wandering forbearers, but some fortunates had ancestors notable enough to leave a mark which can be traced. Denton, whose head rose above the crowd, can symbolize all those anonymous settlers who made the same westering trek to Texas. By studying one family, we can see the movement of which they were a part, and by that token, better understand how we got here, and who we are as a people. That's why, whether tall tales prove to be as false as buried bones, John B. Denton still matters.

Afterword

If I have any regret about this book it is that I was not successful in making a conclusive link between John B. Denton and the illustrious line of Rev. Richard Denton of Hempstead, New York. As I have mentioned previously, there are many genealogies that make this connection by assuming that Denton's parents were James and Elizabeth Clarkson Denton of Jennings County, Indiana. I spent a considerable amount of time following this line of ancestors and their fascinating trek west. In the end, it became a question of conflict between these genealogies and the few recollections of the Denton family. I chose to believe Denton's immediate family, and although they admittedly didn't know very much about their father's family, I was not prepared to assume they were completely wrong.

I have been fortunate in having many more resources available to me than previous Denton researchers. I am going to assume that even more resources will become available and that future historians will have the luxury of using these to correct and embellish my recording of Denton's history. It is my sincere hope that at some point a definitive

link can be made between Rev. John B. and Rev. Richard Denton because
I believe that link exists: I just could not prove it to my satisfaction. It has
taken me decades to gather the information used to write this history.
To make it easier for any future Denton historians, I will be depositing all
of my notes in the collection at the Denton County Courthouse Museum.
Good luck.

Appendix 1

Alfred W. Arrington:
Preacher, Poet, Lawyer, Scoundrel

In many ways, the life story of Alfred W. Arrington was every bit as entertaining as the tales he told about others. He was born in 1810 in North Carolina, but in 1819, he and his family moved to the frontier in Arkansas. His father was a Methodist minister and at the age of eighteen, Arrington followed his father by becoming an itinerant Methodist preacher assigned to the southern Indiana circuit.

As previously mentioned in Chapter 23, Arrington's verbal abilities were well known and respected; it was just his character that caused him problems.

> His language and voice rose in musical cadence on ornate key, and gradually expanded into rapturous rhythm and a wilderness of splendor. He carried his auditory on magnetic wing in a tireless flight, and then, with the greatest facility and without the slightest friction, passed to a grave argument and resistless logic.[1]

Yet he had a spotty record in the Methodist Church in Arkansas, having been several times ejected from the rolls of the ministry for seducing the wives of his parishioners. Contemporary writers would refer to Arrington having been involved in a "*crim. con. scandal*" a nineteenth century legal euphemism for adultery.[2] After being forced from the church, he became a frontier lawyer in Arkansas, entered politics and continued to spellbind with his use of the language. In politics he was elected to the legislature as a Whig, but became dissatisfied with their policy towards the annexation of Texas, which he favored. In 1845, like many a rapscallion and scoundrel before him, he abandoned his wife and children, and with his mistress, he absconded to Texas to start a new life.

In 1850 Arrington was elected to the judiciary of the 12th Judicial District and moved to Brownsville, Texas. Although growing in respectability in his adopted State of Texas, Arrington's reputation from his Arkansas days still followed him. An Arkansas paper, upon hearing of his successful election had this to say:

> This infamous character, so well known in Washington county, and other portions of this State, has recently been elected a Circuit Judge, in a Judicial District on the Rio Grande, in Texas. If they pollute the temple of Justice, in Texas, by elevating such shameless fellows as Arrington, to the bench, we can form but a new low estimate of the respectability of the people who elected him ...[3]

In 1856, citing ill health Arrington left Texas and moved to New York where he took up writing full time as Charles Summerfield, and published more books of life on the frontier: *Sketches of the South and South West; Rangers and Regulators of the Tanaha*; and an obtuse philosophical tract entitled, *The Mathematical Harmonies of the Universe*, which was translated and published in French and German.[4]

In 1857, Arrington moved to Chicago where he resumed his career as a lawyer with great success. He became a highly respected member of the Chicago Bar and was involved in a number of important legal cases, where once again his superior verbal skills were held in high esteem. Although his days of writing fanciful stories of western desperadoes were over, he continued to write poems that were gathered and published by his wife after his death.

Though he spent the Civil War in the North, his sympathies still lay with the Southern cause and towards the end of the war, as the defeat of the South was imminent, Arrington became involved in an odd enterprise to form a colony of defeated Southerners in Northern Mexico. Arrington became a director of the American and Mexican Emigrant Company, an organization on its face seemed to encourage general immigration to Mexico, but was in fact intended to be an escape route for bloody but unbowed Southerners after their defeat.[5] The prospectus for the company mentioned that the settler would find, "whole communities of the same race and language springing up all around him."[6]

After Lee's surrender at Appomattox on April 9, 1865, it was obvious to all the that support for the Confederacy was a literal "lost cause." Arrington's plans for a colony in Mexico became more real a few weeks later when the contract for the venture was signed by Emperor Maximillian of Mexico on April 27, 1865.[7] There were several groups of Southerners with colonial aspirations in Mexico after the Civil War. Empress Carlota encouraged these as she was said to have been sympathetic to the Confederate cause and indeed some were referred to as "Carlota Colonies." Although many of these Mexican emigration colonies merely existed on paper, Arrington's American and Mexican Emigrant Company was actively selling parcels from a tract of a thousand square miles in northern Mexico.[8]

The concentration of historical events in this brief span of time must have weighed heavily on the Confederate sympathizing Arrington, and any hopes for a post-war time of peace were dimmed with Lincoln's assassination on April 15, 1865. On April 26, 1865, John Wilkes Booth had been killed while fleeing capture by Union authorities. Arrington was so despondent that he again put his considerable talents to poor use and penned an elegy for his fallen "hero." It was reported that "a man with a pale face and disordered attire, his breath laden with alcohol and enthusiastic anger in his eyes"[9] dropped off a poem entitled, "To John Wilkes Booth," at office of the Chicago Times. It was published the next day, but the paper had a small circulation and no one seemed to notice.[10]

O, give him a sepulcher broad as the sweep
of the tidal wave's measureless motion;
Lay our hero to sleep in the arms of the deep,
Since his life was free as the ocean.

It was Liberty slain that maddened his brain,
To avenge the dead idol he cherished;
So it's meet that the main, never curbed by a chain,
Should entomb the last freeman, now perished.

He has written his name in letters of flame
O'er the archway of Liberty's portal,
And serfs that now blame shall crimson with shame
When they learn they have cursed an immortal.

This public declaration, signed by Arrington, was practically heresy in Lincoln's home of Illinois. That evening, a noticeably drunk Arrington showed up at the Sherman House Bar, in one of the finest hotels in Chicago, where he was well known as an able lawyer. The bar was filled with Union officers, drinking heavily and celebrating the end of the war. They were still likely mourning the assassination of their president two weeks before and celebrating Booth's death the day before.

Arrington joined them for a few drinks, but then, ever the rascal and seemingly unable curb his instinct for self-destruction, he volunteered to recite a poem. He climbed up on a table and started to recite his "Elegy for Booth."[11] And "with a roar the men were upon him. He was dragged from the table, hurled to the floor ..."[12] Only the intercession of the bartender saved his life by picking him up and throwing him out onto the street.

Arrington's contract with Emperor Maximillian was nullified when he was captured by the forces of Benito Juarez and executed on June 19, 1867. Six months later Alfred W. Arrington died on December 31, 1867. In spite of his erratic behavior, in his eleven years in Chicago he had developed such a stellar reputation as a lawyer and gained such respect from his peers that the Chicago Law Institute called a special meeting when they heard the news. There, he was eulogized by no fewer than fifteen notables of the legal community whose speeches were later included in a book entitled, *Memorial of Alfred W. Arrington*.[13] Adlai E. Stevenson, Sr.,[14] writing forty years later recalled that Arrington was one of the finest lawyers he had ever seen, his arguments on dry points of law were, "as if touched by the enchanter's wand."[15]

Even after his death Arrington continued to impress. His wife Leora Arrington gathered his poems and posthumously published *The Poems of Alfred W. Arrington*. Though he had only lived in Texas for twelve years, he was included in *Poets and Poetry of Texas*, his work introduced with the declaration: "Few men have made a more lasting impression upon the people of Texas than Judge Arrington."[16]

While that may be debatable, Alfred W. Arrington certainly had a lasting effect on the history of John B. Denton. With his story of Paul Denton and later the fanciful tale of the murder trial in Fayetteville, Arrington could have had no idea that these fictional pieces would work their way into the biography of the real Denton and be taken for truth, but he might have been amused. It may well be that he saw in Denton a brother, a fellow preacher and lawyer, with a powerful way of speaking, and only by chance borrowed his good name for literary embellishment, but in the end it worked out well for all concerned.

Post Script:

One last piece of irony concerning Arrington: in 1871, just four years after his death, a short story was published in a San Francisco paper entitled, "The Case of Summerfield," under the pseudonym Caxton. Summerfield, if you will recall was the pen name Alfred W. Arrington used when he wrote his famous article; the "Apostrophe to Water" and immortalized Paul Denton. This new story was actually written by William Henry Rhodes and in it Summerfield's life is eerily reminiscent of the life of Arrington. Like the real Arrington, the character of Summerfield moved to Arkansas as a boy, became a lawyer, moved to Texas, wrote a book entitled *Desperados of the (South)West*, wrote about mathematics, and became a judge in Brownsville, Texas. It is obvious that Rhodes did to Arrington, what Arrington had done to John B. Denton: that is to create a fictional character borrowing some of the elements from the life of a real person.

Summerfield, the character, had an interest in chemistry and had invented a chemical that would cause all the water in the world to burst into flames. He became insane with power shouting, "I feel like God! and I recognize my fellow-men but as pygmies that I spurn beneath my feet."[17] He then demanded $1,000,000 from the City of San Francisco, threatening, "scenes too terrible even for the imagination to conceive, will surely be witnessed by every living human being on the face of the globe." It is a long, complicated, and convoluted story, but the irony is that the story based on the life of a man who made up a famous story about a glass of pure Godly water is turned into a character who threatens to burn up all the water on earth. His last words were "For God's sake, give me a drop of water!"

Appendix 2

Tarrant Expedition Muster Roll

Tarrant Expedition Muster Roll of Captain James Bourland, Company of Volunteers Provided to the Pilot Point Signal by Mrs. W. B. Merrill
May 23, 1901

As previously discussed, there has been some disagreement over the exact number of participants in the Tarrant Expedition. Various historians have weighed in on this question with other credible estimates, but I have decided to just include the official muster roll, as submitted and certified by Captain James Bourland. Two notable exceptions to the official roll are General Edward Tarrant and young Andrew Davis, who were in unpaid positions and thus not listed in this document.

James Bourland, Capt.
William C, Young, 1st Lieut.
Samuel Johnson, 2nd Lieut.
Samuel (Lem) Cochran, 1st Sgt.
McQuincy H. Wright, 2nd Sgt.
Wm. N. Porter
Henry Stout
Holland Coffee
Robt. Madden
Silas C. Colville
John Gentry
Elbert Early
Calvin Sullivan
Littleton Ratton
Caswell Russell
John Ratton
Wiley B. Merrill
Wm. H. Bourland
Alfonso Crowder

Frank Sharp

John Kimball

Sam Moss

John Hunter

Joseph Hunter

Mable Gilbert

William Chisum

James Isham

Alsa Fuller

J. C. Guest

Amos Clark

Jas. R. O'Neal

Thomas Westbrook

James Beaty

John Bourland

Daniel Adam

John Baldwin

Phillip Smith

Lindley Johnson

J. N. Dornstine

Thomas W. Box

John T. Griffin

Randolph Scott

John B. Denton

J. S. Dillingham

Jose Maria Gonzales

Wiley B. Brigham

Ira Stanley

Jackson McFarland

Alexander Webb

C. C. Simons

Jack Dalby (Dolby)

John Watson

Wm. R. Morris

Wm. Pullman
Nathan Petty
William Hemphill
James Crowder
George Dugan
Joseph Spenser
Lee Langford
Samuel Burks
Robert L. Mathews
Josiah Ashley
Lewis Williams
David Waggoner
Thomas Cozzins
William Griner
Green Walden
Jack Ivy
Charles McPherson

Endnotes

Notes for Preface

1. Judge J. M. Deaver, The Life and Death of John B. Denton, http://www. dentonhistory.net/denton/.

Notes for Introduction

1. *Denton County Historical Markers*, accessed December 18, 2019, https:// apps.dentoncounty.gov/website/historicalmarkers/historical-markers. htm#John%20B.%20Denton. There is a discrepancy in his reported birthdates. *The Handbook of Texas* reports his birthdate as July 28, 1806, while his son, Ashley Newton Denton gives July 27, 1806, as his correct birthdate.
2. Many family historians and early biographers have maintained that Denton's middle name was "Bunyan," after John Bunyan, author of *Pilgrim's Progress*. It was confusing because his nickname was "Bun" and he never signed his middle name with anything but his initial. In his will he referred to his son John B. Denton, Jr., as Burnard establishing that as his actual middle name. John B. Denton, Jr's widow also referred to her husband's middle name as Burnard in her Confederate Pension application in 1917. Dr. Ashley Newton Denton referred to his father as John "Bunard" Denton in a letter dated, July 1, 1895.
3. William H. Allen, *Captain John B. Denton, Preacher, Lawyer, and Soldier, his Life and Times in Tennessee, Arkansas, and Texas* (Chicago, IL: R.R. Donnelley and Sons, 1905), 77.

Notes for Chapter 1

1. Letter from A.N. Denton to J. S. Denton, Esq, dated July 1, 1895.
2. The James Denton often linked to John B. Denton, was born in 1774, and died in Jennings County, Indiana, in 1827. James Denton was married to Sarah Clarkson Denton, born in 1775 in North Carolina and died in Jennings County, Indiana, in 1846. Though it is true the children of John B. Denton didn't know much about their family history, it seems like they would have been aware of a living grandmother, who lived for another five years after the death of their father in 1841.
3. Skipper Steely, *The Journey across America 1630–1931* (Paris, TX: Cecile Denton Roden, 1985), Chart 8-B. John Woodson Denton was the son of Thomas Denton and grandson of John Denton.

4. Letter from Jonathan F. Denton to John S. Denton, Washington, D.C., July 16, 1895. Emily Fowler Public Library, Denton Texas. Jonathan Denton's letter mentioned the birthplace of his grandfather, but not his name.

5. Allen, *Captain John B. Denton*, 77.

6. Jonathan F. Denton Letter.

7. Homer Thrall, *History of Methodism in Texas* (Houston, TX: E.H. Cushing, 1872), 15.

8. Macum Phelan, *A History of Early Methodism in Texas, 1817–1866* (Dallas, TX: Cokesbury Press, 1924), 70.

9. John Denton Carter, "John B. Denton, Pioneer Preacher-Lawyer-Soldier," *East Texas Historical Journal* 15, no. 2 (1977), 4.

10. W. L. Newberry, "Genealogy of James H. Crow", *The Arkansas Family Historian* Vol. 27, Arkansas Genealogical Society (June 1989), 54.

11. During the 1831 Choctaw Trail of Tears from Mississippi to the west, Jacob Wells had a government contract to sell cow-bells to the migrating Indians. *The Correspondence on the Emigration of Indians*, 1831–33. Vol. 1. 23rd Congress, 1833–1835, Senate Document N. 512. Washington, DC: 1835, 949–1179.

12. *Biographical and Historical Memoirs of Clark County*, Arkansas published in 1890. In 1831, Wells was paid $40 for providing twenty ox-bells and collars for the government removal of the Choctaws from Arkansas. Ox-bells were crafted by blacksmiths.

13. *Publications of The Arkansas Historical Association*; Edited by John Hugh Reynolds; Vol. 1, 1906.

14. *The Gems of Pike County, Pike County Archives and History Society, Vol. 7, no. 2* (Spring 1996).

Notes for Chapter 2

1. S. Charles Bolton, "University of Arkansas at Little Rock Louisiana Purchase through Early Statehood, 1803 through 1860." *The Encyclopedia of Arkansas*, accessed February 23, 2017, http://www.encyclopediao farkansas.net/encyclopedia/entry-detail.aspx?entryID=398.

2. List of U.S. states and territories by historical population. *Wikipedia*, accessed December 30, 2019, https://en.wikipedia.org/wiki/List_of_U.S._states_and_territories_by_historical_population.

3. Having been previously a part of Missouri Territory.

4. *Arkansas Atlas of Historical County Boundaries*, Dr. William M. Scholl Center for American History and Culture. The Newberry Library, Chicago, IL. https://publications.newberry.org/ahcbp/map/map.html#AR.

5. William Clark. *Wikipedia*, accessed January 7, 2021, https://en.wikipedia.org/wiki/William_Clark.

6. *The Encyclopedia of Arkansas*, https://encyclopediaofarkansas.net/entries/clark-county-754/.

7. Norma S. Arnold (San Antonio, TX) and Wendy Richter (Arkansas History Commission), *The Encyclopedia of Arkansas History & Culture*, accessed February 23, 2017, http://www.encyclopediaofarkansas.net/encyclopedia/entry-detail.aspx?search=1&entryID=754.

8. Mary Greenlee Stewart was born on December 12, 1808 in Natchitoches Parish, La. She died on January 12, 1849 in Mt. Pleasant, Titus Co, Tx. Most histories list Mary Greenlee Stewart's birthplace as Bossier Parish, La., which was not created until 1843. https://lists.rootsweb.com/hyperkitty/list/kygallat.rootsweb.com/2001/8/.

9. Denton Family Bible, https://www.ancestry.com/mediaui-viewer/tree/106381047/person/210050420243/media/2877ae3d-b182-479f-a2e4-b9fd0bc134df?_phsrc=SKc75&_phstart=successSource.

10. Sallie Davis, Admrx. of the Estate of W. Davis deceased, V The Heirs of J.B. Denton, Collin County District Court, November Term, 1870. Texas State Archives, Austin, TX.

11. D. W. Harris and B. M. Hulse, *The History of Claiborne Parish, Louisiana* (New Orleans, LA: Press of W.B Stansbury & Co., 1886), 16.

12. Clark County, Arkansas, 1820 Census. John Stewart.

13. *The Arkansas Gazette* (Arkansas Post, Arkansas), June 14, 1825, 2.

14. Donauschwaben in den USA, "Militia Orders 1825-1848 Arkansas Territory" http://donauschwaben-usa.org/militia_orders_1825-1848_arkansas_territory.htm.

15. Thrall, *History of Methodism in Texas*, 15.

16. Allen, *Captain John B. Denton*, 92.

17. US Census, 1830, Clark County, Ark.

18. Jonathan F. Denton, b. July 30, 1828; Narcissa Jane Denton, b. Sept. 23, 1830; Eldridge H. Denton, b. August 16, 1833; Ashley Newton Denton, b. March 12, 1836; John B. Denton, Jr., b. March 16, 1840. Source, Denton Family Bible.

19. A friend from his early days in Clarksville described Denton in less glowing terms: "He was of medium stature while his personal appearance was not attractive. It was only after an acquaintance of some time that he became familiar and social in his intercourse with persons. There was about his manner a high sense of propriety which amounted to something more than a strict reserve. After a conversation was commenced with him, he entered into it with much fervor and animation, warming up in the subject until he exhibited a degree of eloquence not common to men of his attainments; which were very limited at the time indeed."

Archibald H. Rutherford, *Memorandum*, Nov. 14, 1874, Center for American History, University of Texas at Austin.
20. Old Texan, *Dallas Herald*, Sept. 21, 1867, p. 2, c. 1.
21. Rutherford, *Memorandum*.

Notes for Chapter 3

1. William A. Powell, "Methodist Circuit Riders in America, 1766–1844" (MA thesis, University of Richmond, 1977), 44.
2. Paul Neff Garber, "The Homiletical Heritage of American Methodism," *Duke Divinity School Bulletin* Vol. VIII, no. 2 (1943): 11.
3. Donald M. Scott, *The Religious Origins of Manifest Destiny*, Divining America, TeacherServe©. National Humanities Center. Feb. 27, 2017. http://nationalhumanitiescenter.org/tserve/nineteen/nkeyinfo/mandestiny. htm.
4. Powell, "Methodist Circuit Riders in America," 22.
5. Horace Jewell, *History of Methodism in Arkansas* (Little Rock, Ark.: Press Printing Company, 1892), 104. Dr. Andrew Hunter, described another brilliant orator with an unfavorable comparison to Denton. "He never had a peer west of the Mississippi as a pulpit orator except John B. Denton, of whom I wrote in a former communication."
6. Skipper Steely, *Forty Seven Years: a New Look at Early Texas History 1930–1877*, Kindle Edition, Loc. 817. Stevenson moved to Missouri in 1806, settling near Moses and Stephen F. Austin.
7. Walter N. Vernon, *Methodism in Arkansas, 1816–1976* (Little Rock, AR: Joint Committee for the History of Arkansas Methodism 1976), 24.
8. Often called Mound Prairie.
9. Vernon, *Methodism in Arkansas, 1816–1976*, 18.
10. S. Charles Bolton, *Arkansas, 1800–1860: Remote and Restless* (Fayetteville: University of Arkansas Press, 1998), 111.
11. Jeannie M. Whayne, *Arkansas: A Narrative History* (Fayetteville: University of Arkansas Press, 2002), 113.
12. Vernon, *Methodism in Arkansas, 1816–1976*, 21.
13. Ibid.
14. Horace Jewell, *History of Methodism in Arkansas* (Little Rock, AR: Press Printing Company, 1892), 404.
15. Ibid., 48.
16. Powell, "Methodist Circuit Riders in America," 51.
17. Ibid., 48.
18. In this sense, "location" means being removed from a traveling circuit and "located" or placed, as a permanent preacher at a specific church.
19. Ibid., 49.

20. Vernon, *Methodism in Arkansas, 1816–1976*, 26.
21. Thomas Nuttall, *Nuttall's Journal of Travels into the Arkansa Territory October 2, 1818-February 18, 1820*, vol. 30 (Applewood Books, Carlisle, MA, 1821), 222. "Spanish Territory," i.e., Texas.
22. Vernon, *Methodism in Arkansas, 1816–1976*, 37.
23. Thrall, *History of Methodism in Texas*, 15.
24. Rutherford, *Memorandum*.
25. Ibid.
26. Ibid.
27. Powell, "Methodist Circuit Riders in America," 30.
28. Arkansas had previously been under the jurisdiction of the Missouri Conference of the Methodist Episcopal Church.
29. Thomas F. Ruffin, "The Elusive East Texas Border," *East Texas Historical Journal* 11, no. 1, Article 5 (1973). The border was finally settled in 1841 to the advantage of Texas.
30. James A. Anderson, *Centennial History of Arkansas Methodism*, (Benton, AR: L.B. White Printing Company, 1935), 61.
31. Jewell, *History of Methodism in Arkansas*, 90.
32. Ibid.

Notes for Chapter 4

1. Hubert Freeman Mills, "The Methodist Circuit Rider in Texas, 1865–1900" (MA thesis, The Rice Institute, Houston, TX, 1953), 4. McMahan's Chapel was not a purpose-built church, but the name given to the preacher's home where the illegal Methodist services were held.
2. Joseph Martin Dawson, "The Protestants of East Texas" chapter 26, in Dabney White, ed., *East Texas, its History and Makers Vol 1* (New York: Lewis Publishing Company, 1940), 695.
3. "4th–The families which are to compose this Colony besides being industrious as he offers in his petition must be Cat[ho]lics, and of good morals proving these qualifications by the documents required by the 5th Article of the said Law of Colonization of the 24th March." Stephen Austin's contract to bring settlers to Texas, June 4, 1825, (The Gilder Lehrman Collection, GLC01160), accessed June 19, 2020, https://www.gilderlehrman.org/sites/default/files/inline-pdfs/01160_FPS.pdf.
4. John W. Storey, "Religion," *Handbook of Texas Online*, accessed August 31, 2014, http://www.tshaonline.org/handbook/online/articles/izrdf.
5. Phelan, *A History of Early Methodism in Texas*, 70.
6. Ibid.
7. An account in the history of the Fowler family names Littleton Fowler as the first to volunteer.

8. Dawson, "The Protestants of East Texas," 699.
9. E. G. Littlejohn, *Texas School Journal* 22, no. 11 (Jan. 1906): 21.
10. Nolan Eugene Boles, "Littleton Fowler, Father of Texas Methodism" (MA thesis, Stephen F. Austin State University, 2007), 30.

Notes for Chapter 5

1. Ibid.
2. Glenn Dora Fowler Arthur, *Annals of the Fowler Family* (Austin, TX: by the author, 1901), 125.
3. Ibid., 125.
4. Skipper Steely, *Six Months from Tennessee* (Paris, Texas: Wright Press, 1984).
5. Dora Fowler Arthur, "Jottings from the Old Journal of Littleton Fowler," *Quarterly of the Texas State Historical Association* 2, no. 1 (July 1898), 78.
6. Letter from Martin Ruter to Littleton Fowler. July 5, 1837, Bridwell Library, Bridwell Library Special Collections, SMU, Box 2121B.
7. Boles, "Littleton Fowler," 30.
8. Arthur, *Annals of the Fowler Family*, 196.
9. Steely, *The Journey across America 1630–1931*, 155.
10. *Minutes of the Annual Conferences of the Methodist Episcopal Church, for the Years 1829–1839.* Volume II, Methodist Episcopal Church Conferences, 1840 (New York: T. Mason and G. Lane, for the Methodist Episcopal Church).
11. Phelan, *A History of Early Methodism in Texas*, 75.
12. "Ferry at Fulton, Red River," *The Arkansas Gazette* (Little Rock, AR, Feb. 16. 1836), 3.
13. Max Floman, "Cruel Embrace: War and Slavery in the Texas Border-lands, 1700–1840" (PhD dissertation, University of California, 2018), 196. https://escholarship.org/uc/item/2q08b3nd.
14. *The Encyclopedia of Arkansas History and Culture*, web accessed on February 2, 2018, http://www.encyclopediaofarkansas.net/encyclopedia/entry-detail.aspx?entryID=3793#.
15. Gary L. Pinkerton, *Trammel's Trace: The First Road to Texas from the North* (College Station: Texas A&M University Press, 2016), chap. 2, Kindle.
16. Terry G. Jordan, *Trails to Texas; Southern Roots of Western Cattle Ranching* (Lincoln: University of Nebraska Press, 1981), 86.
17. Allen, *Captain John B. Denton*, 92. The issue of when exactly Fowler and Denton arrived in Texas is complicated by the fact that the land in question was claimed by both Texas and Arkansas. Texas maps of

the period show the area south of the Red River as clearly part of Red River County, Texas, whereas Arkansas maps just as clearly show it to be Lafayette County, Arkansas.

18. Land Office Department, Red River County, Second Class Headrights, Texas General Land Office. https://s3.glo.texas.gov/ncu/SCANDOCS/ archives_webfiles/arcmaps/webfiles/landgrants/PDFs/1/0/6/2/1062475. pdf. John B Denton's official date of entry into Texas was September 30, 1837.

19. Pinkerton, *Trammel's Trace*, chap. 2, Kindle.

20. Ibid.

21. Ibid.

22. Charles F. Deems, *Annals of Southern Methodism*. (New-York: J.A. Gray's printing office, 1856), 358. Note: Duke lived between English and White Rock, in Red River County a few miles northeast of Clarksville. He is buried in the White Rock Cemetery. http://www.redrivercountytx. org/cemetery/Search.cfm.

23. Ibid.

24. Ibid.

25. Ibid., 358.

26. Pinkerton, *Trammel's Trace: The First Road to Texas from the North*, chap. 2, Kindle.

27. Phelan, *A History of Early Methodism in Texas*, 75.

28. Arthur, *Annals of the Fowler Family*, 131.

29. Randolph B. Campbell, *Gone to Texas: A History of the Lone Star State* (New York: Oxford University Press, 2003), 57.

30. In 1729, Los Adaes became the official capital of the Spanish Province of Tejas, and by 1770, when all of Louisiana was under Spanish control, the fort was abandoned. The population of the area had grown to more than four-hundred; a mixture of soldiers, priests, escaped slaves and traders who were forced to move to the San Antonio area. In 1800, the territory was briefly returned to French control when Napoleon traded the Duchy of Tuscany for the return of Louisiana. https://www.texasbeyondhistory. net/adaes/index.html.

31. Sabine River, https://en.wikipedia.org/wiki/Sabine_River_(Texas–Louisiana)#Ferries.

32. *Bay Area Genealogical Society Quarterly* 10, no. 1 (December 2010), 11.

33. Dawson, "The Protestants of East Texas," 701. The first church actually completed was in Washington.

34. Letter from James D. Carter to C.A. Bridges, June 30, 1953.

35. Archie P. McDonald, "Louisiana Origins of Freemasonry in East Texas," *Louisiana History: The Journal of the Louisiana Historical Association* 46, no. 4 (Autumn 2005): 435–448, 443.

36. Ibid., 444.
37. Letter from Littleton Fowler to Missouri M. Porter. May 3, 1838, Bridwell Library, Bridwell Library Special Collections, SMU, Box 2121B.
38. Boles, "Littleton Fowler," 33.
39. Ibid., 36, "*Doggery*" a cheap saloon.
40. Phelan, *A History of Early Methodism in Texas*, 79.
41. Ibid., 80.
42. Littleton Fowler was senior member of the Methodist Mission in Texas only because Martin Ruter had not yet arrived .
43. Arthur, "Jottings from the Old Journal of Littleton Fowler," 79. Fowler's cousin, George W. Wright, was in Congress at the time.
44. Arthur, *Annals of the Fowler Family*, 135.
45. Letter from Jno. B. Denton, San Augustine to Revd Littleton Fowler, Houston; Nov. 15, 1837, Bridwell Library Special Collections, SMU, Box 2121B.
46. Boles, "Littleton Fowler," 37.
47. Ibid., 38. To his defense, Boles speculates that in the cash-strapped Republic of Texas, that land could have formed the basis of a barter economy which Fowler used to support his ministry.
48. *Minutes of the annual conferences of the Methodist Episcopal Church, for the years 1829–1839*. Volume II, by Methodist Episcopal Church (New York: T. Mason and G. Lane, 1840). The Sulphur Forks Circuit included Miller County, Arkansas and Red River County, Texas. TX.
49. Letter from Martin Ruter to Littleton Fowler, Dec. 15, 1837, Bridwell Library Special Collections, SMU, Box 2121B.
50. Letter from John B. Denton to Littleton Fowler, March 29th, 1838, Bridwell Library Special Collections, SMU, Box 2121B.
51. Ibid.
52. Letter from John B. Denton to Littleton Fowler, Feb 16th, 1838, Bridwell Library Special Collections, SMU, Box 2121B.

Notes for Chapter 6

1. Maurice Garland Fulton and Paul Horgan, eds., *Diary & Letters of Josiah Gregg ...: Southwestern Enterprises, 1840–1847* (Norman: University of Oklahoma Press, 1941), 83.
2. The French being generally on the south side of the river in what is today Texas, and Old Miller County in Southeastern Arkansas.
3. Timothy K. Perttula, "Caddo Indians," *Handbook of Texas Online*, accessed June 22, 2020, http://www.tshaonline.org/handbook/online/articles/bmcaj.

4. Rex Strickland, "Miller County, Arkansas Territory, the Frontier that Men Forgot," *Chronicles of Oklahoma* 18, no. 1 (March 1940), 14.

5. Max Floman, "Cruel Embrace," 188. George Gray to James Barbour, June 13, 1827, TPUS, *Volume 20: The Territory of Arkansas, 1825–1829*, 480.

6. Rex W. Strickland, "Pecan Point, TX," *Handbook of Texas Online*, accessed June 22, 2020, http://www.tshaonline.org/handbook/online/articles/hrp20.

7. Jack Jackson, "Nicholas Trammell's Difficulties in Mexican Texas," *East Texas Historical Journal* 38, no. 2 (2000). Available at: https://scholarworks.sfasu.edu/ethj/vol38/iss2/1.

8. Rex Strickland, "Miller County," *Chronicles of Oklahoma* 18, no. 1 (March 1940), 12.

9. Rex Strickland, *Red River Pioneers: Anglo-American Activities in Northeast Texas, Southeast Oklahoma and Southwest Arkansas*, (Kindle Locations 2615–2627). George W. Smythe to Samuel Gragg, November 23, 1833, George W. Smythe Papers, University of Texas Library.

10. J. Williams, "The National Road of the Republic of Texas," *Southwestern Historical Quarterly* 47, no. 3 (1944): 207–224. A few years later this crossing would become the last Texas crossing on the old Republic of Texas National Road.

11. Letter from John B. Denton to Littleton Fowler, Feb 16th, 1838, Southern Methodist University, Bridwell Library, Box 2121B. This letter was started in Choctaw Nation on February 16, 1838, and finished on February 18, 1839, on the Sulphur Fork, at the home of Brother Simpson. The hand-written postmark was April 26, 1838, by the "Politeness of A. J. Fowler."

12. Ibid.

13. Letter from John B. Denton to Littleton Fowler, March 29th 1838, Southern Methodist University, Bridwell Library, Box 2121B.

14. Phelan, *A History of Early Methodism in Texas*, 70.

15. Letter from John B. Denton to Littleton Fowler, Feb 16th, 1838, Southern Methodist University, Bridwell Library, Box 2121B.

16. Binger Hermann, *The Louisiana Purchase and Our Title West of the Rocky Mountains: With a Review of Annexation by the United States*. U.S. Government Printing Office, 1900. As part of the terms for the return of Louisiana to France, Spain would receive in exchange the Duchy of Tuscany.

17. Thomas F. Ruffin, "The Elusive East Texas Border," *East Texas Historical Journal* 11, no. 1 (1973), 4.

18. Ibid., 7.

19. Rex Strickland, *Red River Pioneers*, Kindle Locations 2697–2699.

20. Deems, *Annals of Southern Methodism*, 358.

21. Letter from John B. Denton to Littleton Fowler, March 29th 1838, Southern Methodist University, Bridwell Library, Fowler Family Papers, Box 2121B.

22. Allen, *Captain John B. Denton*, 113.

23. Land Office records No. 303, Conditional 2nd class March 23, 1838. https://s3.glo.texas.gov/ncu/SCANDOCS/archives_webfiles/arcmaps/ webfiles/landgrants/PDFs/1/0/6/2/1062491.pdf. Denton filed his claim on March 23, 1838 (based on his Sept. 30, 1837 entry into Texas) and had it surveyed on October 16, 1838. The Certificate #303, was the conditional certificate number. He received his final approval for his headright grant No. 24, on May 4, 1841. The land description indicates that Denton's land was ten miles southeast of Epperson's Ferry on the Sulphur River, the route he and Littleton Fowler had taken when coming to Texas. Present day location near Linden, in Titus County.

24. The League and Labor were Spanish units of measure that remained in use in former Spanish possessions. They are based on the "vara" (33 1/3 inches). They became obsolete in Spain when they adopted the metric system, but can still be seen on old land descriptions in Texas.

25. Terry Cowan, "History of the Texas Public Domain," Texas Society of Professional Surveyors Annual Convention & Technology Exposition October 11, 2015, Sheraton Dallas Hotel, 45, RPLS #4139.

26. Deems, *Annals of Southern Methodism*, 358.

27. Letter from John B. Denton to Littleton Fowler, Jan. 17th, 1839, Southern Methodist University, Bridwell Library, Fowler Family Papers, Box 2121B.

28. *Minutes of the Annual Conferences of the Methodist Episcopal Church*, 1839–1845, Volume 3, 22.

29. Letter from John B. Denton to Littleton Fowler, Jan. 17th, 1839, Southern Methodist University, Bridwell Library, Fowler Family Papers, Box 2121B.

30. Allen, *Captain John B. Denton*, 103.

31. Letter from John B. Denton to Littleton Fowler, March 29th 1838, Southern Methodist University, Bridwell Library, Fowler Family Papers, Box 2121B.

Notes for Chapter 7

1. Gunnar M. Brune, *Springs of Texas, Volume 1* (Fort Worth, TX: Branch-Smith Inc., 1981), 381.

2. Linda Jordan, "Stout Family Biography," *The Mesquite Tree* 20, no 1, http://genealogytrails.com/tex/pineywoods/wood/biographies.html

3. Selen Stout was at the Battle of San Jacinto and one of the three soldiers charged with guarding Generalissimo Antonio Lopez de Santa Anna after the battle, https://www.ancestry.com/mediaui-viewer/tree/16589700/person/28669044494/media/ab7a608d-5cc6-4f55-9cd4-1c28429a9a93?_phsrc=SKc18&_phstart=successSource.

4. "Stories of Henry Stout," *Dallas Morning News*, Feb, 28, 1909.

5. https://www.findagrave.com/memorial/7049134/henry-stout.

6. Wavell's Colony, Register of Families, https://s3.glo.texas.gov/ncu/SCANDOCS/archives_webfiles/arcmaps/webfiles/landgrants/PDFs/1/0/7/3/1073963.pdf#page=15.

7. Richard B. Marrin and Lorna Geer Sheppard, *The Paradise of Texas: Clarksville and Red River County, 1846–1860* (Westminster, MD: Heritage Books, 2007), 258.

8. Pat B. Clark, *The History of Clarksville and Old Red River County* (Dallas, TX: Mathis, Van Nort & Co., 1937), 8. Note: Although various reports mention that James Clark bought to the land from Stout in 1833, the title was no doubt encumbered and the actual sale, to Clark's widow Isabella H. Clark, did not take place until 1838.

9. Atlas of Historical County Boundaries, The Newberry Library Dr. William M. Scholl Center for American History and Culture. https://publications.newberry.org/ahcbp/pages/Texas.html.

10. *Volume 1 of Early Laws of Texas. General Laws from 1836 to 1879 ...: Also Laws of 1731 to 1835, as Found in the Laws and Decrees of Spain Relating to Land in Mexico, and of Mexico Relating to Colonization; Laws of Coahuila and Texas; Laws of Tamaulipas; Colonial Contracts; Spanish Civil Law; Orders and Decrees of the Provisional Government of Texas John Sayles, Henry Sayles, St. Louis, Gilbert Book Company, 1891.*

11. Ibid.

12. N. Doran Maillard, Esq., *The History of the Republic of Texas* (London: Smith, Elder, and Co. Cornhill, 1842), 205.

13. *Clarksville and Red River County*, Red River County Historical Society, Arcadia Publishing, 2010.

14. Steely, *Six Months from Tennessee*, 26.

15. Judy Watson, "The Red River Raft," *East Texas Historical Journal* 5, no. 2 (1967), Article 8. Available at: https://scholarworks.sfasu.edu/ethj/vol5/iss2/8.

16. *Clarksville and Red River County*, Red River County Historical Society, Arcadia Publishing, 2010, 7.

17. Texas General Land Office, Land Grant Registry, https://s3.glo.texas.gov/ncu/SCANDOCS/archives_webfiles/arcmaps/webfiles/landgrants/PDFs/3/3/0/330135.pdf

John B. Denton's headright was about thirteen miles north of Linden, Texas, in present day Cass County, and about ten miles southwest of Epperson's Ferry, a ferry crossing on the Sulphur River.

18. Susan Katcher, "Legal Training in the United States: A Brief History," paper was especially prepared for the International Conference on Legal Education Reform: Reflections and Perspectives, held at National Taiwan University College of Law (September 16–17, 2005), 343.

19. P. B. Bailey, *From the Texas Christian Advocate*, a clipping found in old family scrapbook, ancestry.com.

20. Ibid.

21. General Land Office, Land Certificate Record, https://s3.glo.texas.gov/ncu/SCANDOCS/archives_webfiles/arcmaps/webfiles/landgrants/PDFs/1/0/6/2/1062475.pdf.

22. *Telegraph and Texas Register* 6, no. 5, ed. 1, Houston (Wednesday, December 23, 1840), 4.

23. Thomas W. Cutrer, "Fowler, Andrew Jackson," *Handbook of Texas Online*, accessed February 16, 2018, http://www.tshaonline.org/handbook/online/articles/ffo23.

24. Ibid.

25. Arthur, *Annals of the Fowler Family*, 200. Letter to Littleton Fowler from Bradford Fowler (Clarksville, TX, Aug. 29, 1838).

26. Allen, *Captain John B. Denton*, 113.

27. Deed Records of Lamar County, Texas, Vol. 1, 29–30.

28. Aldon S. Lang and Christopher Long, "Land Grants," *Handbook of Texas Online*, accessed January 27, 2019, http://www.tshaonline.org/handbook/online/articles/mpl01.

29. Linda Lavender, *Dog Trots and Mud Cats, the Texas Log House* (Historical Collection, North Texas State University, 1979), 22.

30. Arthur, *Annals of the Fowler Family*, 199. Letter to Littleton Fowler from Bradford Fowler (Clarksville, TX, April 13, 1838).

31. *History of Texas Public Lands*, p. 9, accessed February 25, 2018, http://www.glo.texas.gov/history/archives/forms/files/history-of-texas-public-lands.pdf Texas General Land Office, revised January 2015.

32. Ibid.

33. Campbell, *Gone to Texas*, 159.

Notes for Chapter 8

1. *The Caddo Indians of Louisiana*, Second Edition, Second Printing March 1990, Department of Culture, Recreation and Tourism, Louisiana Archaeological Survey and Antiquities Commission, by Clarence Webb and Hiram F. Gregory https://www.crt.state.la.us/dataprojects/archaeology/virtualbooks/CADDO/hist.htm.

2. Jim Tiller and Gang Gong, "July 1, 1835: What did the Caddo Believe they were Selling, and was the Price Paid Fair?", *Index of Texas Archaeology: Open Access Gray Literature from the Lone Star State* Vol. 2012, Article 8. https://doi.org/10.21112/.ita.2012.1.8.

3. Carol A. Lipscomb, "Cherokee Indians," *Handbook of Texas Online*, accessed February 27, 2018, http://www.tshaonline.org/handbook/online/articles/bmc51.

4. Campbell, *Gone to Texas*, 166.

5. Ibid.

6. Ibid., 169.

7. Ibid.

8. Walter Prescott Webb, *The Texas Rangers* (Austin: University of Texas Press, 1935), 31.

9. Mirabeau B. Lamar to the Texas Congress, December 20, 1838. House Journal, Third Congress. Archives and Information Services Division, Texas State Library and Archives Commission.

10. Stephen L. Moore, *Savage Frontier Volume II: Rangers, Riflemen, and Indian Wars in Texas, 1838–1839* (Denton: University of North Texas Press, 2006), Kindle loc. 4025–4030.

11. Ibid., location 4110.

12. Webb, *The Texas Rangers*, 31.

Notes for Chapter 9

1. "The Indians, settled along our frontier, upon the north side of the Red River, by the Government of the United States, has become the source of serious annoyances to our citizens. Since the first settlement upon our borders, neither the property nor the lives of Texans have been respected by them in the various descents they have made into Texas under the guise of wild Indians. They have carried out a series of depredations of the most daring and outrageous character. The frequency and boldness of these occurrences have compelled our citizens in many instances to take summary justice upon those thieves ... The tribes principally engaged in these outrages are the Chickasaws and Choctaw ..." *Northern Standard*, Oct. 22, 1842. Lorena Geer Sheppard, *An Editor's View of Early Texas* (Austin, TX: Eakin Press, 1998), 59.

2. Three Forks of the Trinity: an area north and west of Dallas and Ft. Worth comprising the land between the three branches of the Trinity River, from which the river gets its name.

3. Dorman Winfrey and James M. Day, *The Texas Indian Papers, 1825–1843. Four Volumes* (Austin, TX: Austin Printing Co., 1911), 1:23.

4. Charles Adams Gulick, Katherine Elliott, Winnie Allen, and Harriet Smither, eds., *The Papers of Mirabeau Buonaparte Lamar by Lamar*,

Mirabeau Buonaparte, 1798–1859; no. 842, Texas State Library, J.H. Dyer to J.S. Mayfield, October 21, 1838, "I have ordered 100 rangers on the frontier and expect every day to have to call out my whole force to protect the frontier against the Caddoes and other different tribes ...."

5. *The Telegraph and Register*, Houston, Texas November 10, 1838, http://genealogytrails.com/tex/prairieslakes/redriver/news.html.

6. Gulick, et al., *The Papers of Mirabeau Buonaparte Lamar by Lamar, Mirabeau Buonaparte, 1798–1859*; no. 842, J.H. Dyer to J.S. Mayfield, October 21, 1838.

7. Ibid.

8. Ibid., 270.

9. Ibid., 270. The tribes deemed exempt from extermination were the Shawnees, Delawares, Cherokees, Kickapoos, and Choctaws.

10. Ibid., 308.

11. Arkansas Territorial Militia, accessed December 28, 2019, https://ipfs.io/ipfs/QmXoypizjW3WknFiJnKLwHCnL72vedxjQkDDP1mXWo6uco/wiki/Arkansas_Territorial_Militia.html.

12. The Caddo were credited with the raids which killed nine settlers on the Sulphur in 1836; an attack on the Crooker Family near Bonham in 1837; and the murder of the James Pearson family near Marshall in 1838. https://library.uta.edu/borderland/tribe/caddo.

13. Moore, *Savage Frontier Volume II*, Kindle loc. 4420.

14. Letter from Hugh McLeod to M.B. Lamar, November 24, 1838.

15. Ibid.

16. Cecile Elkins Carter, *Caddo Indians: Where We Come From* (Norman: University of Oklahoma Press, 2001), 273.

17. William B. Glover, "A History of the Caddo Indians," reprinted from *The Louisiana Historical Quarterly* 18, no. 4 (Oct. 1935), http://www.beereadys.com/history_of_the_caddo_indians_chap5_1.htm.

18. Ibid.

19. Statement of the Indian Wars on the Red River Border, Furnished by Capt. Wm. B. Stout [c.1850?] Item No. 2465, 12 pages, *The Papers of Mirabeau Buonaparte Lamar*, Texas State Archives.

20. Carter, *Caddo Indians*, 273.

21. Ibid., 293.

22. Gulick, et al., *The Papers of Mirabeau Buonaparte Lamar by Lamar, Mirabeau Buonaparte, 1798–1859*; no. 884, Letter from Hugh McLeod to M.B. Lamar, November 21, 1838.

23. Ross Phares, *Texas Tradition*, (Lone Star Publishing, Gretna, LA, 1954), 168.

24. Mabilyn McAdams Sibley, "The Texas Cherokee War of 1839," *East Texas Historical Journal* 3, no. 1 (1965) : 24.

25. "Old Texan," *Dallas Herald*, Vol XV, no. 43 (July 11, 1868).

26. *The Papers of Mirabeau Buonaparte Lamar*, McLeod to Lamar, letter of January 18, 1838, 424.

27. *Statement of the Indian Wars on the Red River Border*, Furnished by Capt. Wm. B. Stout [c.1850?] Item No. 2465, 12 pages, The Papers of Mirabeau Buonaparte Lamar, Texas State Archives.

28. *The Papers of Mirabeau Buonaparte Lamar*, McLeod to Lamar, letter of January 18, 1838, 424.

29. Ibid.

Notes for Chapter 10

1. Washington Land Office, Doc. No. 3365, United States, Bureau of Land Management. *Arkansas, Homestead and Cash Entry Patents, Pre-1908* [database on-line]. Provo, UT, USA: Ancestry.com Operations Inc, 1997.

2. Carol A. Lipscomb, "Cherokee Indians," *Handbook of Texas Online*, accessed July 21, 2020, http://www.tshaonline.org/handbook/online/articles/bmc51.

3. Sibley, "The Texas-Cherokee War of 1839," Article 6.

4. An Empresario was a land agent under the Mexican Imperial Colonization Law of 1823, in which the Empresario was granted the right to bring in settlers to encourage colonization of Texas. Among other requirements, the colonists were required to be at least nominal Catholics and within six year pay a fee for their grant. http://www.sonsofdewittcolony.org//empresarios.htm.

5. Carter, *Caddo Indians*, 293.

6. Hampson Gary and Randolph B. Campbell, "Neches, Battle of the," *Handbook of Texas Online*, accessed June 26, 2020, http://www.tshaonline.org/handbook/online/articles/qen02.

7. Moore, *Savage Frontier Volume II*, Kindle loc. 7956.

8. The Long Ago–A Half Hour's Chat with Mr. Henry Stout of Wood County One of the Texas Veterans, *Ft. Worth Weekly Gazette*, July 1, 1887, 7.

9. Moore, *Savage Frontier Volume II*, Kindle loc. 9004.

10. Cecil Harper, Jr., "Wyatt, Peyton Sterling," *Handbook of Texas Online*, accessed March 08, 2018, http://www.tshaonline.org/handbook/online/articles/fwy01.

11. Sibley, "The Texas-Cherokee War of 1839," Article 6.

Notes for Chapter 11

1. Jordan, *Trails to Texas*, 87.

2. Acts of Fifth Congress, 1840–41, Art. 935. Dec. 17, 1840, p. 97.

3. Mortgage signed September 24, 1840, John B. Denton; Probate Records, Red River Texas County Records. Exhibit A Filed May 28th AD 1844, J.C. Hart, Clerk. File number OLD-000-974. For years after Denton's death, his old home was locally known as the King Place after J. C. King. Mrs. King was reported to have been related to the Denton family.

4. Probate Records, Red River County, Texas. File number, OLD-000-974.

5. Ibid. Paid July 9, 1842.

6. Ibid. Paid April 30, 1842.

7. Martha Sue Stroud, *Gateway to Texas: History of Red River County* (Austin, TX: Nortex Press, 1997), 43.

8. "Death of Denton," *Dallas Morning News*, July 30, 1916, part 2, p. 3.

9. "Old Warren, TX," *Handbook of Texas Online*, accessed January 27, 2019, http://www.tshaonline.org/handbook/online/articles/hvo27.

10. Rex Wallace Strickland, "History of Fannin County, 1836–1843," *Southwestern Historical Quarterly* 34, no. 1 (July 1930), 38–68.

11. Judge J. M. Deaver, "The Life and Death of John B. Denton," *Frontier Times* (December 1931), retrieved from http://www.dentonhistory.net/denton/, Feb. 10, 2019.

12. Strickland, "History of Fannin County, 1836–1843," 65.

Notes for Chapter 12

1. Skipper Steely, *War in the Redlands: The Regulator-Moderator Movement 1838–1844* (Skipper Steely and Wright Press, Kindle Edition, 2012), Kindle loc. 825–826.

2. Alfred W. Arrington, *The Rangers and Regulators of the Tanaha, or, Life among the Lawless: A Tale of the Republic of Texas*. (New York: R.M. De Witt., 1856). Ironically, in his fictional account the life of "Paul" Denton, Alfred W. Arrington borrowed heavily from the life of real-life John B. Denton and one story featured "The incarnate fiend … Col. Watt Foeman (Moorman), chief hangman of the Shelby Lynchers," who Denton vanquished in a battle of wits before heroically dying and having a county named for him. Arrington apparently did not realize that Denton and Moorman were on the same side.

3. Lawrence Meir Friedman and Harry N. Scheiber, eds., *American Law and the Constitutional Order: Historical Perspectives* (Cambridge, MA: Harvard University Press, 1988), 179. "… there were four major waves of vigilantism occurring in the early 1830s. the early 1840s, the late 1850s, and the late 1860s. The first wave was from 1830 to 1835, and it took place mainly in the lower southern states of Alabama and Mississippi … The second wave took place in the Bellevue vigilante war in Iowa, the east Texas regulator-moderator conflict, the northern

and southern Illinois regulators and the Slicker War of the Missouri Ozarks."

4. William S. Speer and John Henry Brown, *The Encyclopedia of the New West* (Marshall, TX: United States Biographical Publishing Company, 1881), 283.

5. Probate Records, Red River County, Texas. File number, OLD-000-974. July 9, 1842.

6. William Allen, *Five Years in the West* (Nashville, Tenn.: Southern Methodist Publishing House, 1884), 46.

7. (2018, May 6). Robert Potter (U.S. politician). In *Wikipedia, The Free Encyclopedia*. Retrieved 12:12, January 29, 2019, from https://en.wikipedia.org/w/index.php?title=Robert_Potter_(U.S._politician)&oldid=839923121.

8. James R. Norvell, Lewis v. Ames–An Ancient Cause Revisited, 13 Sw L.J. 301 (1959) page 304, https://scholar.smu.edu/smulr/vol13/iss3/1.

9. Joe E. Ericson, "Potter, Robert," *Handbook of Texas Online*, accessed January 29, 2019, http://www.tshaonline.org/handbook/online/articles/fpo31.

10. James L. Haley, *Sam Houston* (Norman: University of Oklahoma Press, 2015), 122.

11. Ernest G. Fischer, *Robert Potter: Founder of the Texas Navy* (Pelican Publishing, 1976), 110.

12. "Old Texan," *Dallas Herald* (Sept. 21, 1867), p.2, c.1., *The American Sketch Book, An Historical and Home Magazine*, 1880. The Texas State Archives, Austin, Texas pages 201 through 213. SKETCH OF DENTON COUNTY, TEXAS (copied by Polly Harmonson) Compiled by Laura Irvine.

13. "Old Texan," *Dallas Herald*, Vol XV, no. 43 (July 11, 1868). This is possibly an apocryphal story as it does not sound like something Potter might say.

14. Margaret Stoner McLean, "Rose, William Pinckney," *Handbook of Texas Online*, accessed January 30, 2019, http://www.tshaonline.org/handbook/online/articles/fro74.

15. C. L. Sonnichsen, *Ten Texas Feuds* (Albuquerque: University of New Mexico Press, 2000), 58.

16. Charles Dickens, *American Notes for General Circulation: In 2 Vol*, Volume 2 (Chapman and Hall, 1842), 271.

Notes for Chapter 13

1. Strickland, "History of Fannin County, Texas, 1836–1843," 288.

2. Walker Demarquis Wyman, *The Wild Horse of the West* (Lincoln: University of Nebraska Press, 1963), 68.

3. John Frair, "Warren-Fannin County first county seat," *Bonham Daily Favorite*, September 6, 1992, Fannin County Historical Commission, https://www.fannincountyhistory.org/fort-warren.html, Retrieved February 6, 2019.

4. Campbell, *Gone to Texas*, 171.

5. *Journals to the House of Representatives, Fifth Congress*, Report on the Council House Fight, by Hugh McLeod, March 1840, 3.

6. Earl Henry Elam, "Anglo-American Relations with the Wichita Indians in Texas, 1822–1859: A Thesis in History" (MA thesis, Texas Technological College 1967), 64.

7. Ibid., 70.

8. J.W. Wilbarger, *Indian Depredations in Texas* (Austin, TX: Hutchings Printing House, 1899), 435. The young son of William Cox and another boy were captured by Indians while driving milk cows a few miles north of present-day Bonham, Fannin County, Texas. The boys were later ransomed, and reported witnessing acts of cannibalism while they were prisoners.

9. "Border Land: The Struggle for Texas, 1820–1879," Center for Greater Southwestern Studies UTA Libraries https://library.uta.edu/borderland/ retrieved Feb.1, 2019.

10. Examples of these fortified and stockaded forts were Ft. Shelton at Roxton, Texas and Fort Lyday, near present day Ladonia, Texas, and there is a replica of Ft. English in Bonham.

11. James De Shields, *Border Wars of Texas* (Tioga, TX: The Herald Company, 1912), 337–341.

12. Ibid., 344.

13. Ibid., 345.

Notes for Chapter 14

1. The *Paris News* (Paris, TX), 7 Nov 1937, Sun, Page 11, Downloaded on Jan 23, 2019.

2. Steely, *Forty Seven Years*, Kindle loc. 10605. The Cherokee Trace was an early trail, attributed to the Cherokee, which ran from the vicinity of Nacogdoches, north through East Texas and on up into Oklahoma and Arkansas. https://tshaonline.org/handbook/online/articles/exc06.

3. Formerly Red River, this became Titus County in 1846.

4. Gunnar Brune, *Major and Historical Springs of Texas*, 429. The spring is located about 1.5 miles south of Mt. Vernon, Texas.

5. *The Paris News* (Paris, Lamar, Texas), Nov. 7, 1937, 11. Downloaded on Jan 23, 2019.

6. Steely, *Forty Seven Years*, Kindle loc. 10626.

7. MUSTER ROLL of Captain W B Stout Company of the Rangers 1st Regiment Red River Commanded by Colonel Saml N Simms of the fourth Brigade of the Militia of the Republic of Texas. https://tshaonline. org/supsites/military/t/stouwb1t.htm.

8. Probate Records, Red River County, Texas. File number, OLD-000-974. J.B. Craig, Administrator: Ambrose Ripley—Debt Status, "Doubtful."

9. Stephen L. Moore, *Savage Frontier III: Rangers, Riflemen, and Indian Wars in Texas, 1840–1841* (Denton: University of North Texas Press, 2007), 236.

10. Steely, *Forty Seven Years*, Kindle loc. 11312. There were stories of a second posse of retribution which sought to avenge the Ripley massacre. "Apparently on April 11 or 12, there was a second posse formed at the Ripley place. These men moved out west to hunt the killers. They were led by Joel Arrington and supposedly traveled as far as the present day Greenville area before turning back."

11. Ironically, on the same day the Tarrant Expedition was forming, and Denton left Clarksville for the last time, he finally received the title for the headright he had claimed three years before. "John B. Denton is entitled to Six hundred and Forty acres of Land by virtue of certificate No 303 dated Oct. 4th 1838 granted to him by the Board of Land Commissioners for the County of Red River he having proved to us that he has resided in the Republic Three years and performed all the duties required of him as a citizen" May 4, 1841, Red River County Probate Records. He would not enjoy his property long.

12. Current maps refer to this as Choctaw Creek. Note: The term "*bayou*" comes from the Choctaw word "*bayuk*."

13. "Old Warren, TX," *Handbook of Texas Online*, accessed June 26, 2021, https://www.tshaonline.org/handbook/entries/old-warren-tx.

14. "The Long Ago," *Ft. Worth Weekly Gazette* (July 1, 1887), 7.

15. Moore, *Savage Frontier III*, 238.

16. Edward Smith, *Account of a Journey Through North-eastern Texas, Undertaken in 1849* (London: Hamilton, Adams & Company, 1849). "In Titus county, labour costs $15 per month. In Hopkins county, labour costs $8 to $12 per month, and is plentiful. In Lamar county, labour costs $8 to $10 per month, and is plentiful."

17. "The Long Ago," *Ft. Worth Weekly Gazette*, July 1, 1887, 7.

18. William N. Porter, Acting Brigade Inspector, *The Texas Sentinel*, (July 8, 1841), 1.

19. See Appendix.

20. Steely, *Forty Seven Years*, Kindle loc. 10709.

21. Jose Enrique de la Pena, *With Santa Anna in Texas* (College Station: Texas A&M University Press, 1975), 67.

22. Miguel Ángel González-Quiroga, *War and Peace on the Rio Grande Frontier, 1830–1880* (Norman: University of Oklahoma Press, 2020), 10.

23. The Archives of Alamo de Parras, http://www.sonsofdewittcolony.org// adp/archives/archives.html.

24. "General Austin's Order Book for the Campaign of 1835," *Quarterly of the Texas State Historical Association* 11, no. 1 (July 1907), 1–55.

25. Ibid.

26. Ibid.

27. *The Texas Almanac*, 1857, 44.

28. *The Galveston Daily News* (Galveston, Tex.), Vol. 36, no. 217, ed. 1 Saturday, December 1, 1877.

29. Moore, *Savage Frontier Volume II*, Kindle loc. 10757). Captain Gonzales Mounted Volunteers, Sept. 8-Nov. 21, 1839.

30. Including Frederic Chopin who arrived in Paris in 1831 and never returned to Poland.

31. Stefan Nesterowicz, *Travel Notes: Visiting Polish Settlements in Arkansas, Louisiana, Mississippi and Texas: A Translation of Notatki Z Podrozy*, ed. Teana Sechelski and Virginia Felchak Hill (Polish Genealogical Society of Texas, 2007).

32. Gerald S. Pierce, *Texas Under Arms* (Austin, Texas: The Encino Press, 1969), 80. Fort Johnston was named for Brigadier General Albert Sydney Johnston, commander of the Texas Army, and architect of the plan for frontier defenses which caused this fort to be built. Some sources, including the historical marker at the site, maintain that this fort was named Fort Johnson, after Francis Johnson, an early leader in the Texas Revolution. But in 1836, Johnson quit the army over a dispute with Sam Houston, and in 1839 he fled Texas, abandoning both his family and his creditors and it is unlikely that a fort would have been named in his honor.

33. John Henry Brown, *Indian Wars and Pioneers of Texas* (Austin, TX: L.E. Daniell Publisher, 189-?), 85.

34. Robert L. Jones and Pauline H. Jones, "Edward H. Tarrant," *Southwestern Historical Quarterly* 69 (July 1965-April, 1966), 300.

35. Brown, *Indian Wars and Pioneers of Texas*, 87.

36. Ibid., 85.

37. Ibid.

38. "The Long Ago," *Ft. Worth Weekly Gazette*, July 1, 1887, 7.

39. Gunnar Brune, *Major and Historical Springs of Texas*, 49, Texas Water Development Board, 1975.

40. "The Long Ago," *Ft. Worth Weekly Gazette*, July 1, 1887, 7.

41. The Village Creek Historical Marker is by the 7th Tee, Lake Arlington Golf Course, 1516 Green Oaks Boulevard, Arlington, Texas.

42. Rev. Andrew Davis, "The Story of the Fighting Captain Denton's Death," *The Dallas News*, October 6, 1900.

Notes for Chapter 15

1. Strickland, "History of Fannin County, 1836–1843," 38. Note: Although this battle is mentioned by William Porter in his report on the Battle of Village Creek to the Secretary of the Army, a number of historians believe it is hard to verify.

2. Gary Clayton Anderson, *The Conquest of Texas: Ethnic Cleansing in the Promised Land, 1820–1875* (Norman: University of Oklahoma Press, 2005), 193.

3. H. Allen Anderson, "The Delaware and Shawnee Indians and the Republic of Texas, 1820–1845" *Southwestern Historical Quarterly* 94 (1991), 245. That some of the tribes reportedly at Village Creek were Algonquin speaking tribes (Shawnees and Delawares) should indicate how far they had been pushed west by encroaching Anglo settlements.

4. Janet Suzanne Claeys-Shahmiri, "Ethnohistorical Investigation of the Battle of Village Creek, Tarrant County, Texas, in 1841" (MA thesis, University of Texas at Arlington, 1989).

5. Brown, *Indian Wars and Pioneers of Texas*, 85.

6. Davis, "The Story of the Fighting Captain Denton's Death," *The Dallas News*, October 6, 1900.

7. "The Long Ago," *Ft. Worth Weekly Gazette*, July 1, 1887, 7.

8. Porter, *The Texas Sentinel*, 1.

9. Davis, "The Story of the Fighting Captain Denton's Death," *Dallas Morning News*, October 7, 1900, 17. Note: the phrase, "every man ... to do his duty," is a reference to a call to arms made by Governor Henry Smith, during the Battle of the Alamo: "Texas Expects every man to do his duty." This in turn may have been a reference to Lord Nelson's famous words at the Battle of Trafalgar.

10. Jones and Jones, "Edward H. Tarrant," 300–323. "The boy who General Tarrant had taken in May, 1841 at the battle of Village Creek, was ... turned over to his uncle, Jose Maria, a chief of the Anadarko tribe."

11. Porter, *The Texas Sentinel*, 1.

12. Davis, "The Story of the Fighting Captain Denton's Death," 17.

13. Ibid.

14. Brown, *Indian Wars and Pioneers of Texas*, 85.

15. Strickland, "History of Fannin County, Texas, 1836–1843," 45.

16. "The Long Ago," *Ft. Worth Weekly Gazette*, July 1, 1887, 7.

17. Davis, "The Story of the Fighting Captain Denton's Death," 17.

18. Ibid.

19. Jose Maria figured prominently in a later incident involving the Denton family. In 1858, Ashley Newton Denton was a young medical student living in Weatherford, Texas, west of Ft. Worth. At that time it was commonly believed that Jose Maria had been personally responsible for the death of his father, John B. Denton at Village Creek. Responding to various depredations in the area and the murders of the Mason and Cameron families, a small ranging force was organized to pursue the Indians and Denton volunteered. Though they had no encounters with Indians, young Denton did receive intelligence that, "Jose Maria had boasted of killing his father." Vowing revenge, "the young man determined upon 'life for life,' and resolved to go to the lower Indian reservation, at or near the present site of Graham, and kill his father's assassinator."

Subsequently Denton received new information that Jose Maria was definitely not his father's killer and he declined to join the next expedition of marauding settlers. Weatherford had descended into some political factions over the Indian question, with one side favoring pursuing them in the field and the other side seeming to favor a defensive force to protect the town. Denton, having changed sides in this debate drew some criticism, including a comment from Mayor John W. Curtis, which implied that Denton was a coward. In response Denton got a pistol and returned to face Curtis, stating, "I fear you no more than I fear a child," and began shooting at Curtis. Denton's first shot hit Curtis in the wrist and subsequent shots pierced his neck and left breast while he himself was barely touched. Denton ran from the injured Curtis who followed cursing and calling his assassin a coward, before dropping dead in the street. Denton stood trial for murder and after being acquitted removed to Ft. Worth where he finished his studies, married and lived until after the Civil War. He went on to have a distinguished career, as a doctor, member of the legislature and director of the State Lunatic Asylum in Austin.

Henry Smythe, *Historical Sketch of Parker County and Weatherford, Texas* (St. Louis, MO: Louis C. Lavat, Book and Job Printers, 1877), 87.

20. "The Long Ago," *Ft. Worth Weekly Gazette*, July 1, 1887, 7.
21. Ibid.
22. Ibid.
23. E. (Elbert) Early, "One of Denton's Men," *Dallas Morning News*, October 17, 1900, 6.
24. Porter, *The Texas Sentinel*, 1.
25. Ibid.
26. Anderson, *The Conquest of Texas*, 193.
27. John R. Swanton, *Source Material on the History and Ethnology of the Caddo Indians*, Smithsonian Institution Bureau of American

Ethnology Bulletin 132 (U.S. Government Printing Office, Washington, D.C.: 1942), 124.

28. The boy whom General Tarrant had taken in May 1841, at the battle of Village Creek, was taken to the treaty ground at Bird's Fort and turned over to his uncle, Jose Maria, a chief of the Anadarko tribe. It was arranged to have the boy returned to the general when he was eight or ten years of age to be educated. The child's mother was reported to be in the Choctaw Nation, and General Tarrant sent some articles belonging to her with the clothes and trinkets worn by the child when he was captured.

Jones and Jones, "Edward H. Tarrant," *Southwestern Historical Quarterly* 69 (July 1965-April 1966), 313.

29. Bird's Fort Treaty Ratification Proclamation, 10, https://www.tsl.texas.gov/treasures/indians/birds-10.html.

30. Porter, *Texas Sentinel*, 1.

31. "The Long Ago," *Ft. Worth Weekly Gazette*, July 1, 1887, 7.

32. Ibid.

33. *The Telegraph and Register*, Houston, June 23, 1841 (About $54,000 today, which would have been divided amongst the soldiers.).

34. Porter, *Texas Sentinel*, 1.

35. A. J. Sowell, "Captain John B. Denton," *The Houston Post* (Oct. 16, 1904), 37.

36. Davis, "The Story of the Fighting Captain Denton's Death," 17.

37. Ibid.

38. "The Long Ago," *Ft. Worth Weekly Gazette*, July 1, 1887, 7.

39. Davis, "The Story of the Fighting Captain Denton's Death," 17.

40. "The Search for John B. Denton's Body," *Denton Record Chronicle* (June 19, 1960), sec. 1, 5.

41. Deaver, "The Life and Death of John B. Denton," http://www.dentonhistory.net/denton/.

Notes for Chapter 16

1. *The Sunday Gazetteer.* (Denison, Tex.), Vol. 19, no. 28, ed. 1 (Sunday, October 28, 1900).

2. Sowell, "Captain John B. Denton," 37.

3. *The Dallas Weekly Herald.* (Dallas, Tex.), Vol. 21, no. 36 (May 23, 1874).

4. Brown, *Indian Wars and Pioneers of Texas*, 92.

5. G. Gerdes, "Death of John B. Denton," *Dallas Morning News*, part 2, July 30, 1916, 3.

6. Moore, *Savage Frontier Volume III*, 264.

7. Lorena Geer Sheppard, *An Editor's View of Early Texas* (Austin, TX: Eakin Press, 1998), 59. "The Indians, settled along our frontier, upon the north side of the Red River, by the Government of the United States, has become the source of serious annoyances to our citizens. Since the first settlement upon our borders, neither the property nor the lives of Texans have been respected by them in the various descents they have made into Texas under the guise of wild Indians. They have carried out a series of degradations of the most daring and outrageous character. The frequency and boldness of these occurrences have compelled our citizens in many instances to take summary justice upon those thieves ... The tribes principally engaged in these outrages are the Chickasaws and Choctaw ..." *Northern Standard*, Oct. 22, 1842.

8. Thought to be J. N. Dornstin. "A Dutchman in our party got ten head of horses that were stolen from him previously." Henry Stout, *Ft. Worth Gazette*, July 1, 1887.

9. Strickland, "History of Fannin County, Texas, 1836–1843," 52.

10. Campbell, *Gone to Texas*, 185.

11. Herbert Gambrell, "Lamar, Mirabeau Buonaparte," *Handbook of Texas Online*, accessed February 19, 2019, http://www.tshaonline.org/handbook/online/articles/fla15.

12. William Carey Crane, *Life and Select Literary Remains of Sam Houston, of Texas* (Dallas, TX: William G. Scarff and Co.,1884), 348.

13. Red River, Lamar, Fannin and Bowie Counties. Texas State Library and Archives Commission, https://www.tsl.texas.gov/ref/abouttx/annexation/voters.html#images.

14. *Acts of the First Legislature, 1846*, Art. 1606, "An Act to create the County of Denton," April 11, 1846, 57.

15. *Southern Historical Research Magazine*, Worth S. Ray, editor, Vol. 1, no. 1, Dallas, TX, Feb. 1936.

Notes for Chapter 17

1. Deaver, "The Life and Death of John B. Denton": "Dr. Pat B. Clark, though a small boy, remembered in the early morning of the cries and screams that awoke the citizens of that town when the first courier arrived with the sad news that the Indians had killed Captain Denton."

2. *The Northern Standard*, (Clarksville, Tex.), Vol. 3, no. 5, ed. 1 (Thursday, December 12, 1844).

3. Last Will and Testament of John B. Denton, from Probate Records, Red River County; http://www.dentonhistory.net/denton/page15/

   The Last Will and Testament of John B. Denton, The Republic of Texas, County of Red River Know all now by these present–That I John B. Denton, in view of the mortality of man do make this my last will and Testament. First I will that my debts be paid out of my property. 2nd, I will that my beloved wife Mary Denton, have and hold all my personal property during her life. 3rdly I will to my beloved wife Mary six hundred and forty acres of land which I obtained as a head right from the government of Texas. And also three hundred and twenty acres of land part of an undivided section of land belonging to Craig and Denton west of Dekalb, on Mud Creek-in fee simple to her and her heirs for ever. 4th, I will to my Daughter Elizabeth in fee simple, one thousand acres of land to be taken out of the land held by Craig and Denton in partnership. 5th The balance of my undivided interest in land held with J.B. Craig to be equally divided with my son Johnothan Denton, My Daughter Nancysu (J?) Denton. My son Eldredg(e) H. Denton, My Son Ashley N. Denton and My son Burnard P. Denton, to be held by them and their heirs in fee simple, for Ever.

Lastly I appoint, constitute and ordain, my friends William N. Porter, and John B. Craig the Executors of this my last will and testament in Testimony where of I have hereunto set my hand and seal this the 15th day of July 1840. Test Richard Miller, John B. Denton, J.B. Cassidy.

4. *The Northern Standard*, (Clarksville, Tex.), Vol. 1, no. 26, ed. 1 (Thursday, March 9, 1843).
5. *The Northern Standard*, (Clarksville, Tex.), Vol. 6, no. 29, ed. 1 (Saturday, November 11, 1848).
6. John D. Osburn, "McKenzie College," *Southwestern Historical Quarterly* 63 (July 1959-April 1960), 548.
7. Lawrence L. Crum, "Banks and Banking," *Handbook of Texas Online*, accessed February 17, 2019, http://www.tshaonline.org/handbook/online/articles/czb01.
8. Probate Records, Red River County, Texas. File number, OLD-000-974.
9. Pleading, May 31, 1842, Probate Court, John B. Denton Estate, Red River County Records.
10. Ironically an $8.00 debt owed Denton from Ambrose Ripley, the settler whose great loss Denton died trying to avenge, was deemed "uncollectible."
11. *The Northern Standard*, (Clarksville, TX), Vol. 1, no. 26, ed. 1 (Thursday, March 9, 1843).
12. P. B. Bailey, *Texas Christian Advocate*, A clipping found in old family scrapbook. Craig died, Sept. 23, 1869.
13. Collin County History Website. https://www.collincountyhistory.com/davis-william.html.
14. Sallie Davis, Admrx. of the Estate of W. Davis deceased, V The Heirs of J.B. Denton, Collin County District Court, November Term, 1870. Testimony of John L. Lovejoy, Jr.

15. Sallie Davis, Admrx. of the Estate of W. Davis deceased, V The Heirs of J.B. Denton, Collin County District Court, November Term, 1870.

16. In Texas, illegitimate children could not inherit from their parents until 1991. http://www.texasinheritance.com/inheritance-mainmenu-28/children-inherit-mainmenu-40/278-read-about-the-inheritance-rights-of-illegitimate-children.

17. Her first husband Bernard Hill had died around 1847, and she had remarried W. C. Baker.

18. Washington Land Office, Doc. No. 3365, United States, Bureau of Land Management. *Arkansas, Homestead and Cash Entry Patents, Pre-1908* [database on-line]. Provo, UT, USA: Ancestry.com Operations Inc, 1997.

19. Thomas Denton was the son of another John Denton who lived in Southwest Arkansas. Some genealogies have imputed that this Thomas Denton is an uncle of John B. Denton, but the evidence is weak.

20. Letter from J. H. Fowler to Littleton Fowler, Feb 16th, 1838, Southern Methodist University, Bridwell Library, Box 2121B.

21. Charles H. Barnard and John Jones, *Farm Real Estate Values in the United States by Counties, 1850–1982*, (Washington, D.C.: U.S. Dept. of Agriculture, Economic Research Service, 1987), 92 http://hdl.handle. net/2027/uiug.30112046854219. Based on the average cost of agricultural land in Collin County in 1870.

22. Sallie Davis, Admrx. of the Estate of W. Davis deceased, v. The Heirs of J.B. Denton, Collin County District Court, November Term, 1870.

Notes for Chapter 18

1. E. D. Odom, "The Economic impact of Railroads on Denton County, Texas," *East Texas Historical Journal* 29, no. 2 (1991), Article 9.

2. A Jollification Meeting, *Denton County News*, (Denton, Tex.) Vol. 7, No. 49, Ed. 1, https://texashistory.unt.edu/ark:/67531/metapth503879/ m1/1/zoom/?q=Massjolification&resolution=32&lat=-409.4875869212 1373&lon=7559.693555041929.

3. Edmond Franklin Bates, *History and Reminiscences of Denton County* (Denton, TX, McNitzky Printing Company, 1918), 174.

4. Ibid., 175.

5. Ibid., 176.

6. *1900's New Century Hype was Millennial*, accessed, February 20, 2019, https://abcnews.go.com/US/1900s-century-hype-millennial/story? id=89978.

7. Ibid.

8. *The Post Signal* (Pilot Point, TX, May 10, 1901).

9. Allen, *Captain John B. Denton*, 17.

10. Allen, *Five Years in the West*.
11. "The Search for John B. Denton's Body," *Denton Record Chronicle*, sec.1 (June 19, 1960), 5.
12. W. Allen, *Erudia, the Foreign Missionary to Our World; or The Dream of Orphanos* (Nashville, TN: Publishing House of the M.E. Church South, 1890).
13. "The Search for John B. Denton's Body," 5.
14. "Remains of Captain John B. Denton," *Dallas Herald* (February 23, 1859), 2.
15. "The Long Ago," *Ft. Worth Weekly Gazette*, July 1, 1887, 7.
16. "Sketch of the Life of John B. Denton," *Dallas Weekly Herald*, Sept. 21, 1867.
17. Rev. L. M. White served from 1872–1876 and also 1878–1880 as pastor of the Methodist Episcopal Church of Grapevine. Personal correspondence from Rhonda Rodman.
18. "Denton's Remains," *The Sunday Gazetteer*. (Denison, TX), Vol. 19, no. 28, ed. 1 (Sunday, October 28, 1900).
19. "To Honor a Texas Pioneer," *Dallas News*, September 9, 1900.
20. *Dallas News*, Sept. 23, 1900.
21. *Dallas News*, Sept. 12, 1900.
22. James Chisum was John Chisum's brother. John Chisum was often confused with Jesse Chisholm for whom the Chisholm Trail is named.
23. "Col. Peter Smith's Version, He Says John B. Denton's Grave Was Never Found," *Dallas News*, Sept. 26, 1900, 8.
24. Note: While Mayor of Fort Worth, John Peter Smith was responsible for having the county seat of Tarrant County moved from Birdville to its present location at Fort Worth. Kristi Strickland, "Smith, John Peter," *Handbook of Texas Online*, accessed February 22, 2019, http://www.tshaonline.org/handbook/online/articles/fsm29.
25. "Col. Peter Smith's Version," *Dallas News*, 8.
26. John L. Lovejoy, http://www.dentonhistory.net/page26/page48/.
27. "John B. Denton's Grave—Two Denton County Citizens Assert Positively They Know Where It Is," *Dallas Morning News*, Sept. 27, 1900, 10.
28. Ibid.
29. "John Denton's Bones–John S. Chisum, Who Buried Them Tells Where They Can Be Found, and Gives Diagram," *Dallas Morning News*, Oct. 2, 1900, 5, col. 2
30. Ibid.
31. Ibid. Original in the Denton County Courthouse Museum.
32. "Bones of John B. Denton–Opinion of a Man Who Helped to Disinter Them," *Dallas Morning News*, Oct. 31, 1900, p. 7, 10.

33. McKittrick remembered going to the site without Bourland, after the bones had been retrieved, not before. *Dallas Morning News*, Nov. 11, 1900.
34. "*Bones of John B. Denton*," *Dallas News*, Oct. 31, 1900, 7. Robert G. Johnson said it was 1860. Other contemporary documents say it was 1861.
35. Phil and Jiles Chisum were African American, presumably slaves who had taken Chisum's name.
36. "Bones of John B. Denton–Opinion of a Man Who Helped to Disinter Them," 7, 10.

Notes for Chapter 19

1. Allen, *Captain John B. Denton*, 41.
2. Ibid., 42. (Note that Rev. Johnathan F. Denton adopted a more conventional spelling of his name. In his father's Will, he is listed as "Johnothan."
3. Ibid., 45.

Notes for Chapter 20

1. Burial of John B. Denton, photograph, November 21, 1901, accessed August 5, 2020), (https://texashistory.unt.edu/ark:/67531/metapth12603/, University of North Texas Libraries, The Portal to Texas History, https://texashistory.unt.edu; crediting Denton Public Library.
2. O. M. Thurman, a Socialist, was the first President of John B. Denton College, which opened its doors at 300 John B. Denton St., on September 10, 1901.
3. Allen, *Captain John B. Denton*, 45.
4. Ibid., 51.
5. Ibid., 53.
6. Ibid., 61.
7. Ibid., 47.
8. *Dallas News*, Nov. 27, 1901.
9. Allen, *Captain John B. Denton*, 63.
10. Ibid., 65.
11. Mike Cochran, "Farsighted Visionary: A. G. Lee, Denton and the John D. Rockefeller Monument," unpublished manuscript by the author. The monument to Rockefeller was to have been the second tallest man-made structure in the world, built of ironstone and placed near the present-day corner of I-35 and Teasley Lane in Denton.
12. Ibid.
13. *Record and Chronicle*. (Denton, Tex.), June 29, 1911.
14. Bates, 176.

Notes for Chapter 21

1. Allen, *Captain John B. Denton*, 1–171.
2. Ibid., 118.
3. Ibid., 121.
4. Ibid., 122.
5. Ibid., 125.

Notes for Chapter 22

1. "Grave Controversy," *Denton Record Chronicle* (May 24, 1941).
2. A. C. Greene, *Sketches from the Five States of Texas* (College Station: Texas A&M University Press, 1998), 82.
3. Barrot Sanders, *Dallas: Her Golden Years* (Dallas: Barrot Steven Sanders Press, 1989), from the manuscript.
4. Letter from Dr. Bullitt Lowry to Barrot Sanders. Denton County Historical Museum files.
5. *The Dallas Morning News*, September 9, 1900, 9.
6. *The Dallas Morning News*, October 19, 1900.
7. Porter, *Texas Sentinel*, 1. Col. William Porter was a friend, a business associate, and a co-executor of John B. Denton's will.
8. "Remains of Captain John B. Denton," *Dallas Weekly Herald* (February 23, 1859), 2.
9. "Col. Smiths Version. He Says John B. Denton's Grave Was Never Found," *The Dallas News*, September 26, 1900, 8.
10. I believe he is referring to Bird's Fort, which is often confused with Birdville. Bird's Fort, on the Trinity, was abandoned and the town of Birdville settled about ten miles west of the original site of the fort.
11. "Col. Smiths Version," 8.
12. *Christian Messenger* (Bonham, Tex.), Vol. 5, no. 45, ed. 1 (November 12, 1879).
13. Henry Stout, *Ft. Worth Gazette*, March 12, 1887.
14. White's Chapel UMC website: https://www.whiteschapelumc.com/our-story.html.
15. Davis, "The Story of the Fighting Captain Denton's Death," *The Dallas News*, October 6, 1900.
16. Ibid.
17. *The Dallas Morning News*, October 27, 1900.
18. John Peter Smith, quoting Stouts report.
19. Mrs. Thelma (Bailey B.) Ray, *The History of Birdville* (Fort Worth, TX: self-published, 1965).
20. Brown, *Indian Wars and Pioneers of Texas*, 92.

Notes for Chapter 23

1. Mary Whatley Clarke, *John Simpson Chisum, Jinglebob King of the Pecos* (Austin, TX: Eakin Press, 1984), 11.
2. 1856 in John W. Gober's account, or 1860 according to Robert Johnson.
3. Etienne Cabet, *Travels in Icaria*, translated by Leslie J. Roberts (Syracuse, NY: Syracuse University Press, 2003), xxx.
4. Albert Shaw, *Icaria: A Chapter in the History of Communism* (New York: G. P. Putnam's Sons, 1884), 38. From a letter dated, Sept. 2, 1848, "Almost all those who survive are sick. Four are dead; the first was Guillot, the second, Collet, who was killed by lightening, the third was Guerin, and the fourth Tange."
5. Paula Selzer and Emmanuel Pecontal, *Adolphe Gouhenant: French Revolutionary, Utopian Leader, and Texas Frontier Photographer* (Denton: University of North Texas Press, 2019), 191.
6. Geri Walton, "Edward Maynard: Dentist and Firearms Inventor," Geri Walton Unique Histories from the 18th and 19th Centuries, July 3, 2021, https://www.geriwalton.com/edward-maynard-dentist-and-firearms-inventor/.
7. Harry Schenawolf, "History of Dentistry in the 18th Century," Revolutionary War Journal, July 3, 2021, https://www.revolutionarywarjournal.com/dentistry/.
8. Dr. Harrell Gill-King, Director of Institute of Forensic Anthropology & Human Evolution, University of North Texas. Phone conversation with the author.
9. Ibid. Mitochondrial DNA is passed through the female line and it would be technically possible to test the DNA in the bones retrieved by Chisum, by comparing it to the DNA of any direct female descendant of John B. Denton's sister. None are known at this time.

Notes for Chapter 24

1. Early on in my research on John B. Denton I had heard vague reports that the life of Denton had been turned into a fanciful tale and published as an old "pulp western." Initially I searched for this in libraries and later on the internet, but I could find nothing involving John B. Denton and pulp westerns. Every few years I would try it again, hoping for a different result. In 2009, by chance I came across the British website of a man named Arthur Nathan, who had posted fragments of an article about a "Paul" Denton, a Methodist preacher from Texas who spoke about the evils of alcohol. The fragment was collected by Nathan's great-great-grandfather, George Burgess (1829—1905), who had visited America in the 1850s and had saved

interesting newspaper articles. The name "Paul" Denton was the link to everything else I learned about Alfred W. Arrington. I am indebted to Mr. Burgess for his meticulous preserving of over five hundred newspaper articles spanning the entire Victorian era from 1845 to 1901, and to his great-great grandson, for being so meticulous as to post them online. https://www.nathanville.uk/religion/paul-denton-19th-century-methodist-preacher-in-the-wild-west-of-america.

2. See Appendix for a brief biographical sketch of the life of Alfred W. Arrington.
3. Pat Ireland Nixon, "Judge Alfred W. Arrington, Judge William H. Rhodes, and the Case of Summerfield," *Southwestern Historical Quarterly* 55, no. 3 (Jan. 1952): 341–357.
4. Judge William F. Pope, *Early Days in Arkansas; Being for the Most Part the Personal Recollections of an Old Settler* (Frederick W. Allsopp, 1896), 141.
5. Ibid.
6. John Hallum, *Biographical and Pictorial History of Arkansas* (Albany, 1887), 280–281.
7. *Arkansas Gazette*, Feb. 4, 1834.
8. *Minutes of the Annual Conferences of the Methodist Episcopal Church for the Years 1773–1881*, Methodist Episcopal Church, (New York, NY), 1840.
9. John Hallum, pp. 280–281.
10. Arrington, Alfred W., *The Lives and Adventures of the Desperadoes of the South West*, W.H. Graham, New York, 1847.
11. John Hallum, pp. 280–281.
12. *History of Texas: From Its First Settlement in 1685 to Its Annexation to the United States in 1846, Volume 2*, Yoakum, H. (Henderson K.), p. 540, New York, 1855.

Notes for Chapter 25

1. Thrall, *History of Methodism in Texas*, 15.
2. *The Daily Journal*, Evansville, Indiana, Feb. 23, 1850, 1.
3. Handbook of Texas Online, Michael Moorman Fricke, "Moorman, Charles Watt," accessed March 15, 2016, http://www.tshaonline.org/handbook/online/articles/fmo39.
4. *The Galveston Daily News* (Galveston, TX), Vol. 39, no. 50, Ed. 1 Thursday, May 20, 1880.
5. John Hallum, p. 281.
6. *The Standard* (Clarksville, TX), Vol. 7, No. 37, Ed. 1 Friday, July 23, 1886.

7. *Band of Hope Record and Children's Friend*, July 27, 1861, Melbourne, Australia.

8. The Brussels Model United Nations, conference encourages youth from around the world to engage in a model UN meeting. One of the suggested speeches in the Declamation Contest for the 2020 conference, is "Apostrophe to Water" by Paul Denton. http://model-united-nations-of-brussels.mozello.com/declamation-competition/sa/28-apostrophe-to-water/.

9. Henderson K. Yoakum, *History of Texas from Its First Settlement in 1685 to Its Annexation to the United States in 1846*, (New York, Redfield, 1855), 540.

10. *The Belton Independent.*, Vol. 3, no. 20, Ed. 1 Saturday, September 18, 1858 (Belton, TX).

11. Thrall, *History of Methodism in Texas*, 16.

12. *Reminiscences, sketches and addresses selected from my papers during a ministry of forty-five years in Mississippi, Louisiana and Texas*, Hutchison, J. R., E.H., (Cushing, Houston, Texas), 1874.

13. *The Galveston Daily News* (Galveston, TX), May 20, 1880.

14. *The Standard*, A Letter from Charles De Morse, (Clarksville, Texas) June 15, 1883.

15. *The Galveston Daily News* (Galveston, TX), Vol. 39, no. 290, February 24, 1881.

16. *Transactions of the Texas State Medical Association*, Volume 33, by Texas State Medical Association, Von Boeckmann, Schultz & Co., Printers, Austin, Texas.

Notes for Chapter 26

1. *Denton Record Chronicle*, January 31, 1971, Denton, TX.

2. Wendy Gamber, *The Female Economy: The Millinery and Dressmaking Trades, 1860–1930*, University of Illinois Press, 1997, 18.

3. Ibid., p. 18.

4. Capt. J. C. Terrell, *Reminiscences of the Early Days of Ft. Worth*, (Fort Worth, TX), 1906.

5. Ibid.

6. *Denton Record Chronicle*, January 31, 1971, Denton, TX.

7. Capt. J. C. Terrell, *Reminiscences of the Early Days of Ft. Worth*, (Fort Worth, TX), 1906.

8. Capt. J. C. Terrell, *Reminiscences of the Early Days of Ft. Worth*, (Fort Worth, TX: Texas Printing Company), 1906.

9. *Centurama History of Denton*, Denton Centennial Commission, 1957.

10. Letter from Patsy Cross [Patterson] to Mrs. Annie Baker, August 21, 1956.

11. *Denton Record Chronicle*, (Denton, Texas) February 3, 1957.
12. Ibid.
13. J. B. Keith, actor.
14. *Reminiscences of the Early Days of Ft. Worth*, by Captain J. C. Terrell Texas Printing Company, Fort Worth, Texas, 1906.
15. *The Mountain Sentinel* (Ebensburg, PA) April 18, 1850, by Charles Summerfield–Timon in this case referring to *Timon of Athens*, Shakespeare, "... I, Timon, who alive, all living men did hate.")
16. Ibid.
17. *Erie Observer*, Erie, PA, March 16, 1850, p. 1.
18. Ibid.
19. Ibid.
20. General Albert Pike, "John Taylor," in Hallum, *Biographical and Pictorial History of Arkansas* (Albany, 1887), 70–72.
21. Ibid., 71. General Albert Pike said of Taylor: "He was the most hatable man I ever knew."
22. *The Neenah Bulletin*, (Neenah, Wi) July 30, 1856, 1.
23. Ibid.
24. *Hancock Democrat*, (Greenfield, Ind.), January 12, 1882.

Notes for Appendix 1

1. Hallum, *Biographical and Pictorial History of Arkansas*, 36.
2. Ibid.
3. *Arkansas Gazette*, October 11, 1850.
4. Jay Onofrio, *North Carolina Biographical Dictionary* (Somerset Publishers, 2000), 25–27.
5. *Papers Relating to the Foreign Relations of the United States*, Part 3, by the United States Dept. of State.
6. *Prospectus of the American and Mexican Emigrant Company*, April 27, 1865. Other Confederate colonies were created in Brazil and Mexico, and Brazilian Confederados colonies still exist today.
7. Ibid.
8. *The New York Times* (Mar. 20, 1866), 1.
9. "It is Booth's Elegy," *Chicago Tribune* (June 5, 1898).
10. Ibid.
11. Ibid. In another example of the ironic interconnections between the cast of characters surrounding the story of Denton and Arrington, the poem "Elegy for Booth" was erroneously credited to Alexander W. Terrell, United States Minister to the Ottoman Empire. Alexander W. Terrell was the brother of J. C. Terrell, of Ft. Worth, who revived the fanciful story of Denton and his wife's trial for murder, also written by

Alfred W. Arrington. Alexander W. Terrell is immortalized in Texas law for having written the Terrell Election Laws (1905), which were designed to disenfranchise African-American voters.

12. Ibid.

13. Pat Ireland Nixon, "Judge Alfred W. Arrington, Judge William H. Rhodes, and the Case of Summerfield" *Southwestern Historical Quarterly* 55 (1952), 350.

14. Adlai E. Stevenson, I, Vice President of the United States, 1893–1897, and grandfather of Adlai E. Stevenson II, Governor of Illinois and Democratic Candidate for President of the United States.

15. Adlai E. Stevenson, *Something of the Men I Have Known* (Chicago: A. C. McClurg & Co.,1909), 192.

16. Sam H. Dixon, *The Poets and Poetry of Texas* (Austin, TX: Sam H. Dixon & Co., 1885), 22.

17. W. H. Rhodes, *Western Classics*, Containing the Case of Summerfield, with an Introduction by Geraldine Bonner (New York: Tomoye Press), eBook produced by David A. Schwan.

Bibliography

Government Documents

Acts of the First Legislature, 1846, Art. 1606, "An Act to create the County of Denton," April 11, 1846, p. 57.

The Correspondence on the Emigration of Indians, 1831–33. Vol. 1. 23rd Congress, 1833–1835, Senate Document N. 512. Washington, D.C., 1835.

General Land Office, Land Certificate Record, https://s3.glo.texas.gov/ ncu/SCANDOCS/archives_webfiles/arcmaps/webfiles/landgrants/ PDFs/1/0/6/2/1062475.pdf.

History of Texas Public Lands, p. 9, accessed February 25, 2018. http://www. glo.texas.gov/history/archives/forms/files/history-of-texas-public-lands. pdf Texas General Land Office, revised January 2015.

Journals to the House of Representatives, Fifth Congress, Report on the Council House Fight, by Hugh McLeod, March 1840, p. 3.

Probate Records, Red River County, Texas. File number, OLD-000-974, July 9, 1842.

Statement of the Indian Wars on the Red River Border. Furnished by Capt. Wm. B. Stout [c.1850?] Item No. 2465, 12 pages. The Papers of Mirabeau Buonaparte Lamar, Texas State Archives.

Washington Land Office, Doc. No. 3365, United States, Bureau of Land Management. *Arkansas, Homestead and Cash Entry Patents, Pre-1908* [database on-line]. Provo, Utah, United States: Ancestry.com Operations Inc, 1997.

Wavell's Colony, Register of Families, https://s3.glo.texas.gov/ncu/ SCANDOCS/archives_webfiles/arcmaps/webfiles/landgrants/ PDFs/1/0/7/3/1073963.pdf#page=15.

Books

Allen, William H. *Captain John B. Denton, Preacher, Lawyer, and Soldier, His Life and Times in Tennessee, Arkansas, and Texas*. Chicago, IL: R.R. Donnelley and Sons Company, 1905.

Allen, William H. *Erudia, the Foreign Missionary to Our World; or The Dream of Orphanos*. Nashville, TN: Publishing House of the M.E. Church, South, 1890.

Allen, William. *Five Years in the West,* Nashville, TN: Southern Methodist Publishing House, 1884.

Anderson, Gary Clayton. *The Conquest of Texas: Ethnic Cleansing in the Promised Land, 1820–1875*. Norman: University of Oklahoma Press, 2005.

Anderson, James A.. *Centennial History of Arkansas Methodism.* Benton, AR: L. B. White Printing Company, 1935.

Arrington, Alfred W. *The Lives and Adventures of the Desperadoes of the South West.* New York: W.H. Graham, 1847.

Arrington, Alfred W. *The Rangers and Regulators of the Tanaha, or, Life among the Lawless: A Tale of the Republic of Texas.* New York: R.M. De Witt, 1856.

Arthur, Glenn Dora Fowler. *Annals of the Fowler Family.* Austin, Texas: by the author, 1901.

Barnard, Charles H. and John Jones. *Farm Real Estate Values in the United States by Counties, 1850–1982*, p. 92, Washington, D.C., U.S. Dept. of Agriculture, Economic Research Service, 1987, http://hdl.handle.net/2027/uiug.30112046854219.

Bates, Edmond Franklin. *History and Reminiscences of Denton County.* Denton, TX: McNitzky Printing Company, 1918.

Biographical and Historical Memoirs of Clark County, Arkansas. Chicago, IL: Goodspeed Publishing Company, 1890.

Bolton, S. Charles. *Arkansas, 1800–1860: Remote and Restless.* Fayetteville: University of Arkansas Press, 1998.

Brown, John Henry. *Indian Wars and Pioneers of Texas.* Austin, TX: L.E. Daniell Publisher, 189-?.

Brune, Gunnar M. *Springs of Texas.* Fort Worth, Tex.: Branch-Smith Inc., 1981.

Cabet, Etienne. *Travels in Icaria.* Trans. Leslie J. Roberts. Syracuse, NY: Syracuse University Press, 2003.

Campbell, Randolph B. *Gone to Texas: A History of the Lone Star State*, New York: Oxford University Press, 2003.

Carter, Cecile Elkins. *Caddo Indians: Where We Come From*, Norman: University of Oklahoma Press, 2001.

Clark, Jim. *Clarksville and Red River County.* Mount Pleasant, NC: Arcadia Publishing, 2010.

Clarke, Mary Whatley. *John Simpson Chisum, Jinglebob King of the Pecos.* Austin, TX: Eakin Press, 1984.

Clark, Pat B. *The History of Clarksville and Old Red River County.* Dallas, TX: Mathis, Van Nort & Co., 1937.

Dawson, Joseph Martin. "The Protestants of East Texas." In Dabney White, ed., *East Texas: Its History and its Makers Vol. 1.* New York: Lewis Publishing Company, 1940.

de la Pena, Jose Enrique. *With Santa Anna in Texas.* College Station: Texas A&M University Press, 1975.

De Shields, James. *Border Wars of Texas.* Tioga, TX: The Herald Company, 1912.

Deems, Charles E., D.D. *Annals of Southern Methodism for 1857*. Nashville, TN: Methodist Episcopal Church South, 1858.

Dickens, Charles. *American Notes for General Circulation: Volume 2*. Chapman and Hall, 1842.

Dixon, Sam H. *The Poets and Poetry of Texas*. Austin, TX: Sam H. Dixon & Co., 1885.

Fischer, Ernest G. *Robert Potter: Founder of the Texas Navy*. Pelican Publishing, 1976.

Friedman, Lawrence Meir and Harry N. Scheiber, eds. *American Law and the Constitutional Order: Historical Perspectives*. Cambridge, MA: Harvard University Press, 1988.

Fulton, Maurice Garland and Paul Horgan, eds. *Diary & Letters of Josiah Gregg ...: Southwestern Enterprises, 1840–1847*. Norman: University of Oklahoma Press, 1941.

Gamber, Wendy. *The Female Economy: The Millinery and Dressmaking Trades, 1860–1930*. Champaign: University of Illinois Press, 1997.

González-Quiroga, Miguel Ángel. *War and Peace on the Rio Grande Frontier, 1830–1880*. Norman: University of Oklahoma Press, 2020.

Greene, A. C. *Sketches from the Five States of Texas*. College Station: Texas A&M University Press, 1998.

Gulick, Charles A. Jr., Katherine Elliott, Winnie Allen, and Harriet Smither, eds. *The Papers of Mirabeau Buonaparte Lamar*, 6 Volumes, 1922. Reprint, Austin, TX: Pemberton Press, 1968.

Hallum, John. *Biographical and Pictorial History of Arkansas*. Albany, 1887.

Harris, D. W., *The History of Claiborne Parish, Louisiana*. New Orleans, LA: Press of W.B Stansbury & Co., 1886.

Hermann, Binger. *The Louisiana Purchase and Our Title West of the Rocky Mountains: With a Review of Annexation by the United States*. Washington, DC: U.S. Government Printing Office, 1900.

Hutchison, J. R. *Reminiscences, sketches and addresses selected from my papers during a ministry of forty-five years in Mississippi, Louisiana and Texas*. Houston, TX: E.H. Cushing, 1874.

Jewell, Horace. *History of Methodism in Arkansas*. Little Rock, AR: Press Printing Company, 1892.

Jordan, Terry G. *Trails to Texas; Southern Roots of Western Cattle Ranching*. Lincoln: University of Nebraska Press, 1981.

Lavender, Linda. *Dog Trots and Mud Cats, the Texas Log House*. Denton: Historical Collection, North Texas State University, 1979.

Crane, William Carey. *Life and Select Literary Remains of Sam Houston of Texas*. Dallas, TX: William G. Scarff and Co., 1884.

Littlejohn, E. G. *Texas School Journal*. Houston: Texas Educational Journal Publishing Co., 1906.

Maillard, N. Doran, Esq. *The History of the Republic of Texas.* London: Smith, Elder, and Co. Cornhill, 1842.

Marrin, Richard B. and Lorna Geer Sheppard. *The Paradise of Texas: Clarksville and Red River County, 1846–1860.* Westminster, MD: Heritage Books, 2007.

Minutes of the Annual Conferences of the Methodist Episcopal Church for the Years 1773–1881, Methodist Episcopal Church. New York, 1840.

Minutes of the Annual Conferences of the Methodist Episcopal Church, 1839–1845, Volume 3. New York: T. Mason and G. Lane, 1840.

Minutes of the Annual Conferences of the Methodist Episcopal Church, for the Years 1829–1839. New York: T. Mason and G. Lane, for the Methodist Episcopal Church, 1840.

Moore, Stephen L. *Savage Frontier Volume II: Rangers, Riflemen, and Indian Wars in Texas, 1838–1839.* Denton: University of North Texas Press, 2006.

Moore, Stephen L. *Savage Frontier Volume III: Rangers, Riflemen, and Indian Wars in Texas, 1840–1841.* Denton: University of North Texas Press, 2007.

Nesterowicz, Stefan. *Travel Notes: Visiting Polish Settlements in Arkansas, Louisiana, Mississippi and Texas: A Translation of Notatki Z Podrozy.* Edited by Teana Sechelski and Virginia Felchak Hill. Polish Genealogical Society of Texas, 2007.

Nuttall, Thomas. *Nuttall's Journal of Travels into the Arkansa Territory October 2, 1818-February 18, 1820.* vol. 30. Carlisle, MA: Applewood Books, 1821.

Onofrio, Jay. *North Carolina Biographical Dictionary.* Somerset Publishers, 2000.

Phares, Ross. *Texas Tradition.* Gretna, LA: Lone Star Publishing, 1954.

Phelan, Macum. *A History of Early Methodism in Texas, 1817–1866.* Dallas, TX: Cokesbury Press, 1924.

Pierce, Gerald S. *Texas Under Arms.* Austin, TX: The Encino Press, 1969.

Pinkerton, Gary L. *Trammel's Trace: The First Road to Texas from the North.* College Station: Texas A&M University Press, 2016.

Pope, Judge William F. *Early Days in Arkansas; Being for the Most Part the Personal Recollections of an Old Settler.* Frederick W. Allsopp, 1896.

Ray, Mrs. Thelma (Bailey B.). *The History of Birdville.* Fort Worth, TX: Self-published, 1965.

Reynolds, John Hugh. *Publications of The Arkansas Historical Association,* 1: 1906.

Rhodes, W. H. *The Case of Summerfield.* New York: Paul Elder and Company, 1907.

Sayles, John and Henry Sayles. *Volume 1 of Early Laws of Texas. General Laws from 1836 to 1879.* St. Louis, MO: Gilbert Book Company, 1891.

Haley, James L. *Sam Houston.* Norman: University of Oklahoma Press, 2015.

Sanders, Barrot. *Dallas: Her Golden Years.* Dallas, TX: Barrot Steven Sanders Press, 1989.

Scott, Donald M. *The Religious Origins of Manifest Destiny.* Divining America, TeacherServe©. National Humanities Center. Feb. 27, 2017. <http://nationalhumanitiescenter.org/tserve/nineteen/nkeyinfo/mandestiny.htm>.

Selzer, Paula and Emmanuel Pecontal. *Adolphe Gouhenant: French Revolutionary, Utopian Leader, and Texas Frontier Photographer.* Denton: University of North Texas Press, 2019.

Shaw, Albert. *Icaria: A Chapter in the History of Communism.* New York: G. P. Putnam's Sons, 1884.

Sheppard, Lorena Geer. *An Editor's View of Early Texas.* Austin, TX: Eakin Press, 1998.

Smith, Edward. *Account of a Journey Through North-eastern Texas, Undertaken in 1849.* London: Hamilton, Adams & Company, 1849.

Smythe, Henry. *Historical Sketch of Parker County and Weatherford, Texas.* St. Louis, MI: Louis C. Lavat Book and Job Printers, 1877.

Sonnichsen, C. L. *Ten Texas Feuds.* Albuquerque: University of New Mexico Press, 2000.

Speer, William S. and John Henry Brown. *The Encyclopedia of the New West.* Marshall, TX: United States Biographical Publishing Company, 1881.

Steely, Skipper. *Forty Seven Years: A New Look at Early Texas History 1830–1877.* Kindle Edition, 2011.

Steely, Skipper. *Six Months from Tennessee.* Paris, TX: Wright Press, 1984.

Steely, Skipper. *The Journey across America 1630–1931.* Paris, TX: Cecile Denton Roden, 1985.

Steely, Skipper. *War in the Redlands: The Regulator-Moderator Movement 1838–1844.* Skipper Steely & Wright Press, Kindle Edition, 2012.

Stevenson, Adlai E. *Something of the Men I Have Known.* Chicago, IL: A. C. McClurg & Co., 1909.

Strickland, Rex. *Red River Pioneers: Anglo-American Activities in Northeast Texas, Southeast Oklahoma and Southwest Arkansas.* Kindle Edition, 2011.

Stroud, Martha Sue. *Gateway to Texas: History of Red River County.* Austin, TX: Nortex Press, 1997.

Swanton, John R. *Source Material on the History and Ethnology of the Caddo Indians.* Smithsonian Institution Bureau of American Ethnology Bulletin 132. United States Government Printing Office, Washington, D.C., 1942.

Terrell, Capt. J. C. *Reminiscences of the Early Days of Fort Worth.* Fort Worth, TX, 1906.

The Texas Almanac 1857. Facsimile edition. Dallas, TX: A.H. Belo, 1966.

Thrall, Homer. *History of Methodism in Texas.* Houston, TX: E.H. Cushing, 1872.

Vernon, Walter N. *Methodism in Arkansas, 1816–1976,* Little Rock, AR: Joint Committee for the History of Arkansas Methodism, 1976.

Webb, Clarence, and Hiram F. Gregory. *The Caddo Indians of Louisiana,* Second Edition. Department of Culture, Recreation and Tourism, Louisiana Archaeological Survey and Antiquities Commission. Second Printing, March 1990.

Webb, Walter Prescott. *The Texas Rangers.* Austin: University of Texas Press, 1935.

Wilbarger, J. W. *Indian Depredations in Texas.* Austin, TX: Hutchings Printing House, 1899.

Winfrey, Dorman, and James M. Day. *The Texas Indian Papers, 1825–1843. Four Volumes.* Austin, TX: Austin Printing Co., 1911.

Wooten, Dudley G., ed. *A Comprehensive History of Texas 1685–1897.* Dallas, TX: William A. Scarff, 1898.

Wyman, Walker Demarquis. *The Wild Horse of the West.* Lincoln: University of Nebraska Press, 1963.

Yoakum, Henderson K. *History of Texas: From Its First Settlement in 1685 to Its Annexation to the United States in 1846, Volume 2.* New York, 1855.

Articles

Anderson, H. Allen. "The Delaware and Shawnee Indians and the Republic of Texas, 1820–1845." *Southwestern Historical Quarterly* 94 (1991).

Arkansas Family Historian, Volume 27. Conway, Arkansas: Arkansas Genealogical Society, 1989.

Bay Area Genealogical Society Quarterly. 10, no. 1 (2010).

Carter, John Denton. "John B. Denton, Pioneer Preacher-Lawyer-Soldier." *East Texas Historical Journal* 15, no. 2 (1977).

Deaver, Judge J. M. "The Life and Death of John B. Denton." *Frontier Times* (December 1931), retrieved from http://www.dentonhistory.net/denton/, Feb. 10, 2019.

Garber, Paul Neff. "The Homiletical Heritage of American Methodism." *Duke Divinity School Bulletin,* Durham, North Carolina 8, no. 2 (1943).

"General Austin's Order Book for the Campaign of 1835." *Quarterly of the Texas State Historical Association.* 11, no. 1 (1907).

Jones, Robert L., and Jones, Pauline H. "Edward H. Tarrant." *Southwestern Historical Quarterly,* 69, no. 3 (1966): 300–323.

McDonald, Archie P. "Louisiana Origins of Freemasonry in East Texas." *Louisiana History: The Journal of the Louisiana Historical Association.* Lafayette: University of Louisiana Press (2005).

"Militia of Arkansas, General Order." *The Arkansas Gazette,* June 14, 1825, accessed February 7, 2017. Little Rock, Arkansas: https://www. newspapers.com/clip/8813706/the-arkansas-gazette/.

"Militia of Arkansas Territory 1825." *The Gems of Pike County* 7, no. 2. (1996).

Strickland, Rex. "Miller County, Arkansas Territory, the Frontier that Men Forgot." *Chronicles of Oklahoma* 18, no. 1 (1940).

Newberry, W. L. "Genealogy of James H. Crow." *The Arkansas Family Historian* 27, no. 2. Arkansas Genealogical Society (June 1989): 54.

Nixon, Pat Ireland. "Judge Alfred W. Arrington, Judge William H. Rhodes, and the Case of Summerfield." *Southwestern Historical Quarterly* 3 (1952): 341–357.

Odom, E. D. "The Economic Impact of Railroads on Denton County, Texas." *East Texas Historical Journal* 29, 2, art. 9 (1991).

Osburn, John D. "McKenzie College," *Southwestern Historical Quarterly* 63 (July 1959-April 1960): 533–553.

Ruffin, Thomas F. "The Elusive East Texas Border." *East Texas Historical Journal* 11, no. 1 (1973): 3–11.

Sibley, Mabilyn M. "The Texas-Cherokee War of 1839." *East Texas Historical Journal* 3, no. 1, (1965): 18–24.

Southern Historical Research Magazine. Worth S. Ray, Editor. Vol.1 Number 1, Dallas, TX, (Feb. 1936).

Transactions of the Texas State Medical Association, Volume 33. Austin: Texas State Medical Association. (1901)

Watson, Judy. "The Red River Raft." *East Texas Historical Journal* 5, no. 2 (1967). Available at https://scholarworks.sfasu.edu/ethj/vol5/iss2/8.

Williams, J. The National Road of the Republic of Texas. *Southwestern Historical Quarterly* (1944): Retrieved July 21, 2020, from www.jstor.org/stable/30236033.

Newspapers

Arkansas Gazette. Little Rock, AR, 1825.
Band of Hope Record and Children's Friend. Melbourne, Australia, 1861.
Belton Independent. 3, no. 20. Texas: September 18, 1858.
Christian Messenger. Bonham, TX: 5, no. 45, 1879.
The Daily Journal. Evansville, IN, 1850.
Dallas Herald. Dallas, TX: 15, no. 43, July 11, 1868.
Dallas Morning News. October 7, 1900.

Dallas Morning News. October 17, 1900, p. 6.

Dallas News. September 28, 1900, p. 8.

Dallas News. October 6, 1900.

Dallas Weekly Herald. September 21, 1867.

Denton Record Chronicle. Denton, TX, 1960.

Erie (PA) Observer. March 16, 1850, p. 1.

Frair, John. "Warren-Fannin County First County Seat," *Bonham Daily Favorite*, September 6, 1992.

Frontier Times 9. no. 3. Bandera, TX, 1931.

Galveston Daily News. Vol. 36, No. 217, Ed. 1 Saturday, December 1, 1877.

Hancock Democrat. Greenfield, IN, January 12, 1882.

Houston Post. October 16, 1904.

"The Long Ago–A Half Hour's Chat with Mr. Henry Stout of Wood County One of the Texas Veterans," *Ft. Worth Weekly Gazette*, Ft. Worth, Texas (July 1, 1887): 7.

Mountain Sentinel. Ebensburg, PA, April 18, 1850.

Neenah Bulletin. Neenah, WI, July 30, 1856.

New York Times. March 20, 1866, p. 1.

Northern Standard. Clarksville, TX, Vol. 3, No. 5, Ed. 1, Thursday, December 12, 1844.

Paris News. Paris, Texas, 7 November 1937: 11 (accessed January 23, 2019).

Porter, William N. *The Texas Sentinel.* Austin, TX, July 8, 1841, 1.

Post Signal. 23. no. 37. Pilot Point, TX: May 10, 1901.

Sunday Gazetteer. Denison, TX, Vol. 19, No. 28, Ed. 1 Sunday, October 28, 1900.

Telegraph and Register. Houston, TX, November 10, 1838, http://genealogytrails. com/tex/prairieslakes/redriver/news.html.

Telegraph and Texas Register. 6, no. 5. Houston, TX, December 23, 1840.

Telegraph and Register. Houston, TX, June 23, 1841.

Unpublished

Boles, Nolan Eugene. "Littleton Fowler, Father of Texas Methodism." MA thesis, Stephen F. Austin University, 2007.

Bolton, S. Charles. "University of Arkansas at Little Rock Louisiana Purchase through Early Statehood, 1803 through 1860." *Encyclopedia of Arkansas*, http://www.encyclopediaofarkansas.net/encyclopedia/entry-detail. aspx?entryID=398, (accessed February 23, 2017).

Claeys-Shahmiri, Janet Suzanne. "Ethnohistorical investigation of the Battle of Village Creek, Tarrant County, Texas, in 1841." MA thesis, The University of Texas at Arlington, 1989.

Cochran, Mike. "Farsighted Visionary: A. G. Lee, Denton and the John D. Rockefeller Monument." Unpublished manuscript by the author.

Cowan, Terry. "History of the Texas Public Domain." Texas Society of Professional Surveyors Annual Convention & Technology Exposition October 11, 2015, Sheraton Dallas Hotel. Retrieved from http://c.ymcdn. com/sites/www.tsps.org/resource/resmgr/Convention15/TexasPublic Domain.pdf. (accessed February 9, 2018).

Elam, Earl Henry. "Anglo-American Relations with the Wichita Indians in Texas, 1822-1859." MA thesis, Texas Technological College, 1967.

Floman, Max. "Cruel Embrace: War and Slavery in the Texas Borderlands, 1700–1840." PhD diss. University of California, 2018. https://escholarship. org/uc/item/2q08b3nd.

Katcher, Susan. "Legal Training in the United States: A Brief History." Paper was especially prepared for the International Conference on Legal Education Reform: Reflections and Perspectives, held at National Taiwan University College of Law, September 16–17, 2005.

Mills, Hubert Freeman. "The Methodist Circuit Rider in Texas, 1865–1900." MA thesis, The Rice Institute, Houston, Texas, 1953.

Powell, William A. "Methodist Circuit Riders in America, 1766–1844." MA thesis, University of Richmond, 1977.

Rutherford, A. H. "Rev. Jno Denton, Forty Years Ago in Arkansas." Memorandum, November 14, 1874. Center for American History, University of Texas at Austin. Transcribed by Mike Cochran. January 13, 2001.

Online Resources

Archives of Alamo de Parras. http://www.sonsofdewittcolony.org//adp/ archives/archives.html.

Atlas of Historical County Boundaries. The Newberry Library Dr. William M. Scholl Center for American History and Culture. https://publications. newberry.org/ahcbp/pages/Texas.html.

Border Land: The Struggle for Texas, 1820–1879, Center for Greater Southwestern Studies UTA Libraries. https://library.uta.edu/borderland/tribe/ caddo.

Brussels Model United Nations, 2020 Declamation Contest. "Apostrophe to Water." http://model-united-nations-of-brussels.mozello.com/declamation-competition/sa/28-apostrophe-to-water/.

Collin County History Website. https://www.collincountyhistory.com/davis-william.html.

Denton County Historical Markers. https://apps.dentoncounty.gov/website/ historicalmarkers/historical-markers.htm#John%20B.%20Denton.

Encyclopedia of Arkansas History & Culture. https://encyclopediaofarkansas. net/media/entrance-view-14990/.

Fannin County Historical Commission. https://www.fannincountyhistory.org/ fort-warren.html.

Handbook of Texas. https://www.tshaonline.org/handbook.

Jordan, Linda. Stout Family Biography, Wood County Biographies. http://
genealogytrails.com/tex/pineywoods/wood/biographies.html.

Norvell, James R. *Lewis v. Ames–An Ancient Cause Revisited*, 13 Sw L.J. 301
(1959) page 304, https://scholar.smu.edu/smulr/vol13/iss3/1.

Schenawolf, Harry. "History of Dentistry in the 18th Century." Revolutionary
War Journal. July 3, 2021, https://www.revolutionarywarjournal.com/
dentistry/.

Walton, Geri. "Edward Maynard: Dentist and Firearms Inventor." Geri Walton
Unique Histories from the 18th and 19th Centuries. July 3, 2021, https://
www.geriwalton.com/edward-maynard-dentist-and-firearms-inventor/.

Index

Page numbers with an *f* refer to a figure or a caption; *n* indicates an endnote. JBD denotes John Burnard Denton. MGD denotes Denton's wife, Mary Greenlee Denton.

Montague's attack on, 72
at Village Creek, 85
DeMorse, Samuel, 107, 166
Denton, Ashley Newton (son)
  birth of, 187n18
  as doctor, 160f, 161
  inheritance, 103, 105, 208n3
  Jose Maria, Chief, as innocent
    of JBD's killing, 92,
    206n19 obituary
    of, 163
Denton, Charlotte (sister), 2
Denton, Eldridge H. (son)
  birth of, 12, 187n18
  inheritance, 103, 105, 208n3
Denton, Eliza (sister), 2
Denton, James (purported father;
    1774–1827), 1, 2,
    185n2 (ch1)
Denton, Jane (sister), 2
Denton, John Burnard
  Arrington-generated
    confusion, x. See also
    Arrington, Alfred W.
  background
    Allen's biography of, 114f,
     131–32
    birthdate uncertainty,
     185n1 (intro)
    early life, 1–3
    family history, 2
    name uncertainty,
     185n2 (intro)
    physical appearance of, 8,
     187n19
    qualities, x
    death and burial, 90, 91f,
     94–95, 103, 208n1
  in Clarksville, 44

county named after, 64–65,
  100–101
Denton, Richard, unlinked,
  173–74
educational transformation of
  education by wife, 8, 13
  Fowler as mentor, 22f,
   30–31
  legal studies, 59
  Rutherford's loan of books,
   13–14
fictionalized. See Arrington,
  Alfred W.
land grants
  in Arkansas, 109
  in Texas, 37–38, 203n11
legacy of, 171–72
Master Mason in St.
  Augustine, 28
Methodist Church employment
  letters to Fowler, 30–31,
   32, 37, 44
  location of, 14
  mission meetings, 35,
   193n11
  at Mount Prairie circuit, 11
  at Nacogdoches and San
   Augustine, 29, 30, 32
  in Old Warren, 65
  request to locate, 37
  on Sulphur Forks Circuit,
   31, 35–36, 192n48
military involvement
  Captain Denton's Mounted
   Volunteers, 62
  as Indian fighter, 171–72
  military campaigns, 55,
   86, 88, 89–90
  military rank, 62